THE BILL OF RIGHTS: A BICENTENNIAL ★ ★ ★ ASSESSMENT ★ ★ ★

THE BILL OF RIGHTS: A BICENTENNIAL ★ ★ ★ ASSESSMENT ★ ★ ★

EDITED BY

Gary C. Bryner and A. D. Sorensen

BRIGHAM YOUNG UNIVERSITY

To Jane and Necia

Library of Congress Cataloging-in-Publication Data

The Bill of Rights: a bicentennial assessment / edited by Gary C. Bryner and
  A. Don Sorensen.
       p. cm.
    Includes index.
    ISBN 0-7914-2225-9
    1. United States—Constitutional law—Amendments—1st–10th.
  2. Civil rights—United States.   I. Bryner, Gary C., 1951–
  II. Sorensen, A. Don (Alma Don), 1935–
  KF4749.A2B54   1994
  342.73'085—dc20
  [347.30285]   94-1729
                                                                      CIP

Brigham Young University, Provo, Utah 84602
"Toward a Feminist Regrounding of Constitutional Law," © 1991 by Gayle Binion
© 1993 by Brigham Young University. All rights reserved
Printed in the United States of America

Distributed by State University of New York Press
State University Plaza, Albany, New York 12446–0001

Contents

Acknowledgments

M ost of the essays in this volume were developed from papers presented at a lecture series at Brigham Young University during the 1990–91 academic year. The series was funded through a grant from the Commission on the Bicentennial of the United States Constitution's College-Community Forum lecture program. We appreciate very much the support of the commission in helping to bring to our community these thoughtful and provocative speakers and in encouraging discussion of constitutional rights. Additional funding was provided by the College of Family, Home, and Social Sciences and the Department of Political Science at Brigham Young University.

This volume is the fourth in a series published by Brigham Young University to celebrate the bicentennial of the United States Constitution and to engage faculty members, students, and the surrounding community in an examination of constitutional ideas and ideals. Earlier volumes include *Constitutionalism and Rights, The Constitution and the Regulation of Society,* and *Toward a More Perfect Union: Six Essays on the Constitution.*

The ideas expressed in these essays are solely those of the authors and are not necessarily endorsed by the U.S. Commission on the Bicentennial of the Constitution or by Brigham Young University.

Introduction

In September 1789 Congress submitted to the states for ratification twelve amendments to the Constitution, in response to the demands of several states that the Constitution include a bill of rights. The first ten amendments were eventually accepted by the states, and the Bill of Rights officially became part of the Constitution on 15 December 1791, when Virginia voted to ratify. Three of the original thirteen states—Massachusetts, Georgia, and Connecticut—did not vote to accept the Bill of Rights as part of the Constitution until 1939, the sesquicentennial anniversary of their submission to the states. Although they were added four years after the Constitution was written and some states chose to embrace them much later still, the ten amendments making up the Bill of Rights reflect some of our most prized political ideals and are at the heart of our expectations for constitutional government.

The bicentennial of the ratification of the Bill of Rights provides a particularly fitting opportunity to reflect on how—and on how well—individual rights are secured in our democracy. The Declaration of Independence's charge that governments are instituted to secure the unalienable rights of all persons has become for many the central expectation for government. But while there is a general commitment in American politics and society to the ideal of rights, the securing of rights is anything but uncontroversial. Competing conceptions of rights are central to many of the most contentious public issues in the United States, such as free speech and the limits of public expression; affirmative action and the protection of minorities against discrimination; the role of religion and prayer in public schools and other public forums; capital punishment, searches and seizures, and other rights of the accused; and a host of concerns that have been characterized as personal rights of privacy—abortion, sexual preference, nontraditional forms of human reproduction, and withdrawal from life-sustaining medical technologies.

There is little agreement over what role rights should play in addressing these and other pressing contemporary issues. From one view, rights are a politically powerful way to expand government protection for certain interests. Once those interests are defined as rights, they must be provided for; and allocating the resources required is given priority over other interests. An expanded view of rights is an important means of increasing opportunities for all individuals. Even those who believe that rights as traditionally understood in the Bill of Rights are sufficient to protect individuals today may nevertheless believe that threats to those rights have changed, requiring the development of new means of securing them. Technological advances in monitoring property and communication, for example, require new ways of defending constitutional rights of protection against unreasonable searches.

Critics, however, fear that an expansion of rights threatens traditional ones. New rights of employment, health care, adequate food, or a healthy environment may overwhelm government resources set aside to ensure rights or engulf the polity in a difficult-to-resolve battle over which rights are to be recognized, how they are to be provided for, and how to choose or set priorities when rights collide. An expansive view of rights may give excessive attention to individualist demands at the expense of the interest of broader public or majoritarian interests. Conservatives argue that an excessive commitment to rights prohibits the fostering of religious or moral values that are prerequisites of community life. Liberals fear that an immoderate concern with rights inhibits the pursuit of collective purposes such as education, environmental protection, and investment in public works.

The process of defining, interpreting, and extending rights is almost as controversial as the substantive issues themselves. The judicial process has been championed as a means of developing new interpretations of rights to respond to changing circumstances; but this judicial activism has, in turn, triggered fears of an imperial judiciary fueled by the policy biases of judges rather than rooted in constitutional principle. Each controversial Supreme Court decision generates a new round of calls for statutes and constitutional amendments to curb the courts' powers or reverse their decisions. Legislatures also regularly define rights, but majoritarian processes may be insufficiently sensitive to the rights of individuals and ethnic minorities.

While Americans are wrestling with alternative conceptions of rights, many of the world's inhabitants are looking to the United States for ideas about how to secure rights. Citizens of eastern European nations have been suddenly thrust into a position of trying to define for themselves political and civil rights and to establish means of securing them. The collapse of communism there has left a void that threatens to be filled—as in the case of former Yugoslavia—with disorder and violence unless means can be devised to secure individual rights and the other values of democratic government that these people seek. Residents in the less developed world also seek ways of protecting human rights in the face of corrupt, incompetent, and authoritarian governments. The experience of the United States in defining and securing rights can serve as an important source of ideas for these countries as they grapple with these issues.

The purpose of this book is to explore the state of rights in America: to reexamine their roots, assess their effectiveness, and consider their future. By celebrating and assessing the Bill of Rights, we seek to engage in a free and open discussion of how well they have accomplished their purpose of securing basic individual liberties over the past two hundred years and how well suited they are to protect our rights in the future. We hope to learn from the example of the Framers of the Constitution in encouraging an examination of fundamental principles, studying the lessons of history, and looking toward the future. Several questions provide the overall agenda for the essays in this book:

First, what rights do people have? Possible rights range from political participation and self-government to criminal process protections and personal privacy. Do rights change over time, and are there new rights that need to be recognized or at least new threats to rights that need to be guarded against? Is there a danger of rights inflation—newer rights threatening traditional ones—that might jeopardize our commitment to fundamental, historic rights that are rooted in conventional interpretations of the Bill of Rights?

Second, how are rights determined? Legislative bodies, courts, political referendums, and votes can all be means of defining rights, although we have traditionally looked to the Supreme Court as the ultimate authority on rights. The specific provisions of the Constitution, the intent of the Framers, political theories, policy goals, and a number of other factors compete for consideration in defining and interpreting constitutional rights. How can competing values be effectively addressed and balanced and what political mechanisms are best suited to do that?

Third, how do rights shape and define the powers of government? If government is limited to specific delegated powers, then rights can serve to restrict governmental interventions beyond those express limits. But governmental power may also be defined much more broadly to permit any kind of action that is not explicitly prohibited by individual rights. In the first case, the presumption is that individuals will be left alone to conduct their lives according to their own choices except for limited areas of public involvement; in the second case, the presumption is that the majority, acting through its government, can legitimately pursue any public purpose as long as specific individual rights are not infringed. Rights can limit what policies are pursued, as well as limiting the way in which government officials act. Do the rights provided in the Bill of Rights effectively balance the protection of individuals with the prerogatives of the majority to create or foster values that they feel are essential to achieve public purposes such as education, environmental protection, investment in public facilities, or social order?

Fourth, what particular challenges does the protection of minority rights pose? For many, the key test of the Bill of Rights is how it protects ethnic minorities, women, children, those accused of crimes, and others who are not part of the political, economic, and social power structure. Individual rights are perhaps most severely tested when they are called on to protect unpopular or unempowered members of society. For example, should laws be colorblind and gender-neutral, or must they be based on a consideration of the particular challenges confronting people of color and women and the past discrimination aimed at them?

Fifth, how are rights secured? An independent judiciary has generally been viewed as critical. But the separation of powers in the federal government, federalism and the independent power of states, political culture and public virtue, and other characteristics of our political system play some role. A commitment to securing individual rights may not be a natural or inevitable outgrowth of political life; it may need to be cultivated and nourished. What kind of public commitment is required for rights to be protected, and how can that commitment be fostered when so much emphasis is given to individualism? Are individual rights and a sense of community incompatible?

Finally, what is the future of rights? We invoke a discourse of rights for many of our most important public debates. Rights can be an important expression of our common concerns and shared commitments to each other. But their emphasis on individuals may also inhibit collective decisions and the cultivation of community. Does the idea of rights provide a useful framework in confronting hunger and poverty, environmental pollution and scarce natural resources, crime, disease, international debt, and the other challenges confronting humankind, or do other ways of discussing public choices make more sense?

The essays that follow address these and related questions. Part One provides an overview of some of the major conceptions underlying the Bill of Rights. Carl Wellman's essay, "Interpreting the Bill of Rights: Alternative Conceptions of Rights," reviews and critiques the work of several theorists who have tried to define the nature of rights. Different conceptions of rights have important implications for the way in which we interpret the Bill of Rights.

In "Civil Rights and the U.S. Constitution," Rex Martin distinguishes civil rights from other rights, arguing that they are universal political rights that are recognized by law. He traces the evolution of constitutional rights, defining them as civil rights that are given high priority, and emphasizes the way in which the Bill of Rights has come to dominate state and federal governments. He examines the traditional argument that majority rule is a threat to individual rights, as well as the idea that rights reflect a high degree of social commitment.

Christopher Wolfe's essay, "Interpreting the Bill of Rights: What? Who? Why?" takes up the issue of how to interpret the

Constitution and the amendments and offers an explanation of the original understanding of the Bill of Rights. He criticizes the expansive form of judicial interpretation of constitutional provisions that gives the courts broad powers to "balance" competing principles and interests.

The essays in Part Two focus on the current debate over specific constitutional rights. Rex E. Lee's essay on the religion clauses reviews leading Supreme Court cases that have grappled with the tension between the guarantee of religious freedom and the prohibition against the establishment of religion, as well as the confrontation between the free exercise rights of individuals and those of religious organizations.

"Abortion, Ethics, and Constitutional Interpretation," an essay by Leslie P. Francis, explores abortion and privacy rights from the perspective of mother, moral theorist, and legal theorist. Francis explores the conflict between fetal rights and maternal liberties in the leading Supreme Court cases on abortion and examines the role that religious beliefs play in debates over public policy, concluding specifically that the trimester doctrine espoused by the Court in *Roe v. Wade* should not be altered or discarded.

Camille Williams's essay, "Abortion and Equality under the Law," focuses on individual rights, equal protection, and abortion. She argues that contemporary theories of equal protection and individual rights fail to account for the obligations both men and women have to their families and children and that current constitutional doctrines and societal views of abortion fail to reflect a consideration of these obligations.

Gayle Binion traces the evolution of feminist constitutional theory in "Toward a Feminist Regrounding of Constitutional Law." She argues that, while conservative feminism seeks gender neutrality in constitutional law and liberal feminist thought emphasizes the impact of law on women, progressive feminism calls for the incorporation of women's experiences and values into constitutional decision making.

Gary Bryner's essay, "Minority Rights under the Constitution," looks at how the Fourteenth Amendment's guarantee of the "equal protection of the laws" has been used to promote the right of equality of opportunity for women and people of color. He contends that race and gender neutrality has not been enough and examines the role affirmative action has played in ensuring equal opportunity for all persons.

In Part Three, the essays turn to the future of rights. A. D. Sorensen's essay, "Rights and Human Flourishing," outlines a theory of the relationship between rights and self-directed life. He proposes that political societies can be assessed, ultimately, by how well they provide for the preconditions for freedom and personal choice by their members.

In "The Future of Rights," Bryner and Sorensen consider what remains to be done to actualize the free life for all citizens. The future of rights will, they assert, depend in part on our ability to ensure that all persons enjoy the preconditions for the free life.

I

INTERPRETING THE BILL OF RIGHTS: ALTERNATIVE CONCEPTIONS OF RIGHTS

Carl Wellman

The Bill of Rights constitutes an immensely valuable part of our constitutional law. Presumably, this is why we have celebrated its two hundredth anniversary. But what is constitutional law, really? Let us begin by recalling two diametrically opposed views.

Probably the traditional view, and certainly the more respectable view, is that our constitutional law consists of a historical document. Our great country is famous in every land for its Constitution, a document that has for more than two centuries made the United States of America the most successful democracy the world has ever known. This is a historical document, for it was created at a certain time and in a certain place and has continued to influence the historical development of our great nation. If we wish to discover our constitutional law, then, we must read this text and interpret its meaning in terms of what its wise

Carl Wellman is a professor of philosophy at Washington University.

authors intended. Unfortunately, we can no longer ask the Framers of our Constitution precisely what they meant by some of its enigmatic clauses because they are now dead. And how can the document they wrote more than two centuries ago remain a living constitution applicable to the radically different circumstances of contemporary life if we cling rigidly to their original intentions?

The opposite view, somewhat less reputable but, as one would expect, widely accepted by practicing lawyers, is known as American Legal Realism. Real law is not to be found in written documents but in legal practice, especially the practices of our courts. Is the human fetus a person endowed with constitutional rights? One cannot find the answer by reading the Constitution—for the word "fetus" does not occur in that text—or by guessing the intentions of those who originally wrote the due process clause—for they probably never thought of the legal issue we are now raising, and if they did we certainly have no evidence of what they might have intended to say about it. No, our Constitution means what our courts say that it means; real law, law as it really functions in our legal system, consists of judicial decisions, especially the decisions of the Supreme Court. This theory is very useful to any practicing lawyer wondering what to advise a client about how to act to avoid going to jail or paying damages, but it remains a mystery how the judges themselves could use this theory in trying to decide any hard case before their courts.

A more moderate view, one that captures the insights but avoids the errors of both the Historical School and American Legal Realism, has been proposed by Stephen Munzer and James Nickel in an immensely suggestive journal article. They defend the thesis that the Constitution is a text-based practice.[1] They agree with the legal realists that real law is an institutional practice. They are using the word "practice" in the sense defined by Rawls as "any form of activity specified by a system of rules which defines offices, roles, moves, penalties, defenses, and so on, and which gives the activity its structure."[2] Paradigm examples are games and rituals, trials and parliaments. Nevertheless, they reject the legal realist's notion that our written Constitution is not law but merely a source the courts may, if they so choose, use to make law. Constitutional law is and ought to be based upon this document, for within our legal practice any legally valid judicial decision must be based on and justified by one or more legally authoritative texts. At the same time, our legal practices permit—and may even require—our courts to give legally authoritative interpretations of the Constitution, including new interpretations to fit changing circumstances. Therefore, this document is not an unchanging text with a meaning fixed in past history to be interpreted in terms of the original intentions of its authors; it is a living document to be continually reinterpreted in contemporary legal practices based upon it.

This view strikes me as very close to the truth. Still, I think that it misses the mark in two significant respects. First, Munzer and Nickel seem to agree with the legal realists that law consists in its applications, primarily in the courts. This is why they think of constitutional law as "based on" the text of the Constitution. But law is also a text-creating practice, for essential parts of our legal system are legislatures that enact statutes and courts that write judicial decisions which constitute precedents in our common law. A broader and more accurate conception of law would view it as a text-*centered* practice rather than merely a text-based practice. Second, the text or texts central to our constitutional law include more than the original Constitution together with subsequent amendments. The text includes all the judicial opinions, especially of the Supreme Court justices, on any issue of constitutional import.

Since the Bill of Rights is a text central to many of our most important legal practices, it is obviously a very valuable part of our legal system. It can function as a real factor in our legal practices, however, only insofar as it can be effectively interpreted by all those who apply it in their activities—judges deciding cases before their courts, legislators enacting statutes, administrators setting policies and carrying out the business of government, and private citizens attempting to live their lives in legally permissible or even required ways. As the gap between the text of the United Nations Declaration of Human Rights and the legal practices in all too many countries reminds us, an inspiring list of rights acquires legal force only as it is embodied in effective institutions, such as the European Court of Human Rights. And in the United States the Bill of Rights can give practical direction to our conduct and secure protection to our citizens only if we can validly ascribe some articulate meaning to this terse text.

In interpreting the real meaning of our constitutional rights, two problems at once confront us. The obvious problem is to define the content of any specified right. The First Amendment clearly affirms "the right of the people peaceably to assemble." What is less clear is the precise scope of this right. When the police arrested those protesting the Vietnam War by "sitting in" at the premises of the Selective Service Office in Ann Arbor, were they violating this right? Does my constitutional right to "the freedom of speech" include my right to burn the flag of the United States? Legislators and judges, too, have interpreted the language of the Bill of Rights differently on this issue in recent years. And does the Fourth Amendment right of the people "to be secure in their persons, houses, papers and effects, against unreasonable searches and seizures" prohibit university officials from searching a dormitory room without the student's permission to find suspected drugs or stopping and searching my car to see whether I am transporting a half-consumed bottle of vodka? Finally, does the right to "life" presupposed by the due process clause of the Fifth and Fourteenth Amendments encompass the lives of the unborn fetus or the irreversibly comatose patient? The text of the Constitution defines our fundamental legal rights in terms of mere labels or short descriptions. Until we can define the meaning of these phrases in much more detail, we cannot use them to guide or regulate our legal practices in any effective way.

A much less obvious, but equally urgent, problem is interpreting the expression "the right to" or "a right to" as it is used in the Constitution and in the many court decisions that spell out the legal import of this basic text. Thus, not only is it as difficult as it is important to define the scope of life when one deliberates on the practical meaning of our constitutional right to life, but one must also decide precisely what it is to have a right to something, whether it be life or liberty or property. Those who think of rights as claims against others will interpret one's right to life primarily as a claim against others not to take one's life; those who think of rights as freedoms of choice and action may interpret this constitutional right as one's freedom to choose whether or not to continue living. On the former interpretation, one's right to life implies a duty of physicians and others not to put a terminally ill patient out of her misery no matter how urgently the patient begs for this merciful release; on the latter interpretation, the patient's right to life implies a right to die if and when the patient, if fully informed and still competent, so chooses.

Now it just so happens that jurists and philosophers have been pondering the language of rights for the past few decades and have attempted to explain the meaning of the expression "a right" as it occurs in legal and moral contexts. I have been actively involved in these jurisprudential and philosophical discussions and am in a position to make some observations on them. Let us see whether any of the more plausible recent conceptions of rights can help us to interpret the Bill of Rights.

Wesley Newcomb Hohfeld made a careful study of legal language, especially of the written opinions of the courts and the publications of the most influential jurists, and concluded that the expression "a right" is used ambiguously to refer to a legal liberty, a legal claim, a legal power, or a legal immunity. One party X has a legal liberty in face of some second party Y to do some action A if and only if X has no legal duty to Y not to do A. For example, I have a legal liberty in face of Professor Bryner, who arranged for me to speak at a conference, to pause and moisten my lips now because I have no legal duty to him not to do so. X has a legal claim against Y that Y do some act A if and only if Y has a legal duty to X to do A. Professor Bryner has a legal claim against me to deliver a lecture on the Bill of Rights at the conference because I have a contractual duty to him to deliver the lecture. X has a legal power over Y to bring about some legal consequence C for Y if and only if X is able to perform some voluntary action that would be recognized in the law as having this consequence for Y. Thus, Professor Bryner has the legal power of extinguishing my legal duty to lecture at the conference because he is able to release me from our contract by an act that would be recognized by a court of law as terminating my contractual duty to lecture. X has a legal immunity in face of Y against some legal consequence C if and only if there is no voluntary act of Y that would have legal consequence C for X. For example, I have a legal immunity against Professor Bryner's extinguishing my claim for remuneration because no matter how worthless he may consider my lecture there is nothing he can do that would be legally recognized as terminating my claim to be paid for lecturing.

Hohfeld argued that this ambiguity in the language of legal rights is unfortunate because it causes us to fail to distinguish between these four very different fundamental legal conceptions of four distinct irreducible legal relations. He also argued that, in the strict sense, the expression "a right" refers to a legal claim of one person against some second party because only the conception of a claim preserves the logical correlativity of rights and duties. He recommended, therefore, that we conceive of rights as simple claims.[3] On this view, what others would think of as my right that my audience not pelt me with rotten tomatoes is really a number of distinct but very similar rights, each of which is my claim against one or the other of the individuals comprising my audience not to throw any tomatoes at me.

Does Hohfeld's conceptual analysis help us to understand the language of the Constitution? In one respect I believe that it is very valuable indeed. He warns us that the expressions "a right" and "the right to" are highly ambiguous. Moreover, he encourages us to distinguish between those phrases in the Bill of Rights that refer to legal claims and those that refer instead to legal liberties or powers or immunities. Thus, he both helps to protect us against misreading this text and provides conceptual resources for a more accurate and precise interpretation of our fundamental legal rights.

Should we also adopt his proposal to reform our legal language and henceforth to use the expression "a right" only to refer to a single legal claim? I think not. Although this improved technical terminology might be useful in philosophy and jurisprudence where precision is at a premium, it might at the same time undo Hohfeld's valuable contribution to the art of interpreting the law by causing us to read our reformed use of the expression "a right" back into the Bill of Rights and thus overlook the ambiguities in its own language. It threatens thereby to tempt us to misconstrue some of our most important rights. On Hohfeld's conception of rights, for example, any genuine right to free speech must be primarily a claim against the government, and perhaps other individuals, that they not interfere with our public speaking; it could not be a liberty of speaking out in public on controversial issues. But it is the latter that is more central to this right and that gives point and purpose to the former. There would be little or no value to one's claim against interference with one's speaking if one were not at liberty to exercise this right by speaking publicly when one cares to do so.

Joel Feinberg accepts Hohfeld's contention that in the strict sense a right is a claim. But what is a claim? One does not find claims in the surrounding countryside as one finds clams along the beach or chairs around a table. What one does find are not claims, some mysterious sort of legal or moral objects, but claimings, acts of demanding what is due to one. Thus, I claim my coat when I present my claim check to the cloakroom attendant after the concert, and you might claim your money back if you have purchased a ticket to a play that was never performed. Accordingly, to have a claim is to be in a position to claim, to demand something as due to one.

Not every claim, however, is a right. There are often conflicting claims where there is only one right. If I have increased my potential income by contracting with two universities, Brigham Young and Harvard, to lecture at a conference on the same date, both institutions have legal claims that I lecture on their respective campuses on that date. But only one institution—presumably the one with whom I contracted first—can have a legal right that I deliver my lecture as promised, because it is impossible for me to keep both promises. Although both Harvard and Brigham Young had claims to my services, only the latter was a legally valid claim. This is shown by the fact that Harvard lost its case when both claimants sued for performance, which is why I lectured at Brigham Young. Therefore, Feinberg defines a right as a valid claim.[4] What makes a claim valid is that its recognition and satisfaction are called for by the relevant set of rules—legal rules in the case of legal rights and moral rules for moral rights.

Feinberg asks us to consider what would be lost in a community without rights. There might be values and virtues and even duties in Nowheresville, but no one would be in a position to claim anything as her due. To be sure, one could beg or petition for some favor, but there is all the difference in the world between appealing to the kindness or generosity of someone and insisting that another treat one as he is morally or legally obligated to do. This can be seen most dramatically in the history of black Americans. Slaves could, and sometimes did, request their masters to feed and clothe them adequately and not to abuse them. No doubt compassionate and conscientious masters did so without being asked. But when they did not, black Americans were not in a position to insist that their masters treat them as they ought to be treated. Later, free blacks became employees in a position to demand the salary or wages due to them whether or not their employers wished to pay them as contracted. Rights enable someone to insist on what is due, to stand on her rights, and to live as an equal with others in the community.

Feinberg's explanation of the value of rights, or at least *one* value of rights, can help us to interpret the Bill of Rights. It does not define any of the vague or ambiguous terms in that central legal text or directly settle disagreements over any of the essentially contested conceptions implicit in its language. What it can and does do is to show us the importance of adding a set of constitutional rights to a legal system already containing duties and obligations. By pointing to the distinctive value of rights to individual rightholders and to their society, it reminds us of what we need to preserve and enhance in our interpretation of our legal language if the Bill of Rights is to remain a valuable part of our constitutional law and not become a merely historical document that has outlived its usefulness to us and to our nation.

At the same time, Joel Feinberg's conception of a legal right as a legally valid claim shares the defect of Hohfeld's conception in that it requires us, or at least encourages us, to force all constitutional rights into the one mold of legal claims. If we succumb to this temptation, we will overlook the specific differences between our various fundamental rights—for example, the First Amendment liberty right peaceably to assemble, the Fifth Amendment immunity right not to be twice put in jeopardy of life or limb, and the Fifteenth Amendment power right to vote.

H. L. A. Hart recognizes the diversity of rights and attempts to formulate a general theory of rights by defining what is common to legal liberties, claims, powers, and immunities. Within this genus, he hopes to identify the specific differences between these four species of rights. Hart conceives of a legal right as a legally protected choice.[5] At the center of every right is a bilateral liberty, a liberty of acting or not acting in some specific manner. Around this core is a protective perimeter of duties of others not to interfere with the rightholder's exercise of her bilateral liberty. My legal right to scratch my head now, for example, consists of my legal liberty of scratching my head or not scratching my head as I choose, together with various legal duties of others not to interfere with my scratching or not scratching. These include Professor Bryner's legal duty not to tie my hand to my side to prevent me from scratching while I lecture at the conference, and a conference attendee's legal duty not to force me to scratch my head by threatening to shoot me if I refrain from so doing, and the legal duty of all others not to deprive me of my choice to scratch or not scratch by knocking me unconscious.

My legal right to scratch my head is an ordinary or garden variety of liberty right. A power right is a special kind of liberty right, one in which the rightholder has a bilateral liberty of exercising or not exercising some legal power. Thus, an attendee's legal right to give me the shirt off his back, assuming that he is not wearing a shirt that belongs to someone else, consists of his bilateral legal liberty of giving or not giving me this item of his property together with a protective perimeter of duties such as my duty not to force him to give me his shirt by twisting his arm, Professor Bryner's legal duty not to prevent him from giving me his shirt by gluing it to his back, and the duty of the other members of the audience not to threaten to tear him limb from limb if he selfishly chooses to retain his shirt. A legal claim right is in turn a special case of a power right, typically including three bilateral liberties at its center. My legal claim right to be reimbursed for the lecture consists of my bilateral liberty to cancel or not cancel Brigham Young University's legal duty to tender remuneration to me, my bilateral liberty to sue or not sue for compensation in the event that Brigham Young University fails or refuses to reimburse me as contracted, and my bilateral liberty to waive or not waive any payment ordered by the court when it decides in my favor, together with a protective perimeter of duties of others not to prevent me from exercising any of these central bilateral liberties. Finally, an ordinary immunity right consists of a bilateral liberty of waiving or not waiving some immunity—for example, my immunity from Professor Bryner's giving an attendee the shirt off my back—together with the usual sort of protective perimeter of duties. Thus it appears that Hart can conceive of all legal rights as legally respected choices while at the same time recognizing all four distinct species of rights.

What is especially relevant and helpful in Hart's conception when it comes to our interpretation of the Bill of Rights is his insight that what is distinctive about rights is that they concern the *distribution* of freedom in any society. Each right confers some specific freedom of choice and action upon the rightholder but also restricts the freedom of others by imposing duties of noninterference upon them. He thereby avoids both the temptation to think of rights as bare liberties, thus ignoring the duties they impose upon others, and the temptation to think of rights as claims, thus reducing rights to the relative duties of second parties. What we can and should learn from Hart is that the task of interpreting any of our fundamental constitutional rights is at least two-sided; we must define the scope of the liberty any right confers on its possessor *and* the range of duties it imposes on second parties.

Unfortunately, H. L. A. Hart's general theory of legal rights is not general enough to enable us to interpret all constitutional rights. He himself confesses that it does not enable us to interpret some of our fundamental immunity rights, such as our Fifth Amendment right not to be twice put in jeopardy of life or limb and our Thirteenth Amendment right not to be enslaved. The reason his conception cannot fit these rights is that Hart places a legally respected choice at the center of every genuine right. But since one cannot abrogate either of these constitutional immunities, one has no choice at all in these realms of the law. I would add that Hart's general theory also fails to explain any of our mandatory rights—for example, the child's right to a public education. Although every American child does have a legal liberty to attend a primary and then secondary school, this is *not* a bilateral liberty because no child has a liberty of playing truant or dropping out of school before the stipulated school-leaving age. Although the Bill of Rights does not, as far as I know, include any mandatory right—any right to perform a required action—it could do so. It would be quite possible to modify the Fifteenth Amendment by imposing a legal duty upon all citizens to exercise their constitutional right to vote; a mandatory right to vote is already contained in a few other legal systems. Hart's conception of rights would not be adequate to enable us to interpret the language of such a modified amendment.

I believe I can explain both unwaivable rights and mandatory rights because I do not place a choice at the center of his model of rights. I agree with Hart that rights function to distribute freedom but add that they also distribute control. I call one's freedom and control over some area of conduct "dominion." Hence, I conceive of a right as a system of Hohfeldian positions that, if respected, confer dominion on one party in face of one or more second parties in a potential confrontation over a specific domain.[6] In this view, my legal right to scratch my head now has at its core my legal liberty to scratch my head. The other half of Hart's bilateral liberty is not part of the core of *this* right, although it would belong in the core of my right to scratch or not scratch my head; it is one of the associated elements that function to confer freedom and control regarding this core upon the rightholder. Other associated elements include my legal claims against others that they not prevent me from scratching my head by physical restraint or beating me up or even threatening to do so, my legal powers to waive each of these claims, my bilateral legal liberties of exercising or not exercising each of these legal powers, and my legal immunity against other individuals that they not extinguish my liberty to scratch my head by any unilateral action. In addition to legal liberty rights, like my right to scratch my head, I recognize claim rights, power rights, and immunity rights.

The obvious virtue of my conception of a right is that it enables us to interpret all four species of constitutional rights in a way in which the theories of Hohfeld, Feinberg, and Hart cannot. This is because I hold that the modality of a right is determined by its core and that any of the four Hohfeldian legal advantages can constitute the core of a genuine right. Thus, the core of a liberty right can be either a bilateral liberty or a unilateral liberty. And a complex of legal positions with a claim or power or immunity at its core can also be a right in the very strictest sense as long as the entire structure functions, if respected, to confer dominion upon one party in some possible conflict of wills with one or more second parties.

There are, I am confident you will agree, no serious defects in this conception of a right. Still, some critics allege that it misses the point of our fundamental constitutional rights. I adopt an adversarial conception of rights. What is distinctive about a right is its relevance to some potential confrontation between two parties in some specific domain—for example, a conflict between some lecturer and some university about whether to tender reimbursement for a lecture of debatable value. But the primary function of

basic constitutional rights is not at all to distribute dominion—
what Hart called "small-scale sovereignty"—between the members of any society; it is to limit the sovereignty of the state over
its citizens and so protect each individual citizen from mistreatment at the hands of her government. Why was there all that
fuss back in 1791 about adding the Bill of Rights to an otherwise acceptable constitution? There was a very widespread distrust of the proposed strong federal government and a fear that it
would abuse the powers conferred upon it in the new Constitution.
And the gross violations of human rights by various governments
in recent years serve as constant reminders of our continuing
need for constitutional rights if we are to remain secure from
governmental mistreatment.

Ronald Dworkin advises that if we are to take our fundamental constitutional rights seriously, we should conceive of a right
as an individual trump over social goals.[7] All state action requires justification because every action of the government will
harm some members of the society. Thus, when the street on
which I live was made a one-way street, my interest in being able
to drive home from Washington University quickly and easily
was damaged because I am now legally required to use a more indirect and inconvenient route. Still, this state action was justified
because it resulted in a more efficient flow of traffic in my neighborhood and thereby benefitted most of my neighbors and many
of the visitors to my neighborhood more than it harmed me.
Now suppose that some governmental action not only injures
one of my interests but also invades one of my fundamental
rights—for example, taking my property without compensation
in order to enlarge the tiny park adjacent to my lot. Could this
action be similarly justified by the fact that the interests of the
many persons who will use the park outweigh the interest of a
single individual in retaining possession of or receiving compensation for his property? If the state could justify this invasion of
my individual right by an appeal to the public welfare, then my
right would make no difference to how the state ought to treat
me. It would be legally empty because it would impose no additional limitation upon governmental action and afford no special
protection to me. Therefore, the rights of individuals are worth
taking seriously only if they trump social goals so that they outweigh the appeal to social utility in political justifications.

What conceivably could trump social utility, the sum total of the interests of all the members of a society? Dworkin suggests that this could be only human dignity or political equality. He virtually combines these two considerations when he argues that all our specific political rights must be grounded upon and derived from a fundamental right to be treated with equal concern and respect, a foundation very different from that proposed by any utilitarian moral philosopher.

How might Dworkin's conception of a right help us to interpret the Bill of Rights? To apply any right to the case at hand, one must define the applicable right in the original sense, derived from the Latin verb *definire,* of setting boundaries to or drawing the limits of that right. Does the First Amendment right to free speech apply to political speech only or does it also apply to novels and movies and even to actions such as burning the American flag? Dworkin insists that it will devalue our individual right and undermine its essential purpose if the courts decide to include publicly useful speech within its scope but exclude socially harmful speech per se. Rather, the courts should ask whether prohibiting or restricting some controversial form of speech would involve giving less concern to the interests of and according less respect to the persons of those who might wish to speak in this way than to the interests and persons of other individuals in the society. Thus, he provides—or tries to provide—a criterion we can and should use in defining the scope of any constitutional right.

There are, however, some clauses in the Bill of Rights to which this criterion seems inapplicable because they confer rights quite alien to Dworkin's conception. If all rights, or at least all political rights, are *individual* trumps over *social* goals, then only individuals can possess constitutional rights and all constitutional rights hold against society or the state. How, then, shall we interpret the words "nor shall private property be taken for public use, without just compensation" in the Fifth Amendment? At first glance, the answer is obvious. This confers upon an individual owner a right against the government that it not take her property without providing her fair compensation for her loss. True enough, but that is not the whole story. This clause is also the constitutional basis for eminent domain, the right of the government to appropriate private property for public use.

Now this is a right of the state holding against some individual, surely no individual trump over social goals. Again, how shall we interpret the meaning of the Tenth Amendment? It reads, "The powers not delegated to the United States by the Constitution, nor prohibited by it to the States, are reserved to the States respectively, or to the people." This is one of the traditional sources of the doctrine of states' rights, and I believe that it does give constitutional recognition to some rights of the several states joined together in our federal government. But we can hardly use Dworkin's conception of rights of the individual holding against the state to help us to understand these constitutional rights.

Although Joseph Raz agrees with Dworkin that all rightholders must be individuals, he does not conceive of rights as necessarily holding between individual members of a society and their government. He conceives of a right as an interest-based reason for one or more duties.[8] More precisely, to say that someone has a right is to say that some interest of that individual is a sufficient reason for holding some other person or persons to be under a duty. Duties grounded upon rights may be negative duties not to damage or destroy the interest upon which they are based or positive duties to *do* something to preserve or promote that interest. Thus, rights function in practical reasoning, whether moral or legal, as intermediate terms between the interests upon which they are grounded and the duties which they in turn ground. By an interest, Raz means an aspect or component of someone's well-being; our interests normally include things like life, health, wealth, reputation, opportunity, and personal security.

Such interests are often in and of themselves not sufficient to justify the imposition of any duty upon second parties. Nevertheless, they may ground rights if they have a great importance derived from additional factors. For example, the interest of the average citizen in speaking freely on political issues is often less than his interest in receiving a large raise beginning next payday. Still, the former grounds a right to free speech, while the latter is an insufficient basis for any right, legal or moral, to a large raise. This is because the former interest has an importance derived from the fact that it is an interest in something necessary for, or at least highly conducive to, a viable democracy, a common good for all the members of the society. Accordingly, only the most important individual interests ground rights, and their importance need not be a function of their contribution to the well-being of the individual rightholder alone.

Raz can explain the constitutional rights of the states because in his theory states are individuals in the sense relevant to the capacity to be rightholders. It is an accepted principle of law, just as acceptable in morals, that corporate bodies are artificial persons equally capable with natural persons of possessing rights and being under duties. Whether or not it is true that what is good for General Motors is good for the United States, both private and public corporations have interests and can, therefore, possess moral and legal rights. It would appear that Raz has a more general conception of rights than Dworkin and can, therefore, interpret a broader range of our constitutional rights.

I very much doubt, however, that his conception is general enough. He defines a right as an interest-based ground for one or more duties. Powers and immunities seem to have no place in his theory of rights, but any adequate conception of rights must incorporate these essential Hohfeldian positions. How could Raz interpret the right to property presupposed by the due process clause of the Fifth and Fourteenth Amendments? I could hardly be said to own my pen or any other item of property if I lacked the legal power to dispose of it by selling it or giving it away and a legal immunity against being divested of my ownership by any unilateral action of another. Again, how can he explain our Fifteenth Amendment right to vote? Presumably this must be more than the ground of duties of others, private citizens and public authorities, not to prevent citizens from voting and even to assist them in so doing. At the core of this right must be their power to vote. Finally, how could Joseph Raz interpret the words, "Congress shall make no law abridging the freedom of speech," in which the Bill of Rights recognizes our fundamental right to free speech? Surely this clause must confer upon us a legal immunity from legislation that would unduly limit our liberty to speak publicly on controversial issues.

What can and should we learn from our cursory survey of alternative conceptions of rights? At the very least, that how one conceives of a right makes a difference to how one interprets the Bill of Rights. If one had no idea what the expressions "a right" and "the right to" mean, one literally could not read many portions of this text central to so much of our constitutional law.

And readers, whether they be judges deciding cases before their courts or administrators seeking to exercise their powers within the Constitution, will reach very different conclusions depending upon what they take rights to be. These differences will not be merely verbal or rhetorical; they will be substantial and will affect legal and political practice in important ways.

Unfortunately, we cannot find in the literature of philosophy or jurisprudence any fully adequate conception of rights. Each of the theories of rights that we have examined—and I am not aware of any that are more promising—proves unable to explain some of the provisions in the Bill of Rights. Since each conception selects certain aspects of the language of rights for special emphasis, it ignores other features of our ordinary language of rights. Hence, it fails to capture the full richness of our legal language. Worse yet, each conception tempts us to misread the legal text either by requiring some inappropriate meaning or by excluding the soundest interpretation.

Nevertheless, it would be a mistake to turn our backs on these alternative conceptions of rights. There is, as we have seen, something to be learned from each of these philosophical analyses of the language of rights. Since none is perfect and many are illuminating, we should use them all when we are interpreting the Bill of Rights. They contribute to our understanding of the text in a way analogous to, but not quite the same as, the *Oxford English Dictionary*'s several definitions of the expression "a right." They alert us to possible ambiguities in the language of rights and help to guard against confusing one meaning with another. But they also suggest divergent directions for the future development of our legal practices and thereby enable us to improve our constitutional law. Since law is a text-centered practice, new directions should grow out of the traditions we celebrated during this bicentennial; since law is a practice important in our individual lives and social welfare, we should interpret old texts in a way that will make the most of our living present and our future possibilities. If we use their contributions critically and imaginatively, philosophers and jurists can assist us in this common enterprise that means so much to us as individual citizens and to the United States as a constitutional democracy.

Notes

1. Stephen R. Munzer and James W. Nickel, "Does the Constitution Mean What It Always Meant?" *Columbia Law Review* 77 (1977): 1029, 1045.

2. John Rawls, "Two Concepts of Rules," *Philosophical Review* 64 (1955): 3.

3. Wesley Newcomb Hohfeld, *Fundamental Legal Conceptions as Applied in Judicial Reasoning* (New Haven, Conn.: Yale University Press, 1919), 23–114.

4. Joel Feinberg, *Rights, Justice, and the Bounds of Liberty: Essays in Social Philosophy* (Princeton, N.J.: Princeton University Press, 1980), 143–55.

5. H. L. A. Hart, *Essays on Bentham: Studies in Jurisprudence and Political Theory* (Oxford, Engl.: Clarendon Press, 1982), 162–93.

6. Carl Wellman, *A Theory of Rights: Persons under Laws, Institutions, and Morals* (Totowa, N.J.: Rowman and Allanheld, 1985), 81–119.

7. Ronald Dworkin, *Taking Rights Seriously* (Cambridge, Mass.: Harvard University Press, 1977), 184–205, 266–78.

8. Joseph Raz, *The Morality of Freedom* (Oxford, Engl.: Clarendon Press, 1986), 165–92.

II

CIVIL RIGHTS AND THE
U.S. CONSTITUTION

★

Rex Martin

SECTION ONE: BACKGROUND

In 1791, after initiation by the First Congress of the United States, the first ten amendments (familiarly called the Bill of Rights) were ratified by the states and thus were added to the U.S. Constitution. With this action, the momentous events of 1787 were brought to conclusion. In these four years a new U.S. Constitution (to replace the Articles of Confederation) had been written, argued about, ratified, and put into effect (with the inauguration of George Washington as first president, the meeting of the First Congress, and the appointment of the original cabinet and Supreme Court). And a Bill of Rights had been added.

Even though the Bill of Rights is technically a set of amendments to the Constitution of 1787, the rights identified there (in particular, in the First through Eighth Amendments) are conventionally regarded as part of the "original" Constitution of the United States. For not only did the Bill of Rights pick up the theme of rights of individual persons expressed in the Declaration of Independence, but it was also widely understood, after the ratification debates, to be on the agenda as a piece of unfinished business demanding early attention. This anticipated completion to

Rex Martin is a professor of philosophy at the University of Kansas.

the construction of the original Constitution was rapidly accomplished. At this two hundredth anniversary of the Bill of Rights, some reflection on the character of these rights and on their continuing significance is in order.

I want to begin with what I take to be a characteristic view—indeed, perhaps, the standard or prevailing view—of the relationship of majority-rule democracy to the rights of individual citizens, in particular those rights enshrined in the Bill of Rights. This view, for historical reasons, is often associated with James Madison, widely reputed to be one of the principal authors of the Constitution of 1787 and the main architect, in the First Congress, of the Bill of Rights amendments.[1]

Madison put what I have called the characteristic view into play in the *Federalist Papers* (No. 10 especially). Here it is argued that representative democracy, unlike direct democracy, would not readily succumb to the disease of faction—that is, to class-interested majority rule which is contrary to and invades the civil rights of some. But, though more compatible with such rights in point of practice, representative democracy—if my interpretation is correct—has some tendencies to the same abuse and therefore needs additional controls.[2]

External checks, over and beyond those afforded by the representative principle, are required to keep majority rule from mischief. The authors of the *Federalist Papers* suggest several such checks: bicameralism, separation of powers, federalism (all found in No. 51), and judicial review or the power of courts to declare laws unconstitutional and therefore void (found in No. 78). Later, in 1791, the Founders added a Bill of Rights to the U.S. Constitution. So we can include such a device on the list of external checks.[3]

My principal concern in bringing all this up is not so much with the institutional design afforded by the original American Constitution as with the historic rationale offered for it. That rationale, repeated by many subsequent writers down to the present time, is that majority rule is inherently inimical and threatening to civil rights in the long run and that we must control this adverse tendency in two ways: by establishing representative democracy in place of direct democracy, and by implementing external checks (that is, antimajoritarian checks) on representative democracy through devices such as separation of powers, judicial review, and a bill of rights.[4]

This rationale commands wide assent—or, at least, is widely repeated—as affording a sound account of the "republican remedy" to the democratic disease of the tyranny of majority faction. In particular, it gives us a presumably correct account of the relationship of majority rule to individual rights and thereby an accurate understanding of the constitutional status of the rights enumerated in the Bill of Rights as opposed to the lawmaking power of Congress.

SECTION TWO: CIVIL RIGHTS

Even though the rationale I have just described is perhaps prevalent, it has features that give me pause. For one thing, it reflects an estimate of democracy that might not be concurred in so readily today, since the eighteenth century took a less optimistic view of the prospects of a society organized by democratic institutions than perhaps we do at present. Accordingly, people nowadays might tend to allow for a more positive relationship between majority rule and civil rights than did our political forebears. Such an idea at least merits testing. For another—and this is the important point—the exceptional status accorded constitutional rights obscures the fact that such rights are civil rights.

Accordingly, it might be useful to think of constitutional rights (including those enshrined in the Bill of Rights) as, first of all, civil rights—while bearing in mind that civil rights (at least those in the United States) have been formed in an essentially majoritarian political process. Even if one rejects my point about how civil rights have been formed historically in this country, it still seems that a good understanding of constitutional rights in the United States can be gained by first analyzing such rights generically as civil rights and then, after that, by determining wherein they differ from ordinary, garden-variety civil rights. In any event, this is the procedure I follow in the present section and the one next in this essay. We begin, then, with civil rights—with their character as a genus and with the kind of justification appropriate to them, generically.

Civil rights are universal political rights within a given society. They are beneficial ways of acting, or ways of being treated, that are specifically recognized and affirmed in law for each and all the citizens there (or, ideally, for all individual persons there) and that are promoted or maintained by the actions of those on whom directions for conduct have been laid (including at some point, necessarily and always, the actions of government agents).[5]

Civil rights are rights of each and all by design, by express intention. They represent a social commitment. Some civil rights are important because they have a distinctive moral pedigree (of the sort associated with human rights). And the social commitment to them, presumably, reflects this consideration to one degree or another. But social commitment could be there even in cases where that moral pedigree was lacking or was negligible.

Consider, for example, a society that makes not just medical care available to all citizens, as a civil right to a service provided, but also a high level of dental care—or, beyond that, all sorts of other expensive medical procedures (face lifts, hair transplants). The goals of people in doing this are not merely hygienic but largely cosmetic. They put a premium on certain appearances (as most societies do, though few would make it a matter of social commitment). Such cosmetic medical and dental treatment could be a universal political right to a certain kind of treatment (in the case at hand, a provision of service) available to each and all the citizens, promoted and maintained by government action and at considerable cost. I doubt, though, that many people would regard this civil right as a human right; it lacks the appropriate moral backing. Nonetheless, it is important in that society; it represents an express commitment to providing a service for each and all.

Thus, all civil rights are important rights and all reflect a high level of social commitment. But not all can be justified as representing individuated and practicable and universal moral claims which serve as proper conclusions to sound arguments from objective principle(s) of critical morality. Hence, not all can be justified as human rights. Nonetheless, all are susceptible of being justified in a distinctive way, in accordance with one and the same pattern—and we turn to that pattern now.

The governing supposition is that all rights are, in some way, beneficial to the rightholder. Thus, all civil rights (all universal political rights), in being true to this notion, could be represented as identifying ways of acting, or ways of being acted toward, which would upon reflection be claimed by each person; for these claimed ways of acting or of being treated are, arguably, part of the "good" of each person or instrumental to it. A particular line of conduct (or of treatment) might be established, then, on the foundation that it was in the perceived interest of each and all the members. Each could plausibly claim it for herself or for himself and acknowledge it for all others on the very same basis (that it was part of *their* good, or a means to it).

Thus, a given civil right, as found in law, can be regarded as so grounded if it can plausibly be said to be, and could widely be understood to be upon reflection, in the interest of each and all—as constituting a part of the good for them or as a reliable means to it. Of course, we might not ever be in a position to say that literally all civil rights policies are in the interest of each and all, but we do have adequate evidence for saying that many long-established civil rights—assuming here that a concurrent and highly favorable social opinion exists in their case—are justifiable on the regulative standard of mutual perceived benefit. The fact that all civil rights are important, the point with which this discussion began, rides piggyback on the very justifying norm here identified.

Mutual perceived benefit is not as such a moral notion. To be that it would have to be brought into line with overt moral norms—those of conventional morality or, to stay with the case at hand, the principles of a critical morality. And this would involve taking another step, a distinct step beyond the perception of mutual benefit. If this is so, then such benefit can correctly be affirmed (and used as justification) even though the right in question has not been, or cannot be, justified in the way appropriate to a human right. (This was the point of the cosmetic dental care example.)

By *justified* I mean, then, merely that the idea relied on in the case of any civil right is fulfilled. For the presumption of mutual benefit has been cashed in. The presumption holds good here in a given case: what is, legally speaking, a civil right is actually a way of acting (or of being treated) that is plausibly understood to be in everybody's interest—or would be understood to be, upon reflection. Hence, a justified civil right is simply a universal legal right that, in satisfying the criterion of mutual perceived benefit, meets the justifying standard for all civil rights.

It is always feasible to bring this standard to bear on any universal political right, regardless of what other standards (in particular, moral ones) might have bearing in a given case as well.

Thus, the standard of mutual perceived benefit sets an appropriate and uniform justifying pattern for all civil rights.

It follows from this account of civil rights and of mutual perceived benefit as their justifying norm that civil rights are equal rights for each citizen, for each subject of law. They are equal in two respects. First, all citizens (with but a few well-accredited exceptions: children, perhaps prisoners) have these rights fully and have them on the same basis. Second, and more important, these rights are equal in an important respect for each citizen. The rule that formulates the way of acting (or of being treated) identifies the *same* way for each and all of the citizens.

SECTION THREE: CIVIL RIGHTS AS CONSTITUTIONAL RIGHTS

As I suggested in the previous section, all civil rights represent social commitment—some for reasons of moral pedigree (at least that in part) and some for other reasons (and not necessarily bad ones either). Without putting too fine a point on it, we can say that a society that had civil rights would probably afford such rights a fairly high standing, as measured by the resources committed and by the competitive weight of such rights in relation to other considerations. And the whole set of civil rights would reflect a major social commitment.

Let us note one further step. A people might take the making of laws and policies that are in the interest of each and all to be the principal political object in their society. They would thereby give a certain priority to civil rights, individually and as a set, over other possible competing values (over, for example, the common good understood collectively, over the advantage and interests of a certain class, over holiness, and so on).

A definite ordering of options would emerge here. In such a society policies or laws would conform to the following schedule of priorities: (i) those that are in the interest of each and all; and, where (i) is satisfied or, alternatively, not at issue, then next (ii) those interests, such as national defense or the growth of GNP, that are in the corporate or collective interests of the group of which each is a member (though not necessarily in the interests of each); and, where both (i) and (ii) are satisfied or, alternatively, neither is at issue, then finally (iii) those policies that are in the interests of indeterminately many (presumably a majority), though not in the interests of some (presumably a minority).

Let me clarify (iii). Sometimes interests are hurt under this third option (always the interests of a minority) and some of the interests hurt are *not* interests of each and all or interests of the corporate group. The priority ranking I have identified would allow such a possibility. But if the interests hurt here are in fact interests that come under either (i) or (ii), then this would not even be allowed—given the already established priority of the first and second options over the third. Thus, the only policies permissibly involved in option three are those policies that are compatible with policies under the first two options—that is, only (iiia) those policies that concern interests the helping or hurting of which is compatible with serving interests under (i) or (ii). Accordingly, packages of interests (where the interests, say, of group A and of group B are supported by a majority coalition of A and B) are allowable on this account, if they conform to (iiia).

In sum, the ordering of permissible options, put in terms of the interests involved, is (i) over (ii) and (i) or (ii) over (iiia). But some policies—(iiib) policies that concern interests the helping or hurting of which is incompatible with serving interests under the first two options—would be ranked last and ruled impermissible.[6]

Suppose we have, then, a society in which priority (as just described) has been given to civil rights, individually and as a set, over other possible competing values—over collective or corporate goods, such as national defense or the growth of GNP, which are not necessarily in the interest of each and all the members, and over permissible mere-majority interests of the sort identified in (iiia). Here we could say that civil rights are politically fundamental in that society and, in a sense, constitute part of its body politic or "basic structure" (in Rawls's sense).[7] In such a case I think it would be proper to use the terms 'civil rights' and 'constitutional rights' interchangeably.

But the set of civil rights need *not* be given priority (and in many societies is not, even when such rights do exist there). Thus, we have an important ground for differentiating civil rights generically from those civil rights that are constitutional ones.

Constitutional rights are civil rights that—individually and as a set—have priority, within a given political society, over other important norms (such as national security or aggregate welfare) that are not rights and over rights that are not universal, over rights that are not rights of each and all but, rather, rights open only to a few or to a particular class (say, rights that attach to a particular role—like the tenure rights of college and university faculty—or rights that are grounded in some localized and partial undertaking—like the contractual rights of factory workers in industry C or in plant D).

If we were to speak of constitutional rights in the sense just indicated we would mean simply civil rights insofar as belonging to a set of such rights in a situation where that set had a standing priority over other normative considerations—over nonrights and over rights that were not universal. For purposes of ready reference I will call a society in which this priority obtains a system of rights.

But other senses of 'constitutional' would not be implied in the case at hand. Thus, we would not necessarily mean by 'constitutional' those rights that were written down in a document called "The Constitution" (though there would, of course, be nothing wrong with listing all such rights in such a document— adding to, deleting from, modifying the list as time went on).

The notion of 'constitutional' we are contemplating is quite precise. Thus, if a society today was a system of rights (and, hence, civil rights were given the sort of priority described) and cosmetic dental care or facelifting was a civil right in that country's set of rights, then the right to such care would be a constitutional right in the sense intended. Or, to take another example, if education (through age sixteen or age eighteen) was a civil right there, then the right to education would be a constitutional right (in the sense intended) regardless of whether it appeared by name in the national charter or had been endorsed as 'constitutional' within the appropriate traditions of parliamentary or of judicial interpretation.

I do not regard the sense of 'constitutional' developed here to be peculiar (in some bad sense). It reflects the ancient Greek sense of a city-state's constitution (*politeia*) as the correct or prescribed arrangement of the "parts" of that city, emphasizing those parts that were most important. In the same sense, we speak of a person as having a sound constitution (meaning that the parts of that person's body, especially the most important ones, are correctly set up and arranged from the point of view of health and longevity).

The Constitution of the United States (the document) is a part of the American constitution. Its job is to set out the correct or prescribed arrangement of the parts of government (the branches of the federal government and their separation, the division of powers between the federal and state governments, and so on) and explicitly to state some of the other essentials as well. The statement it makes is authoritative and public and agreed-upon; the statement affirms the essentials named and commits the American people to them for an indefinite future.

The important thing, for our purposes, is that the rights enumerated in the Constitution (for example, rights in the body of the Constitution—such as habeas corpus, the right not to be held in involuntary confinement unless charged or sentenced—and the rights in the Bill of Rights, in the First through the Eighth Amendments, and the right to vote, as originally secured in Article I and then modified by subsequent amendments: the Fifteenth, Seventeenth, Nineteenth, Twenty-fourth, and Twenty-sixth) and some other constitutional rights as well (such as the right of privacy) are understood to be among the most important things, to be among the institutional essentials in the (unwritten) American constitution. Thus, at least the beginnings of an argument could be made that, in the United States, some civil rights have priority, individually and as a set, and that such rights are properly called 'constitutional' for that reason.

It follows, though, that the main priority rule for civil rights would undergo an important modification in light of this analysis of the institutional essentials in a system of rights (in the case at hand, the American constitution). Civil rights do not have priority over the *other* institutional essentials, where these essentials had the job either of producing civil rights (as do the democratic institutions, if my earlier suggestion is credited) or of protecting them (as do such checking devices as judicial review or separation of powers). Here civil rights would have to be compatible with these other institutional essentials (just as these institutions would have to be compatible not only with civil rights but with each other as well).

Accordingly, if we were to speak of civil or constitutional rights in the way just indicated—as institutional essentials within the constitution of a well-wrought system of rights (such as I am alleging the American constitution might be, or might be considered to be)—we would mean simply civil rights insofar as belonging to a set of such rights in a situation where that set (i) was compatible with rights-producing and rights-protecting institutional essentials and (ii) had a standing priority over other considerations—over nonrights (such as the corporate good and mere-majority interests) and over rights that were not universal—at least within a certain domain (the public domain).

And if a civil right has the sort of priority indicated, then a certain way of acting, or of being treated, is guaranteed in a given society (that is, specified in law and maintained for all who have the right) over against these other considerations. But such a guarantee is to be understood as involving not simply such a high degree of protection but also the use of the offices of government to harmonize rights in a principled way. For civil rights must be harmonized toward one another if conflict is to be avoided within and between them and a coherent set of rights is to be formed. And such coherence is necessary *if* rights (in turn) are to be compatible with the other institutional essentials and if they are, as a set, to have the requisite priority over these other considerations.

Political agencies ought, in principle at least, to be able—through judicious partitioning and limitation of scope, internal modifications within scopes, and assignment of competitive weight in zones of overlap—to adjust constitutional rights one to another. Where these rights have been satisfactorily balanced definitionally, they cannot conflict with one another. Within its assigned scope and given its determinate weight, a well-defined constitutional right simply governs all applicable situations that arise in the domain of rights.

By the same token, if the relation between a well-defined right (e.g., the right to free political speech or to habeas corpus or to vote) and other important considerations (e.g., the interest in national security) is set up in the same way, then that right would literally govern all applicable situations. The right would dominate the collective concern in the zone where they overlapped, at least under favorable circumstances.

It is important to see even here, however, that the priority I have argued for—the priority of policies in the interests of each and all and, hence, of civil rights—is not absolute. For circumstances are not always favorable, and there are situations in which the priority of individual civil rights would not hold, even after careful scope adjustment and competitive weighting have been given their full due.

Suppose, for example, a crisis situation developed in which national survival could not be assured without restrictions on rights (as, for instance, was presumably the case during the American Civil War when the right of habeas corpus was suspended by Lincoln). In such a case rights as a set and any right within the set can be restricted on an emergency or interim basis and restricted either equally or unequally. But the correct understanding of such a crisis is not that a corporate good (here national security) now takes precedence over rights; rather, the restriction on rights is undertaken here in order that rights as a set can survive.

The two social interests, (a) having a set of civil rights and (b) national security, coincide at this point. Thus, it would be senseless to say that rights as a coordinated set have an absolute priority over corporate aggregative concerns or that particular rights always prevail or always should prevail over corporate goods. There is, then, no all-out priority of rights over such aggregative values. But it is also the case, even in such emergency situations as the one we have envisioned, that such corporate goods are not to be allowed in a system of rights to *supersede* civil or constitutional rights.[8]

SECTION FOUR: BASIC RIGHTS AND CONSTITUTIONAL RIGHTS

In the previous section I have argued that civil rights are constitutional rights if they (as a coherent set) have priority, individually and as a set, over nonrights considerations and over nonuniversal rights. And I have tried to give some content to this notion of priority and to defend, in the course of the discussion, priority as a criterion for constitutionality.

I want now to consider an important challenge to my account. Americans—their judges in particular—seem to distinguish basic rights from other rights and to identify constitutional rights with basic rights in particular. One could say, then, that my analysis was defective on this very point. The tie-in of rights with constitutionality should run only to *basic* civil rights. And priority—which continues, by the way, to attach to basic civil rights—becomes now a secondary and derivative criterion for constitutional status, the first being basicness.

Of course, there is considerable diversity of opinion as to how basicness is to be determined. Accordingly, we should devote some attention to the possible introduction of standards of priority *internal* to the class of civil rights. We could, for example, revert to the earlier distinction (in section two) between those civil rights that were morally based (in a way appropriate to human rights) and those that were not, with priority presumably going to the former, as somehow more basic. Or we could rely on other standards to determine basicness: we could revert to standards of political justice, as with Rawls; or of personhood, as with Nozick; or of natural rights, as with Locke and the Founders (and many early jurists); or of conventional moral or religious judgment or what have you.

Now, the philosophical theories called on here are themselves inherently controversial (when judged by standards of rational coherence and generative power that are appropriate to philosophy); but this is, most likely, going to be true of any philosophical theory and should not be counted against these theories in particular. A more important consideration, though, is that philosophical theory as such is not a primary concern. Theory— be it Locke's or Rawls's or Nozick's—simply was not written into the Constitution.

Of course, there are philosophical ideas in the Constitution and behind it, such as the idea of separation of powers (derived from classical philosophy and from Locke and Montesquieu). But mastery of these ideas, in their mode as philosophical ideas, is not required in constitutional interpretation.

Much—perhaps most—of the interpretation of the rights enumerated in the Bill of Rights, for example—by lawmakers, chief executives, judges, law professors, reflective members of the public—does not rest on a philosophical theory that allegedly justifies these rights as basic. Or, at least, it can be said that no single such theory has been consistently turned to. Rather, what does appear to be relied on (in actual discussion of the Bill of Rights) is such things as historical judgments about "the rights of Englishmen" (rights of the colonists) or common law or the American tradition or political judgments about what is essential to decent or civilized life.

What appears to ground basicness (in this view of constitutional rights) is a common estimate of importance, by the Founders and by us, as mediated in the history of the nation itself. If anything, then, it could be plausibly maintained that the most secure standard for regarding some rights as basic is the conventional judgment—both popular and expert—that they are basic.

At this point, though, a further note is often introduced. For some want to say that it is not basicness as conventionally perceived that counts decisively—not even when that convention constitutes a widely shared and long-running social consensus—but, rather, the Constitution itself. In short, the best ground, on this amended version, for regarding some rights as basic is that they are enumerated in the Constitution, the supreme law of the land. This is still a conventionalist account of sorts, for it does focus on the convention embodied in and expressed in the Constitution, but it limits attention to that one convention, as written down, and to it alone.

Thus, Robert Bork (who exemplifies this view) says that both majority rule and judicial review are profoundly limited by those rights, but only by those rights, that are specified in the *text* of the Constitution or that *derive* "from the governmental processes established by the Constitution." These are the only basic rights Americans have. Save for these rights, majority rule can do anything it wants. And judges (paying attention to the text and to the intentions of the Framers) can hold only these rights, and no others, up as grounds for annulling an otherwise legitimate statute.[9] This radically text-based version does bring certain difficulties in its train, though. For one thing, it calls into question the old rationale of the status of basic rights as *external* checks on majority rule.

Let us recall two points here in setting up this particular consideration. First, the Constitution of 1787 was itself ratified by special conventions, voting on a majority-rule basis, in the several states. Second, every amendment has been passed on a majority-rule basis—indeed, a supermajoritarian basis—by a two-thirds vote in each house of the Congress of the United States and almost all of them ratified (again on a majority-vote basis) by the legislatures of three-quarters of the states. Thus, the rights in the text of the Constitution—including, of course, the rights of the Bill of Rights—are themselves there *by virtue* of majority votes.

So, if one holds a conventionalist view of why some rights are basic and points to their presence in the Constitution (in the way Bork did) as *the* necessary and conclusive ground that they are to be regarded as basic, then one cannot consistently adhere as well to the historic rationale that constitutional rights are external checks (that is, essentially nonmajoritarian checks) to majority rule or that majority rule is itself inherently inimical and threatening to civil rights in the long run.

Let me add, as an aside, that I personally would welcome any such conclusion as going against the historic rationale and as lending support to my earlier suggestion of a positive relationship between civil rights and majority rule. But any such conclusion is not decisive in these matters; for one would still need to show in particular that majority rule is characteristically conducive to rights and is not intrinsically incompatible with them.[10]

In any event, whether the Borkian text-based conventionalist account tells ultimately, and upon reflection, against the historic rationale (often associated, as I said, with the views of Madison) is not our chief concern here. Rather, we want to determine whether such an account affords a good or even an acceptable ground for regarding some rights, namely those enumerated in the Constitution, as basic.

In my judgment, this account has things backwards. We do not say that the rights of the Bill of Rights are basic *because* they are incorporated in the written Constitution; instead, we say that they should be so incorporated because of the inherent importance they have. They cannot have this requisite importance simply by being incorporated into the written Constitution. To put the same point differently, one might believe as an act of Constitutional piety that the rights of the Bill of Rights have importance simply in virtue of their being in the Constitution; but one could not explain or justify their being there in the first place, for that reason.

Thus, to assign importance or basicness to the rights in the Bill of Rights solely on the ground of their being incorporated into the written Constitution, or solely on the basis of appeal to the history of successful constitutions (as Rawls in effect does) is to beg the crucial question.[11] For the crucial question is, what could explain that incorporation in the first place?

Why should the right of habeas corpus and the rights of the Bill of Rights and the right to vote be incorporated into the written Constitution? An appropriate explanatory answer would, I think, include two kinds of considerations: (a) those bearing on the Constitution itself (as a public, authoritative, agreed-on charter having the status of supreme law of the land, designed to lay out the institutional essentials of the American body politic); and (b) those bearing on civil rights as constitutional rights.

Regarding (a), that is, the Constitution itself, an appropriate answer would include the claim that these rights should be incorporated because the written Constitution identifies the institutional essentials and directs the behavior of legislators and administrators and judges. The citizens want the governmental agents to promote certain rights—certain ways of acting and of being treated; they want, so far as practical, to put action hurtful to these matters beyond legislative or judicial reach. So they incorporate the important rights—the rights of the Bill of Rights and so on—into the written Constitution, or include them (in some other way) among the institutional essentials.

Regarding (b), that is, civil rights as constitutional rights, another line of argument would come into play. What *explains* the constitutional status of some civil rights is that they are widely regarded as ways of acting, or ways of being treated, that should be recognized and maintained for everyone—*because* they are perceived (reasonably perceived, we presume, as a matter of social consensus) to be in the interest of each and all. It is the perception of mutual benefit for all (the judgment, upon reflection, that these things really are for the perceived good of each, or a means to it) that makes these particular ways of acting, or of being treated, important. And when people are willing to pay the costs of giving these ways priority over nonrights values and over rights that are not similarly universal, then the civil rights in question have the status—or ought to have the status—of constitutional rights.

Thus, the correct (explanatory) account of civil rights as constitutional rights is wholly consistent with the one given earlier by conventionalism, but with two provisos added. The gloss provided by Constitutional piety (of the Borkian text-based sort) is abandoned as explanatorily (and justificationally) empty. And the conventional judgment of basicness is not taken straight but, rather, is regimented by certain concerns. It is, in fact, structured by considerations familiar from themes developed earlier in this essay.

Specifically, it is structured (i) by the *universal* character of a particular designated way of acting (or of being treated) within the body politic; and (ii) by the satisfaction, by that way, of the justifying criterion of mutual perceived benefit (and, hence, by the *importance* of that way of acting/being treated). It is structured (iii) by the *willingness* (upon due reflection) of the political agencies and of the citizens generally to pay the costs of affording *priority* to that way of acting, or of being treated, and by their commitment to bring that way within the set of rights that, having priority over other kinds of normative considerations, must itself be continuously harmonized. And this last point—involving as it does scope adjustments and competitive weightings, with the goal of adjusting civil rights to nonrights (like national security) and of harmonizing such rights with one another (so as to avoid conflicts and thereby achieve coherence)—is a messy and time-consuming and often frustrating business. So it is structured, finally, (iv) by the citizens' willingness and the political agencies' willingness to *tolerate* and live with such a messy business as this.

These four points (as summarized in the italicized words in the paragraph above) constitute the points of conceptual structure, of rigor, that my analysis of civil rights as constitutional rights introduces into the conventional account of basicness. They identify hurdles that ways of acting/being treated must surmount in order to become constitutional rights. Or, at least, we can say that a successful crossing would *explain* such status in a given case.

What I have tried to suggest in the discussion (in this section) is that a non-question-begging account (one that actually explains why some civil rights are constitutional rights) should focus on what plausibly explains the constitutional status of *some* civil rights. For we can assume that not every civil right will make all the jumps indicated. The civil right to cosmetic dental care and hair transplants, were there such a right, probably would not; but the civil right to an education through age sixteen, say, probably would.

The problem with the Borkian text-based approach to constitutional rights is simply that it is question-begging at the crucial point. And an *unguided* conventionalist approach, minus what little rigor has been supplied it by a text-based approach, is simply too amorphous, too "squishy" to do the job of explaining why certain specific, actual rights are constitutional rights. But a conventionalist approach that has been carefully structured—using the four-point schema I have just been describing—and that has been cut entirely free from the question-begging Bork approach would seem to do the job. And it can do the job without the debilitating liabilities, pointed out at the beginning of the present section, that have attended most philosophical theories of basicness.

Now that this point has been made, let me emphasize that I see no objection to developing an account of basic rights *within* the class of constitutional rights. Indeed, some such move (whether it be engineered by common esteem or by a sound, well-constructed philosophical theory like that offered in Rawls's more recent work) will probably be necessary if the task of harmonization is to be carried out successfully.[12]

It should be noted, however, as we conclude the discussion in this section, that a difference in competitive weight *between* two constitutional rights can be allowed for in the account I have given. It would not disrupt the earlier analysis of the priority of civil rights. For that priority, as we understood in the previous section, was simply the priority of civil rights over nonrights considerations and over rights that are not universal within the body politic—and, we might now add, of civil rights over universal rights that were not themselves constitutional. Hence, the original status of civil rights as constitutional would not be jeopardized where the priority just named persisted, even though the exercise of one constitutional right might yield to another and more basic one, generally or on a given occasion.

We might, for instance, decide to admit something like the following as a standard of basicness: long-term and very widespread esteem, amounting to a concurrent and highly favorable social opinion respecting, say, many old, well-established constitutional rights. These old and time-tested rights, then, would be among our basic constitutional rights. They would, accordingly, have a greater weight in competition with any nonbasic constitutional right. Thus, to cite just a single possible example, the First Amendment right to the nonestablishment of religion (as basic) might outweigh certain features of one's right to an education (as nonbasic).

However, I will not press this idea of differential weights between basic and nonbasic constitutional rights. For it takes us away from what has been our chief concern in this essay: what makes something a *constitutional* right in the first place. Let us stay, then, with that concern.

SECTION FIVE: THE SPECIAL STATUS
OF THE BILL OF RIGHTS

The argument I have conducted has certain problematic consequences for the paradigmatic American constitutional rights: the right of habeas corpus (found in the body of the Constitution), the rights of the Bill of Rights in the First through Eighth Amendments, and the right to vote (as secured in Article I and modified by subsequent amendments). These rights cannot be regarded as constitutional (or basic) simply because they are part of the written Constitution. And, given the analysis I have favored, some of them (for example, some of the rights of the Bill of Rights) may *not* count as constitutional rights at all, nowadays. I say this because political agencies and citizens are unwilling to accord these rights the requisite priority standing.

For example, the Fifth Amendment specifies, among other rights, that "no person shall be held to answer for a capital, or otherwise infamous crime, unless on a presentment or indictment of a Grand Jury." For another, the Sixth Amendment states that "in all criminal prosecutions, the accused shall enjoy the right to a speedy and public trial, by an impartial jury," which shall, by the standards of common law then current, consist of *exactly twelve persons* and which shall reach any verdict of guilty by a *unanimous vote of all twelve.* (And here, it is important to note, the italicized features are necessary elements in the Constitutional idea of trial by jury.) For a third, the Seventh Amendment specifies that "in Suits at common law, where the value in controversy shall exceed twenty dollars, the right of trial by jury shall be preserved."

It is most unlikely that any of these rights would ever be accorded priority, ever be thought important enough to outweigh *any* and all nonrights considerations on every or almost every occasion. Certainly, we can say that such priority has not been accorded—at least not in *state* laws and constitutions, even at the time of adoption of the Bill of Rights amendments or of relevant later amendments (such as the Fourteenth [1868]), or at some later date with such amendments in clear view.[13]

Nonetheless, *most* of these rights—the right of habeas corpus, the *other* rights in the Bill of Rights, the right to vote—would count as constitutional, given the crucial tests of constitutionality outlined in the previous section—though others probably would as well (for example, the right to an education). In any case, though, no special status is accorded to the Bill of Rights per se or to these other rights in the text of the Constitution. For these rights are not the only constitutional rights or even the preeminent ones. The rights of the Bill of Rights are simply some of the constitutional rights—some, among others—that citizens or persons have under American law.

Whence, then, the special status that the Bill of Rights seems to occupy? That status, I would suggest, is largely a matter of history. The Bill of Rights is one of the great rights documents of the eighteenth century. It is, indeed, one of the two most important public manifestos of rights produced by Americans in that century, the other being the famous prefatory paragraphs followed by the catalogue of grievances in the Declaration of Independence.

But the historical importance of the Bill of Rights is not confined to its century of origin or to the incidental fact of its present great age. Rather, two other significant historical events—one in the century previous to our own and one in the present century—have helped change the status of the Bill of Rights and radically transform its character. Hence, the Bill of Rights is not now of *merely* historical significance.

Let me describe these two transforming events briefly and then go into somewhat greater detail. In a very early decision (*Barron v. Baltimore* [1833])[14] the Supreme Court had ruled that the Bill of Rights amendments did not bind the states but only the federal government. However, the Court in this century has begun to "incorporate" certain of the Bill of Rights protections into the Fourteenth Amendment (1868) as holding against the states too.

The Fourteenth Amendment, then, is the first of the two transforming events I spoke of earlier. It is the one that belongs to the
century before our own; it came *after* the decision of 1833 and
substantially changed the picture. And the "incorporation" of
parts of the Bill of Rights into the Fourteenth Amendment as a
standard for *state* laws, an event of our own century, is the second
of the important transforming events.

Let us look at these two events in greater detail, starting with
the Fourteenth Amendment. That amendment is one of three
passed by Congress and ratified by the states in the period immediately after the Civil War. These three amendments radically
changed the American constitution—so much so that the period
after the war, the so-called period of Reconstruction, is sometimes called the Second American Revolution.

The first of these amendments, the Thirteenth (1865), abol-
ished slavery, an institution that had been recognized and protected in the original Constitution of 1787 and that had led to
continual sectional strife from that time on, culminating in the
bloody Civil War itself. The Fourteenth (1868) was complex; it
had several sections. The first and most important section I will
describe in detail below. Finally, the Fifteenth Amendment
(1870) enfranchised the blacks by saying that states could not
disallow people from voting on such grounds as their "race, color,
or previous condition of servitude."

As I said, the various provisions of section 1 of the Fourteenth
Amendment lie at the heart of the matter. The section begins with
a definition of citizenship (both state and U.S. citizenship) and says,
next, that no *state* shall by law "abridge the privileges or immunities of citizens of the United States." Following that came two
other important clauses (as these are often called): the "due process"
clause and the "equal protection of the laws" clause.[15]

There is much debate about what these clauses meant ("privileges and immunities," etc.); but three things do seem reasonably
clear here. The authors of the amendment were trying to state
longstanding American (indeed, human) political values—values
that can be traced back in our own history at least to the Declaration. The authors were trying to address the problem of the civil
status of the freed blacks by making them citizens on a par, in
certain respects, with all other citizens. And finally, the authors
were consciously laying the groundwork for certain *national* stan-

dards that would hold throughout the country and would shape or help shape state as well as federal laws.[16]

Thus, regarding this last point in particular, we should note that there is an interesting duplication of language between the Fifth Amendment (which is binding, as part of the Bill of Rights, on federal action) and the Fourteenth (which explicitly governs state action). Both amendments say, identically, that *persons* shall not be deprived of "life, liberty, or property, without due process of law." In addition, the "privileges and immunities" clause is very similar to (but not identical with) the language of Article IV, section 2, of the Constitution of 1787.

No doubt, part of the intent of the authors of the Fourteenth Amendment, in using these phrasings in the amendment, was to provide backup language in the Constitution in support of the Civil Rights Act of 1866. For the constitutionality of that act had been challenged (even by some of its supporters) and it had been vetoed as unconstitutional by President Andrew Johnson, who had succeeded to that office on the assassination of President Lincoln in 1865.

Now, we do have (in the identical "due process" language of the Fifth and Fourteenth Amendments) loopholes or entry points whereby the protections of the Bill of Rights can be moved over and incorporated into the Fourteenth as holding against the states and the protections of the Fourteenth can, in some appropriate cases, be moved over and incorporated into the Fifth as holding against the federal government. But if we are going to talk about incorporation (which eventually did happen), I would prefer to take a more straightforward, robust approach.

The rights listed in the Bill of Rights are constitutional rights of American citizens (so far as federal law is concerned). They have a self-standing warrant, as specified in the text or in constitutional interpretation of the Bill of Rights, and seem (most of them) to count as important and basic in both popular and official estimate. They mandate a certain standard of equal treatment (under the laws) for all U.S. citizens. And they are certainly "privileges or immunities" of citizens of the United States in virtue of that citizenship, as defined in the Fourteenth Amendment.

Why not simply say, then, that it is the *whole* first section of the Fourteenth Amendment that allows the incorporation? And add that, where the federal government engages in activities substantially identical to state activity (for example, in running elementary and secondary schools in the District of Columbia, as it did at the time of *Brown v. Board of Education* [1954][17]), it is subject to the same constraints (as given in section 1 of the Fourteenth Amendment) as any state. In this way, we remove the appearance of loopholes, of arbitrary entry points, and help relieve suspicion that a dubious doctrine of due process (called "substantive due process") has been resurrected in the implementation of the incorporation thesis.

With these preliminaries in hand, let us move now to our own century, to the second main transforming event in the history of the Bill of Rights: to the details of incorporation. This story can be told quickly enough. In a number of twentieth-century cases, most notably in Justice Black's dissent in the *Adamson v. California* decision (1947), various "incorporationist" theses were advanced. But at no time has the Court said *explicitly* and officially (in a majority opinion) that *all* of the rights in the Bill of Rights (specifically those in the First through Eighth Amendments) have been incorporated into the Fourteenth Amendment as holding against the states. Nor has the Court ever agreed with Black that it was the intent of the original authors of the Fourteenth to effect such a wholesale incorporation.[18]

Rather, the incorporation has been piecemeal, selective. Clearly, the rights of the First, Fourth, Fifth, Sixth, and Eighth Amendments (except for the grand jury provision in the Fifth) have all been incorporated at present. It is not clear, however, whether those rights in the Second, Third, and Seventh Amendments are to be incorporated. To this date they have not been.

Piecemeal, then, the Bill of Rights came to apply to the content of state laws—not all the Bill of Rights, but most of it. This is the first step in our story of the historical transformation of the Bill of Rights in the present century.

Then, second, there has been interpretation of the Bill of Rights itself. One such interpretation led to establishing privacy as a fundamental constitutional right. In the *Griswold v. Connecticut* decision (1965),[19] Justice Douglas (delivering the decision of the Court) said that privacy, while not an express feature of the Bill of Rights, comes along, inevitably, as part of the Bill of Rights package. He reasoned as follows: the right of association, while not mentioned by name in the First Amendment, has been recognized by the Court as a right guaranteed under that amendment (for, without it, the express rights mentioned there would be incompletely specified or inadequately supported). Likewise and by analogy, the right of privacy lies alongside the rights of *several* amendments (not merely the First but also the Fourth and Fifth, as selectively incorporated, and perhaps others as well). It is a sort of background right that holds if the explicit rights recognized in the Bill of Rights themselves hold. Or, to use Douglas's metaphors, the right of privacy is in the "penumbra" of the Bill of Rights; it is an "emanation" from the Bill of Rights.

Not all the judges agreed with Douglas's reasoning, but a majority of them did think that there was a constitutional right of privacy and that it governed the case they were considering. Specifically, there was (as Douglas called it) a right of *marital* privacy which banned the Connecticut statute that had made illegal the use of contraceptive devices by couples (including married ones) or the counseling by others of such use. In his opinion Douglas relied on two considerations in particular: the peculiar intimacy of the marital union and the essential privacy of place of the marital bedroom.

Clearly, the right of privacy is, at the point of its initial enunciation here, a largely unspecified right. Indeed, if, contrary to fact and practice, the Court had simply declared one morning and in no particular context that citizens "had a constitutional right of privacy," that right would simply be an unspecified right (and nothing else) on that curious morning. But in fact we know very little more when we are told in *Griswold* that we have a constitutional right of privacy. Or, to speak more precisely, we have only a partially specified right at this point (given the details of Douglas's opinion): we know merely what the right of privacy means and what it covers in the precise sort of case the Court had in mind in *Griswold*. We know that, but not much else. And it is through further specification of details and elaboration of reasons in subsequent cases that we come to know the specific content of the constitutional right of privacy.

Thus, once it is established that there is such a right, questions of its conditions of possession and of its precise content and scope and competitive weight inevitably arise. What people and situations and things does it cover? Is it a basic constitutional right? This brings us to the final step in our story of the historical transformation of the Bill of Rights in our century.

One very controversial decision, and perhaps the most important to date on the privacy doctrine, is *Roe v. Wade* (1973).[20] Here the right of privacy is extended to cover the right of a woman (whether married or unmarried) to make the decision to terminate her pregnancy (a decision that was incontestably hers to make, in consultation with her doctor, in the first trimester). Thus, the right of privacy here determined a right of abortion on the part of the pregnant woman; the right of abortion, as a specification of the constitutional right of privacy, itself becomes, then, a constitutional right against which no state interest in fact arises (at least in the first trimester).

The right of privacy as specified in *Roe* has lost the connection to the marital state that it had in *Griswold;* indeed, this uncoupling had occurred in an earlier decision (*Eisenstadt v. Baird* [1972]),[21] intermediate between *Griswold* and *Roe.* The reasoning of Justice Blackmun, who wrote the decision for the Court in *Roe,* did not rely on the idea of an intimate union or of a peculiarly private place. Rather, his stress was on the intimacy of the decision to abort and on the personal autonomy of a woman to make such a decision (in a medical context). The essentially personal or self-regarding character of the woman's decision was emphasized in subsequent cases, where it was made clear that the consent of the woman's husband or of the biological father was not required, under the privacy doctrine, for abortions.

In sum, the right of abortion in *Roe*—and withal the privacy right itself—is, like every other right incorporated from the Bill of Rights, a right of individual persons. And its content is essentially one of autonomy—not in all areas but in areas where the decision is unmistakably seen to be intimate and important, touching the very core of personhood and the deep questions of how one's life is to be lived, and where the autonomy of the person centrally involved has been recognized (as in *Planned Parenthood of Missouri v. Danforth* [1976])[22] to be decisive.

Let me hasten to add that I am not concerned here to discuss the right of abortion on its merits or to discuss how subsequent cases (such as *Webster v. Reproductive Health Services* [1989][23]) restrict or are compatible with *Roe.*[24] Rather, I have been interested in this section merely to show that the nationalizing tendency of the Fourteenth Amendment (present at its time of adoption) has been pressed forward in our time to create new standards throughout the nation for *all* laws, both state and federal.

In sum, three things have happened in the present century that, together, have radically transformed the constitutional status and character of the Bill of Rights. First, there has been a piece-meal, selective incorporation into the Fourteenth Amendment of certain rights contained in the Bill of Rights as holding, then, as protections for individual persons against state as well as against federal laws. Second, there has been an ongoing interpretation of the incorporated rights of the Bill of Rights. This has on occasion meant the generation of new, often unspecified rights out of these incorporated rights—thus, we encounter here novel rights not mentioned in the Bill of Rights explicitly (such as the rights of association, expression, conscience [from the First Amendment], privacy [from the First and Fourth and others as well], and human dignity [from the Eighth]). Then, finally, there has been the judicial shaping of these relatively unspecified or only partially specified rights into various determinate specifications—as, for example, the right of privacy has been specified to include or cover a right to abortion—or, to cite another well-known example, to include a right to remove a life-support system (as in the *Quinlan* [1976] and *Cruzan* [1990] cases).[25]

What has happened, in short, in this tying together of the Bill of Rights with the Fourteenth Amendment is that the constitutional status of the Bill of Rights has changed. For these rights, as selectively linked with—incorporated into—the Fourteenth Amendment, now govern state law as well as federal. And the list of rights, along with the content of individual rights, has itself changed in the process. Thus has the Bill of Rights been transformed in character in the present century.

This is an important historical change. But it is not the most important one. The famous rights of the U.S. Bill of Rights (and the same is true of the right to vote enunciated in effect in Article I) were at the time of their adoption merely a "form" of civil rights; they were not civil rights pure and simple. I say this because, though they were nominally rights of all citizens or all persons, they were not really universal within the body politic. Consider here the permanent exclusion from the right to vote of women (and of slaves in the United States) at that time. And the rights of the Bill of Rights, while they are truly enough universal in description, are rights of all persons (*excepting slaves,* of course) *only under federal law.* Thus, they are, given those qualifications, not *the* legal rights of literally all persons.

The really significant transformation of the Bill of Rights (through its linkage with the Fourteenth Amendment), then, has been the making of these rights into true civil rights (that is, into protected ways of acting or being treated that hold for literally all citizens—or literally all persons—within the American body politic). This is the significant change that our century has effected in the ongoing history of the Bill of Rights. And it is *this* transformation that has chiefly made the Bill of Rights into something of more than merely historical significance.

SECTION SIX: AN APPRAISAL

The transformation I have described has been one where constitutional rights have become civil rights and where civil rights are or have become constitutional rights. The attendant result is that the American constitution itself has tended in the direction of becoming a system of rights.

These changes have occurred in a variety of ways, however. No one agency of government has done it all; certainly the Court has not. It is important to see this. In the case of the Bill of Rights the change has occurred through a combination of constitutional amendment and judicial decision. In the case of the right to vote, it has largely come through a series of constitutional amendments, though congressional action (e.g., the Voting Rights Act of 1965) and action by the Supreme Court[26] have of late been factors also. In the case of the right to an education, the change has come largely through constitutional and legislative action by the states themselves, though the constitutional status of this particular civil right (beyond the one issue of desegregated schooling, affirmed by both Court and Congress) still awaits an appropriate ratification as constitutional at the federal level. And, in a few cases, such rights have come through congressional enactment—for instance, the various public accommodation rights set forth in the Civil Rights Act of 1964.[27]

The constitutional rights picture is vastly more complicated than it was two hundred years ago. In the eighteenth century, the usual sources that would be combed for constitutional rights were the constitutions of the individual states (formerly colonies of Great Britain) and common law (that is, judge-made law which relied heavily on the precedent of previous judicial decisions and which dominated the civil and criminal law in Britain and America at that time). And some of these rights in turn (presumably the basic or most important of them) were thought to be grounded in natural rights.

If we stayed with the rhetoric and patterns of thought of our eighteenth-century forebears, one plausible answer to the question, What are constitutional rights? would be that they are the rights endorsed as basic by natural rights—or, as one person has said, constitutional rights are constitutional rights "because they're right."

But the notion of natural rights (except for a brief excursus on human rights in section two) has played almost no role in my account. Rather, my justification for constitutional rights has been some combination of the standard of mutual perceived benefit with a willingness (on the part of citizens and governmental agencies) to accord priority to universal rights, justifiable by that standard, over other considerations.

What, one might be tempted to ask, is wrong with natural rights? Why have they been shunted aside? The main problem, as I see it, is that natural rights cannot form a coherent set and, hence, are ineligible to serve as grounds for constitutional rights. Whatever natural rights are, they are noninstitutional in character. Hence, in one famous formulation, they are the rights we would have in a state of nature.

But I have argued that the scope of rights must be authoritatively set (to preserve their central content) and that, without such setting and adjustment of scope, rights will conflict—conflict internally and with one another and with other (nonrights) considerations. Since such conflict can only be resolved or prevented by the action of agencies that can formulate and harmonize rights (through scope adjustment, competitive weightings, and so on), rights that lack such agencies would necessarily conflict and the set of them could not be coherent. Natural rights, resolutely noninstitutional in character as they are, lack such agencies in principle. Hence, natural rights (as traditionally understood) cannot provide a plausible alternative, or even a useful addition, to the account I have given.

Perhaps the most likely way to save natural rights theory from this crucial disability is to relocate its main thrust somewhat. Thus, we could redescribe such rights as moral norms (reached by sound inferences from the principles of a critical morality). Such norms, which are allowed for in my own account (in the discussion of human rights in section two), provide reasons or grounds for saying that certain ways of acting or being treated *ought* to be civil rights, ought to be formulated in law and maintained for all people in a given body politic.

Such norms, when they are authoritatively acknowledged (as they were in the Declaration of Independence, as the rights to "life, liberty, and the pursuit of happiness") are rather like the unspecified rights (for example, the right to privacy) discussed in the previous section. But, like unspecified rights, these norms or proto-rights, in order to be active civil rights—and hence active constitutional rights—require, as we have seen, specification of content, scope setting and scope adjustment, competitive weighting, institutional devices for the on-site resolution of conflicts, and so on. For, otherwise, such norms will conflict with one another and collapse into an incoherent set. And, equally, they require promotion and maintenance; for, otherwise, they will be mere nominal rights and not active, functioning civil rights.

Accordingly, natural rights (conceived as norms of critical morality that can underwrite some civil rights) do have a place in my account. But we cannot think adequately about such natural rights (where they are correctly thought to be true rights, as distinct from mere norms) by dispensing with the institutional features—scope adjustment, competitive weighting, promotion, and maintenance—I have emphasized throughout. It is these features that are necessary to make such norms into civil rights and, in this very fact, that disqualify them from being rights, when natural rights are understood in the old eighteenth-century way.

I suspect that a lingering hankering for old-style natural rights, or something like them, is the single greatest obstacle that my account of constitutional rights will have to overcome. I hope my remarks in this section will help loosen the hold of this antique idea to a degree.

Two other obstacles are worth mentioning, if only briefly, in conclusion. It might be thought, first, that a system of rights, since it gives priority to civil rights over corporate concerns, leads to an atomistic view of society and encourages a sort of perpetual conflict; and, second, that a system of rights, without the anchor of natural rights theory, will lead to a proliferation of more and more rights, and ever more trivial ones.

It is often alleged, as I have just noted, that liberal societies (societies in which civil rights are given priority) are overcommitted to values such as personal autonomy and the rights of individuals; accordingly, it is further alleged, such societies are atomistic, lack cohesion, and afford no sense of community or of a common good to their members—at least not to those who are clearheaded. The members, then, can have no reasonable sense of identification with or allegiance to a characteristically liberal society. Or, to put the point more precisely, the sense of commitment of persons there is wholly instrumental; it does not go beyond treating the society and the other members (beyond a small circle of family, friends, and associates) as anything but a viable means to the self-interest and personal aggrandizement of the various particular individuals who make it up. Clearly, then, there is no sense in which the body politic or the well-being of its members overall could be an end in itself or a good per se to the individuals involved.

But I have argued that civil rights (the archetypal sort of right in such contemporary liberal societies) are justified there in a characteristic way, by reference to the standard of mutual perceived benefit. It follows that the members (the citizens), insofar as they have civil rights, must have upon reflection a sense of common good and that this must, given the priority of civil rights, restrain self-seeking and the deployment of rights for mere partial or "factional" advantage.

Moreover, I think it could be shown, in view of this pattern of justification, that the members will have a characteristic allegiance to such a society (and a duty to obey many of its laws). This allegiance and its attendant duty are not modeled on voluntary obligations and, in an interesting and recognizable way, are specific to that one particular society (or community) of people with which the members' lot in life has been cast.

Thus, a political system in which civil rights have priority in the public domain (over rights that are not universal within the society and over other—nonrights—normative considerations) is not essentially atomistic. Nor is it antithetical to many of the traditional values associated with communitarianism, with theories of common good, or with republican civic virtue.

Of course, what Aristotle said of Plato's *Laws* (that there are many laws in it—perhaps too many) is also true of a modern system of rights (that there are many rights laws in it). Now, there may indeed be a proliferation of such laws. Are there, then, too many civil rights? I do not know exactly how to address such a contention.

Let us grant that some ways of acting or being treated that arguably would be in the interest of each and all might fail of legal enactment, and some that did secure legal enactment might not meet the standard of according benefits for everyone. But the self-correcting character of democratic procedures would work, over time and given experience, to reduce such likelihoods. Thus, we might not ever be in a position to say that literally all civil rights policies are in the interest of each and all, but we do have adequate evidence for saying that many long-established civil rights—assuming here that a concurrent highly favorable social opinion exists in their case—are justifiable on the regulative standard of mutual perceived benefit.

Clearly, then, it is reasonable to say, at least in the case of such long-established rights, that they meet the justifying standard and constitute a reliable core. And if this is so, then it also seems reasonable, where citizens and governmental agencies have shown a pronounced and longstanding willingness to do so, to accord priority to such rights.

But we must also bear in mind that democratic institutions, though they do afford a reasonably reliable way—given time—to identify and implement justifiable civil rights, constitute at best only an imperfect procedure toward any such end. Inevitably, then, there may be some proliferation of rights, some creations of unnecessary or even undesirable civil rights.

There is no way I know of to prevent this entirely. The better project, rather, is to try to perfect parliamentary democratic institutions, to improve them by moving them in the direction of their own internal goal—that is, by moving these institutions toward the goal of achieving a rough parity between laws and policies approved by a majority of legislative representatives and those approved by a majority of voters; and, within that, the goal of underwriting at least the matters of main priority, or a significant subset of them, with a strong social consensus.

In the end, it is this idea of a strong social consensus, and the willingness of citizens and governmental agencies to accord priority to some rights, that affords the most significant brake (in the account I have given) on any undesirable proliferation of civil rights as constitutional rights.[28]

Notes

1. The association is explicitly made, for example, in Robert A. Dahl's well-known book *A Preface to Democratic Theory* (Chicago: University of Chicago Press, 1956), chap. 1.

One convention which I will follow, and which should be noted at the very beginning, is that I will refer to the document called The U.S. Constitution by using an uppercase "C" in the word "Constitution"; when I mean to refer to the set of institutional essentials that make up the American constitutional system (institutions like separation of powers, federalism, and so on), I will use a lowercase "c" in that same word (hence, "constitutional"). I do not think this will prove confusing.

2. The *Federalist Papers* is a collection of letters published in New York newspapers in 1787–88, under the pseudonym "Publius," advocating New York's ratification of the new U.S. Constitution. The authors were John Jay (5 letters), Alexander Hamilton (51 letters), and James Madison (26 letters plus 3 jointly with Hamilton).

For Madison's celebrated discussion of "faction," see *Federalist* No. 10; also No. 51. The premier philosophical study of the papers is by Morton White, *Philosophy, The Federalist, and the Constitution* (New York: Oxford University Press, 1987). For White's discussion of *Federalist* No. 10, see esp. chap. 5.

3. In the interests of historical accuracy, however, I think a few points should be noted respecting the addition of the Bill of Rights, in particular. *Federalist* No. 84 (by Hamilton) points out that a number of rights are secured in the body of the original Constitution of 1787 (e.g., habeas corpus, no ex post facto law—both in Article I, section 9) and argues that no separate and additional bill of rights was needed. Madison apparently concurred in this judgment at the time of his coauthorship of the *Federalist Papers*— and thus was subject to criticism by his friend Jefferson—but he did later advocate such an addition to the U.S. Constitution and was one of its prime movers in the First Congress (meeting in 1789–91), as we have noted.

The device whereby Madison reconciled his earlier judgment (as to the dispensability of a bill of rights) with his subsequent support for such a bill is afforded by the Ninth Amendment (which states that "the enumeration in the Constitution, of certain rights, shall not be construed to deny or disparage others retained by the people"). This amendment removed the objection that a bill of rights might allow the (incorrect) conjecture that the rights enumerated were the *only* rights the citizens actually had. Such a conjecture would, of course, be intolerable to persons (like Madison) who accepted rights under common law, rights under state constitutions and state laws, and even rights under natural law. In addition, Hamilton and Madison (and others who held the dispensability thesis) wanted to avoid the further incorrect conjecture that without a federal bill of rights Congress did in fact have a constitutional power to control the press, to establish religion, and so on.

4. Thus, a distinguished historian of the United States, Henry Steele Commager, captures the conventional rationale well when he speaks in his Richards Lectures of the "fun-

damentally contradictory" relationship between majority rule and civil rights; the judicial protection of such rights is said to *deny* "the principle of majority rule," and the checking devices themselves are called "impediments" to majority rule government. See his *Majority Rule and Minority Rights* (New York: Oxford University Press, 1943), 4–8. A similar note is regularly struck in the literature of American legal theory, especially regarding the institution of judicial review. John Hart Ely, for example, argues that judicial review, where it acts in support of substantive values (such as by specifying—or specifying further—and then protecting the right of privacy under the Fourteenth Amendment), is antimajoritarian. See his *Democracy and Distrust: A Theory of Judicial Review* (Cambridge, Mass.: Harvard University Press, 1980), chap. 1, esp. pp. 4–7, and chap. 3, esp. pp. 67–69. Ely allows only for a *procedural* type of judicial review, one that helps make the democratic institutions more effectively democratic, say, by extending universal franchise or one person/one vote even further.

And some of the most prestigious contemporary philosophers of politics and law subscribe to the idea of a fundamental conflict in principle between majority rule and universal political or civil rights. See, for one example, John Rawls, *A Theory of Justice* (Cambridge, Mass.: Belknap Press of Harvard University Press, 1971), secs. 36, 37, 53, 54. For another, Ronald Dworkin speaks famously of "rights as trumps over the majority will" in his *A Matter of Principle* (Cambridge, Mass.: Harvard University Press, 1985), 59, and develops a theory of judicial protection of rights, where rights are understood as held, in principle, *against* the majority. See Dworkin, *Taking Rights Seriously* (Cambridge, Mass.: Harvard University Press, 1977), chap. 5; *Matter of Principle,* chap. 2, but also pp. 23–28; and *Law's Empire* (Cambridge, Mass.: Belknap Press of Harvard University Press, 1986), chap. 10, esp. pp. 375–77.

5. See my Internationale Vereinigung für Rechts-und Sozialphilosophie [International Association for Philosophy of Law and Social Philosophy] plenary session paper for the ideas expressed in this paragraph (ideas that provide the supporting background for the entire section): "Explanation in History and the Theory of Rights," in *Human Being and the Cultural Values* [Proceedings of the 12th IVR World Congress, Athens (1985)], ed. S. Panou et al., ARSP Supplementa, vol. 4 (Stuttgart: F. Steiner, 1988), 76–92.

6. The argument for this particular ordering is developed in my book *A System of Rights* (Oxford, Engl.: Oxford University Press, 1993), chap. 7.

For an argument for the priority of civil rights (as in case i) over policies that serve the common good (as in case ii), see also my book *Rawls and Rights* (Lawrence: University Press of Kansas, 1985), 114–20, 125–26.

7. For Rawls's idea of the basic structure of a society, see his paper "The Basic Structure as Subject," in *Values and Morals: Essays in Honor of William Frankena, Charles Stevenson, and Richard Brandt,* ed. Alvin I. Goldman and Jaegwon Kim (Dordrecht, Neth.: D. Reidel, 1978), 47–71; for discussion, see my book *Rawls and Rights,* chap. 1, sec. 2, and p. 240 (for further citations).

8. For further discussion of the priority of a given civil right (e.g., habeas corpus, the right to vote, free speech) over a nonrights concern like national security, see my *System of Rights,* chap. 7; also my *Rawls and Rights,* chap. 3, sec. 2; chap. 7, sec. 5; and p. 148.

9. See Robert Bork, "Neutral Principles and Some First Amendment Problems," *Indiana Law Journal* 47 (1971): 1–35. Some of the key points made here and the passage quoted can be found on p. 17.

10. I have attempted to provide such an argument, specifically, that a *justified* majority rule (hence, majority rule per se) is reliably productive of, and not inherently incompatible with, civil rights. See my *System of Rights,* chaps. 6 and 7; also my paper, "Democracy and Rights: Two Perspectives," in *Law and the State in Modern Times* [Selected Proceedings of the 14th IVR World Congress in Edinburgh, August 1989], ed. Werner Maihofer and Gerhard Sprenger, ARSP Beiheft 42 (Stuttgart: F. Steiner, 1990), 9–18.

11. See John Rawls, "The Basic Liberties and Their Priority," in *The Tanner Lectures on Human Values,* ed. Sterling M. McMurrin (Salt Lake City: University of Utah Press, 1982), 3: 3–87 at sec. 9, esp. pp. 51–53. For discussion, see my *Rawls and Rights,* chap. 6, sec. 1, esp. pp. 111–14.

12. Rawls seems, beginning with his Dewey Lectures in 1980, to be reconfiguring his entire justificatory account. A number of important changes have occurred as he has moved further from positions he occupied in *Theory of Justice* (1971). For example, he now claims that his theory is specifically a *political* theory of justice, which is itself not part of a comprehensive moral theory. In this newer account, comprehensive moral theories (like Kant's or like Mill's utilitarianism) merely "overlap" on the independently justified "political conception of justice." And the values that Rawls uses to do this independent justification of the so-called two principles of justice are themselves said to be latent in the culture of a contemporary democratic society.

The works to consult here would include the three Dewey Lectures themselves, published under the title "Kantian Constructivism in Moral Theory," *Journal of Philosophy* 77 (1980): 515–72. The most important subsequent works, where these newer themes are set out quite fully, are his "Justice as Fairness: Political not Metaphysical," *Philosophy and Public Affairs* 14 (1985): 223–51; "The Idea of an Overlapping Consensus," *Oxford Journal of Legal Studies* 7 (1987): 1–25; and *Political Liberalism* (New York: Columbia University Press, 1993). Rawls's most interesting formulation of his two principles is also found in one of his post-Dewey papers; see "The Basic Liberties and Their Priority," 5.

13. For a detailed state-by-state discussion of the status, in the *states,* of these rights at or near the time of the official adoption of the Fourteenth Amendment, see Charles Fairman, "Does the Fourteenth Amendment Incorporate the Bill of Rights?" *Stanford Law Review* 2 (1949): 5–139, at sec. 12 (pp. 81–132). Fairman's point is that if the Fourteenth Amendment incorporated the entire Bill of Rights as a standard for *state* law, then the states would not have had (or continued to have) laws and constitutions, some of them going back to the time of adoption of the Bill of Rights, that were at variance with the Bill of Rights on these points (on the point of the grand jury indictment rule and the twelve-person criminal-trial jury rule, with a requirement of unanimous votes for verdicts of guilty, and the twenty-dollar common-law suit rule). My point is simply that, since states had and continued to have nonconforming rules on these very points, they could not regard the relevant Bill of Rights rules as matters of high priority, as matters required (over alternative versions) by the standard of mutual perceived benefit.

14. 32 U.S. (7 Pet.) 243.

15. This, in outline, is section 1 of the Fourteenth Amendment. The other sections (all thought to be more important at the time) concerned such matters as (a) reducing the number of representatives a state had in Congress *if* any basis for restricting the vote in a given state was used other than participation in criminal activity (section 2), (b) depriving some former Confederate military officers and politicians of the ability to hold office (section 3), (c) disavowing the debt incurred by the southern states in upholding the Confederacy, as the secessionist government was known, and disallowing any compensation as payment to former slaveowners for the emancipation of their slaves (section 4), and (d) allowing Congress to pass laws to enforce the provisions in these four sections (section 5).

16. The nationalizing point—the third point—is very important. The authors of the Fourteenth Amendment were building a new nation—reconstructing it from the ruins of the old. The former states of the Confederacy were forced to ratify this crucial amendment. For discussion, see Stephen M. Griffin, "Constitutionalism in the United States: From Theory to Practice," *Oxford Journal of Legal Studies* 10 (1990): 200–220, esp. 214, also 215–16 (nationalizing tendency) and 209 (force).

Fairman, in "Does the Fourteenth Amendment Incorporate the Bill of Rights?" agrees about the nationalizing tendency of the amendment. In a brief summary at the end of his article (139) he says, "[Congress] undoubtedly purposed [in the various clauses of the amendment's first section] to establish a federal standard below which state action must not fall."

17. 347 U.S. 483.

18. See the dissent of Justice Hugo Black in *Adamson v. California,* 332 U.S. 46, 68–123. The historical accuracy of Black's contentions has been widely challenged. See here in particular Fairman's "Does the Fourteenth Amendment Incorporate the Bill of Rights?" in which he looks at the expressed intent of the amendment's chief authors, at the public debates at the time, especially in the election of 1868, and at the rather desultory ratification debates in the states. A view roughly similar to Fairman's is reached in Alexander M. Bickel, "The Original Understanding and the Segregation Decision," *Harvard Law Review* 69 (1955): 1–65. In Alfred H. Kelly, "Clio and the Court, an Illicit Love Affair," *The Supreme Court Review* (1965): 119–58, a somewhat more favorable account of Black's history is briefly set forth (132–34).

The account of incorporation developed in the present paper emphasizes, contrary to Black, the idea of selective or piecemeal incorporation and does not require the claim that the authors of the Fourteenth Amendment intended incorporation but, rather, only the weaker claim that they contemplated *some* incorporation as within the scope of section 1. In my account here I have, of course, been influenced by the articles by Fairman and Bickel. I have also been influenced by the Court's decision in the first case it heard on the meaning of the language of section 1 of the Fourteenth Amendment, the *Slaughter-House* cases (83 U.S. [16 Wall.] 36) in 1873. (This decision was written by Justice Samuel Miller—who was, interestingly enough, a physician by training. I should add that I was influenced *negatively* by Justice Stephen Field's dissent in that same case.)

19. 381 U.S. 479.

20. 410 U.S. 113.

21. 405 U.S. 438.

22. 428 U.S. 52.

23. 492 U.S. 490.

24. Nor am I concerned to discuss whether the privacy right was correctly interpreted when it was said in *Bowers v. Hardwick* (478 U.S. 186 [1986]) that under it consenting adults do not have a right to engage in homosexual acts, even in the privacy of one's home. These things are all important matters and must be discussed if one is to engage the issues that arise under the right of privacy. But my concerns in the present paper are quite different from any such focus on privacy per se.

25. *In re Quinlan,* 70 N.J. 10, 355 A.2d 647; *Cruzan v. Director, Missouri Department of Health,* 497 U.S. 261.

26. I have in mind cases bearing on the principle of one person/one vote (and, by extension, on legislative districting). The principal cases here are *Baker v. Carr,* 369 U.S. 186 (1962), on justiciability, and *Wesberry v. Sanders,* 376 U.S. 1 (1964) and esp. *Reynolds v. Sims,* 337 U.S. 533 (1964), on point.

27. Interestingly, the idea that Congress would be the leading body in the construction and maintenance of civil rights as constitutional rights (an idea found in section 5 of the Fourteenth Amendment) has been belied by the relative paucity of such rights actually generated by Congress. Instead, that role has been taken (rather unexpectedly) by the Supreme Court. Ironically, the public accommodations section of the 1964 Civil Rights Act, one of the few pieces of legislation that seemed to fulfil the promise of the Fourteenth Amendment, was passed, not under the authority of that amendment, but, rather, under the Article I power of Congress to regulate interstate commerce.

28. I have not, in this paper, attempted to lay out my characterization of rights in contrast to alternative accounts and to show the grounds on which I think mine is to be preferred. I have, however, done this in my book *System of Rights,* chaps. 2–5.

A careful account of the natural rights philosophy in the eighteenth century, especially in America, can be found in Morton White, *The Philosophy of the American Revolution* (New York: Oxford University Press, 1978). White shows the essential continuity between the view of natural rights in the Declaration of Independence and in the *Federalist Papers* in chap. 13 of his *Philosophy, The Federalist, and the Constitution.*

For the characterization of natural rights used in the present section, see my paper, coauthored with James W. Nickel, "Recent Work on the Concept of Rights," *American Philosophical Quarterly* 17.3 (1980): 165–80, esp. sec. 3. One of the main grounds on which I reject natural rights theory (the inevitability of conflict *within* rights—that is, of the conflict of one exercise of the selfsame right with another—which mandates, in turn, the requirement for agencies of harmonization, which natural rights cannot meet) is laid out in my book *System of Rights,* chap. 5; see also my *Rawls and Rights,* chap. 7. Other grounds—in my judgment, convincing grounds—for rejecting natural rights theory can be found in my paper "Human Rights and Civil Rights," *Philosophical Studies* 37.4 (May 1980): 391–403.

For the point about allegiance to law (made in the short discussion of lesser obstacle 1 at the end of the section) see my paper "The Character of Political Allegiance in a System of Rights," in *On Political Obligation,* ed. Paul Harris (London: Routledge, 1990), 184–217. For the idea of democracy as self-correcting (made in the short discussion of lesser obstacle 2 at the very end of the section) see T. L. Thorson, *The Logic of Democracy* (New York: Holt, Rinehart, and Winston, 1962), esp. chap. 8; also pp. 120–24.

Finally, I want to thank Ted Vagglis for his written comments on an earlier draft of the present paper.

III

INTERPRETING THE BILL OF RIGHTS: WHAT? WHO? WHY?

★

Christopher Wolfe

The bicentennial of the adoption of the Bill of Rights has stimulated much further scholarly interest in examining that important document. A large part of it, unfortunately, brings considerable contemporary baggage along with it, as it goes back to examine what the Framers and ratifiers of the first ten amendments understood themselves to be doing. All too often the Bill of Rights is "celebrated" on the terms of modern commentators themselves—terms that are quite different from the original understanding. In this essay, I hope to give an accurate statement of what that original understanding was—not out of mere historical interest, but because I believe that Americans of this generation can learn much from their forefathers.

I want to examine three questions: What does "interpretation" of the Bill of Rights mean? Who should have the authority, especially the ultimate authority, to interpret the Bill of Rights? And why should authority for that task of interpretation be allocated in that way?

Christopher Wolfe is a professor of political science at Marquette University.

What: The Meaning of "Interpretation"

What is interpretation? The common view today is that some parts of our Constitution are clear but other parts are unclear, partly because they are vague generalities meant to apply not just to their own day but to the distant future as well. Someone therefore must interpret—give meaning to—these generalities to show how they apply to particular circumstances, many of which the Framers could not have foreseen.

I argue that the Framers would reject this view of interpretation. What they meant by interpretation was ascertaining the meaning of a document—the meaning that was inherent in the document, a meaning that the human mind could come to know. Interpretation was not based on the *ambiguity* of the document but on its *knowability*—the fact that it had a content that could be known.[1]

One way to phrase this—and it is a phrase that has occasioned extensive debate in recent years—is to talk about discovering the "original intention" of the lawgiver. The concept of original intention is useful up to a point, but it can be misleading. It is important to recognize that the word "lawgiver" is being used as a kind of legal fiction. In a way we "invent" a single lawgiver as a source of the law. In the case of the Constitution, there were many lawgivers: members of the Constitutional Convention, members of the different state ratifying conventions, and, behind them, the people who elected them. In that sense, there was no single lawgiver; and yet we talk fictionally as if the Constitution were the product of a single mind and therefore consistent and coherent in all its parts. That is the assumption that the interpreter has to begin with—that this is a coherent, understandable document.

What about the specific intentions of those concrete actors back in 1789—or 1866, when Congress framed the Fourteenth Amendment? Are they relevant? The answer is that, for the Founders, they were relevant, but in a quite subordinate way. It is worthwhile paying attention to what they thought and said, because that may help us to understand something about the language in, thought behind, and principles of the document. But when the Founders talked about interpretation, they were talking primarily about a careful examination of the document itself.

It is uncertain just when comprehensive analysis of the debates at the Constitutional Convention of 1787 commenced, but it could not have been earlier than the 1840s, when Madison's notes—the main source we have for the debates of the convention—were first published. The fact that they were not published until after Madison's death (in 1836) shows that they were not regarded as an authoritative source for understanding the meaning of the document. (The fact that Madison's notes were his own personal initiative—essentially a "private" project—and not formally provided for by the convention, suggests the same thing.) The Framers felt that if someone wanted to understand the document there was only one *authoritative* place to go—to the document. That is, after all, what people voted on.

The Framers had some rather elaborate discussions on the *rules* of interpretation, however. These were not technical rules in a narrow sense. As Hamilton describes them in *Federalist* No. 83, "the rules of legal interpretation are rules of *common sense*"[2]—something people use every day when trying to understand how other people speak. For example, if my wife and I go out on a Friday night and tell our children, "You have permission to watch show A or show B on television," we mean implicitly that they *cannot* watch shows C, D, or E. There is nothing "technical" about that; it is simply a common-sense observation—a rule of interpretation—that an enumeration of powers precludes the implication that there is a general power.

Framers and early judges were guided by rules of interpretation that had their origins in English legal practice. A useful summary of those rules is contained in Blackstone's *Commentaries on the Laws of England,* which was published just before the American Revolution and was widely known in this country. Blackstone's discussion of statutory interpretation emphasizes that the goal is to discern the will of the lawgiver, and he says that there are five "signs" of this will.

The obvious starting point is the *words of the law.* Since the law ought to be understandable by the people (especially in a republican government), one should begin by assuming that the words have their ordinary or popular meanings. Occasionally, technical legal terms such as "ex post facto" and "attainder" are used, but these, too, are normally well defined and clearly understood.

The second sign is the *context*—a comparison of one part of the document to other parts of the same document that might shed light on what it means. For example, in *McCulloch v. Maryland* (1819) Marshall places considerable emphasis on the fact that at one point the Constitution uses the word "necessary" and at another point it uses the words "absolutely necessary."[3] There is a difference between the two; "absolutely necessary" is much more emphatic than "necessary." There is a gradation, then, in various meanings of the word "necessary."

There is a broader kind of context as well, derived from studying other, related legislation during the same period. For instance, one can attain a better understanding of both the words and intentions of the framers of the Fourteenth Amendment by reading the Civil Rights Act of 1866, since the Fourteenth Amendment, although it was not ratified until 1868, was drafted close in time to, and with the purpose of giving a constitutional foundation to, the Civil Rights Act of 1866.

A third sign, after words and context, is *subject matter.* In the process of reading, a person is always making certain assumptions based on the context provided by the subject matter. There is, for example, a provision of the Constitution that talks about contracts, saying that states cannot impair the obligation of contracts. Now, everyone agrees that what they had in mind primarily was state debtor laws, such as laws that would permit delays in the payment of debts. But what if somebody were to say that this constitutional provision prohibits divorce, since marriage is a contract and the state cannot therefore impair it? It seems clear that the subject matter of the Constitution, which does not include any references to regulation of marriage anywhere else, does not include that kind of contract. The more typical form of contract is an exchange of goods or services for some kind of consideration—money, for instance, or something else of value. (Marriage seems quite different, because—as it existed in the Founding—it took two individuals and made them one. Afterwards there were not two parties anymore, in some sense, as there were in the case of a typical contract.)

The fourth sign of the lawgiver's will is the *effects* and *consequences* of the law. For example, an interpretation that has an absurd result is an implausible one. The classic case was a law of the Italian city of Bologna that prohibited drawing blood. The law was designed to prevent dueling or stabbing someone, but the question arose of whether it applied to doctors, who performed the medical operation of drawing blood. The answer was no, because the effect of applying it that way was absurd.

The fifth and in some ways the most important sign is the *reason* and *spirit* of the law: what was it that moved the legislature to enact it? This can be discerned from various sources. For instance, the preamble of the law might be useful, or a simple determination of the implicit purposes of a provision. The history of the provision might also be useful; in *Barron v. Baltimore* (1833), as an example, John Marshall noted that the origin of the Bill of Rights was a desire to limit a potentially powerful central government rather than the state governments.[4]

Other rules of interpretation were established by both the Framers and later by justices of the Supreme Court. How are these various rules put together? There is no a priori way of determining that. It depends on the particular case. What are the problems of interpretation in a given case? What are the different possible arguments? What does the nature of that particular case demand? A justice must simply try to put things together reasonably and figure out what the intention of the provision is.

Apart from the particulars of this discussion, perhaps the most important thing to notice is how much the Framers attended to the rules of interpretation. This is an indication of how serious they were to attain the goal: ascertaining the intention of the lawgiver. With these rules for guidance it may be possible to establish a relatively clear meaning of a particular clause of the Constitution. Or it may be possible only to narrow its possible meaning somewhat, leaving the provision unclear. There is no guarantee that interpretation will result in a perfectly clear understanding. Indeed, there *were* defects of language that may have prevented the Framers from saying what they meant as clearly as they wished, or they may have been forced by compromise to be less than precise—both difficulties that might cloud intent regardless of which rules of interpretation were applied, or how zealously. Proper interpretation of such constitutional ambiguities would be to note the existence of the ambiguity.

WHO: THE AUTHORITATIVE INTERPRETER

Let us move on to the second question raised earlier: who should authoritatively interpret the Bill of Rights? What is the common view today? Most people think that it is the job of judges to interpret the Constitution, especially the justices of the United States Supreme Court. The other branches may interpret the Constitution, it is sometimes thought, but only in a preliminary sort of way. (For example, when Congress is considering a bill, some legislators may make arguments regarding its constitutionality. Or the president might instruct his attorney general to carefully determine the constitutionality of a regulatory agency measure before it goes into effect.) But the real or ultimate authority is generally considered to be the Supreme Court. There is some serious truth in this, according to the thought of the Founders, but there are some serious problems with it as well. Some of the problems with that view are indicated by five fairly unknown but rather interesting miscellaneous points that raise questions about the role of the Supreme Court and the judges in interpreting the document.

First, there is a certain irony about the Bill of Rights and judicial review in that those involved in the Founding who were most in favor of judicial review were most likely to be opposed to a bill of rights, while those who were most in favor of a bill of rights were most skeptical of judicial review. Hamilton was a great advocate of judicial review, giving one of the classic expositions and defenses of it in *Federalist* No. 78. But in *Federalist* No. 84 he presented various arguments against having a bill of rights. Jefferson and many of the Antifederalists were much more in favor of the bill of rights, yet many of them were skeptical about judicial review.[5] They had serious misgivings about allowing judges that kind of power. That tension should make us wonder about our own tendency to consider them together, as different aspects of the same principle.

Second, in the Constitutional Convention James Wilson suggests an interesting argument during one of the several debates on a motion to create a "council of revision," which would have brought the president and some of the judges together into a council to exercise the veto power. (These debates, unfortunately, are not well known, because the proposal was ultimately defeated, despite its support from some of the strongest personalities at the Convention, including James Madison, Alexander Hamilton, and James Wilson.) During one of those debates Wilson argues in favor of the council of revision by saying that, although

Congress may pass bad laws, such laws "may not be *so unconstitutional* as to justify the Judges in refusing to give them effect" (emphasis added).[6] What does Wilson mean by "so unconstitutional?" Usually, we think that something is either constitutional or unconstitutional. Apparently, it is not so clear-cut. There is a gradation from clearly constitutional to clearly unconstitutional, with some matters at various points along the continuum. Wilson seems to imply that judges should not strike down laws unless they are *clearly* unconstitutional. That raises the question: who should deal with the constitutional questions where the answers are not clear? If the judges may not have the responsibility for those questions, who does? Maybe there is room for some other entity, besides the courts, to play a larger role in constitutional interpretation.

Third, Hamilton poses an interesting question regarding freedom of speech that appears in the context of his argument in *Federalist* No. 84 rejecting the Bill of Rights. Noting that "there is not a syllable concerning [liberty of the press] in the constitution [of New York]," he asks, "What signifies a declaration that 'the liberty of the press shall be inviolably preserved?' What is the liberty of the press?" That is, Hamilton asks, how efficacious would such a provision be, as a practical matter? For example, the state of New York has the power to tax—and that includes the power to tax publications. If it has the power to tax publications, Hamilton assumes that the "extent" to which that power is exercised is a matter of "legislative discretion." Hamilton concludes that our freedoms ultimately rest, not on constitutional provisions in favor of liberty (to which, in another context, Madison refers as "parchment barriers"), but on "public opinion, and on the general spirit of the people and of the government" (514).

The interesting assumption underlying Hamilton's discussion is that judges cannot authoritatively determine, say, that "small" taxes that do not inhibit the press are admissible and "excessive" taxes that do inhibit the press are not admissible. Why this assumption? A judge is in a difficult position to know what the difference between the two is. As Marshall says in *McCulloch v. Maryland,* the question of the degree of legitimate power is a "perplexing inquiry, so unfit for the judicial department."[7] The judge's typical resources, which involve the interpretation of law, do not provide him with readily available standards for distinguishing between exercises of a power that are "too much" or "just right." Thus, the decision must be left to the legislature, and therefore the real security for rights is not judicial review but public opinion.

Fourth, when Madison gives his first argument for a bill of rights (in a letter to Jefferson on 17 October 1788), he goes carefully through the whole question of whether a bill of rights would be very useful, noting the arguments for and against, without saying a word about the judiciary.[8] The Bill of Rights is very good because it helps to form public opinion, providing a kind of national sentiment in favor of certain rights. It also provides a reference point for political debates, so that defenders of liberties have something to which they can appeal in their struggles. But that occurs in the ordinary political process, not in courts. Jefferson subsequently responded to Madison (15 March 1789), saying that he had omitted another good argument, namely "the legal check which it puts into the hands of the judiciary."[9] Madison dutifully mentioned this argument when he introduced the Bill of Rights in Congress, but the placement of the argument suggests that it was almost an afterthought, or at least a very secondary reason. So, while it is important that Madison believed in the judicial enforcement of the Bill of Rights, it is also worth notice that he did not seem to regard this as the primary way to enforce it. (Later, I come back to the question of what the primary way was.)

The fifth little-known piece of information comes from a statement made by John Marshall. Marshall was not part of the Constitutional Convention, but at the Virginia ratifying convention he was assigned the task of defending the sections of the Constitution dealing with the judiciary. One of the criticisms was that the Constitution did not guarantee sufficiently the right to trial by jury. Part of Marshall's argument is surprising:

> We are satisfied with the provision made in this country [by which he means Virginia] on the subject of trial by jury. Does our [state] Constitution direct trials to be by jury? It is required in our bill of rights, which is not a part of the [Virginia] Constitution. Does any security arise from hence? Have you a jury when a judgment is obtained on a replevin bond, or by default? Have you a

jury when a motion is made for the commonwealth against an individual; or when a motion is made by one joint obligor against another, to recover sums paid as security? Our courts decide in all these cases, without the intervention of a jury, and yet they are all civil cases. The bill of rights is merely recommendatory. Were it otherwise, the consequence would be that many laws which are found convenient would be unconstitutional.[10]

So Marshall describes the Virginia bill of rights as "merely recommendatory." Does this imply that the federal Bill of Rights was regarded in a similar manner (even though, unlike the Virginia bill of rights, it was to be ratified by amendment as part of the Constitution)? Most citizens today would be shocked to hear the Bill of Rights described as "merely" a recommendation to Congress. We consider it to be not a set of recommendations, but as law, as commands. In some respects—that is, when it lays down clear commands—I think it is law; but there are clauses of the Bill of Rights that, owing to their more indeterminate character, might fairly be described as "recommendatory," in line with this different attitude toward bills of rights that seems to have existed alongside the other view (the one more familiar to us) during the Founding. There are some provisions of the Bill of Rights that were left indefinite in a way that is not typical of law—for example, the Fourth Amendment admonition that the "right of the people to be secure . . . against *unreasonable* searches and seizures . . . shall not be violated" or the Eighth Amendment admonition that "*excessive* bail shall not be required." It seems likely that these clauses, though they might be judicially enforceable in the case of egregious abuses, were written primarily with a view to enunciating general political principles rather than specific, judicially enforceable guarantees.

These little-known facts make the point that things that we take for granted were not taken for granted in the Founding. They suggest that we ought to examine the Founders' thought more closely than we sometimes do if we want to understand what they provided for in the Constitution and in the Bill of Rights.

Another historical point that would surprise many today is that judicial review was not the generally accepted power in the Founding Era that it is for us today.[11] Indeed, there was strong opposition to judicial review in the Founding. People today may not like the particular way in which courts exercise judicial review, but few question the authority of the courts to strike down laws. In the Founding, positions other than judicial review were vigorously propounded. One was the position espoused by Pennsylvania chief justice John Gibson, in *Eakin v. Raub* (1825).[12] Gibson argued that judges do not have the power of judicial review, at least respecting acts of coordinate (legislative and executive) branches of government. The ultimate power in our republican form of government is the people, and therefore the ultimate authority for interpreting the fundamental law ought to reside in them, he argued. Judges should no more be able to strike down laws that they consider unconstitutional than legislatures can strike down judicial decisions that they consider to be based on incorrect or unconstitutional reasoning. Gibson's position is ultimately one of legislative supremacy. In a republican government it is the people, through the legislature, that should make the ultimate decisions.

A second alternative to judicial review was based on separation of powers. It might be called "coordinate review" or "departmental review," and it was espoused by Thomas Jefferson and James Madison. Essentially, this position contends that each branch should have the power to decide constitutional issues in questions properly before that branch. No one branch can order other branches to accept its own view of the Constitution in the performance of their duties, since that would destroy the equality that separation of powers creates. The Supreme Court may no more tell the legislature what laws to make or not to make than other branches may tell the Court what decisions to make or not to make in a particular case before it.

Eventually, judicial review won out, and I think rightly so. The arguments for judicial review are strong ones—stronger than the arguments for legislative supremacy or coordinate review. But the fact that there were powerful and influential and articulate opponents of judicial review should be kept in mind when we ask what the power of judicial review is, because it may provide a context that suggests a more limited scope for the power of judicial review than is generally thought today.

Let us look briefly at several examples of how judicial review was limited. Judicial review, it should be remembered, is not an explicit constitutional power but is said to be *implied* in the

Constitution. Judicial review is a derivative power, coming from the fact that judges have a certain kind of function. That function is to decide cases. They should do so according to law, not merely their own subjective opinions; and so they have to interpret the law. Since the Constitution, by its own terms, is a fundamental law, this line of reasoning by implication leads us back to judicial review. Judges must interpret the Constitution, and in cases of conflict between it and ordinary law they must prefer the Constitution, because it is fundamental. But the power of judicial review is something derivative, something judges have to do in order to accomplish their most central task of deciding cases.

Note that judicial review does not consist in the power of "giving content to ambiguous constitutional phrases." The assumption in the Founding was that judicial review is striking down a law that is clearly incompatible with the Constitution. Judicial review was not based on ambiguity or uncertainty about what the Constitution meant, but precisely on the fact that the interpreter knew what the Constitution meant and what a law meant and that those two meanings were not compatible. What this means is that the argument—so common today—that judicial review is a power made necessary by the *ambiguity* of the Constitution dangerously flips things around. From the standpoint of the Founding, as soon as one says that the Constitution is generally ambiguous, one loses the whole basis for judicial review. Why is that?

Hamilton gives the argument in *Federalist* No. 78: Judges "may be truly said to have neither FORCE no WILL but merely judgment. . . . The courts must declare the sense of the law; and if they should be disposed to exercise WILL instead of JUDGMENT, the consequence would equally be the substitution of their pleasure to that of the legislative body" (465, 469). But when the Constitution is assumed to be ambiguous, then by definition we do not have a constitutional meaning to declare. We do not know what the Constitution says—that is the problem. And without that knowledge, the conditions for the exercise of judicial judgment do not exist. Of course, someone will have to make a decision as to which of several legitimate interpretations will be authoritative. I comment about who that should be later in this essay.

Finally, one other point about judicial review and the Founding should be made, namely the limited scope of authority for it. The best example of this point is still Lincoln's discussion of the *Dred Scott* case (*Dred Scott v. Sandford* [1857][13]). Lincoln had a tremendous respect for the Supreme Court. Normally, he said, Supreme Court decisions are authoritative, not only regarding which party wins but regarding the meaning of the Constitution. But he denied that this can be laid down as a universal rule. Why? "If the policy of the Government," he said, "upon vital questions affecting the whole people is to be irrevocably fixed by decisions of the Supreme Court, . . . the people will have ceased to be their own rulers, having . . . practically resigned their Government into the hands of that eminent tribunal."[14]

Interpreting the Constitution is a very important task, since government is based upon the Constitution. How can we turn that task completely over to judges whom we do not even elect? We cannot do that completely. We have to retain the possibility that, if the judges use the power badly, the other branches will have legitimate power to resist the Court's interpretation. Lincoln said that if he were elected to Congress and a bill prohibiting slavery in the territories were introduced, he would feel free to vote for that bill despite the fact that the Supreme Court had declared such a law unconstitutional, because the Court was clearly wrong. He gave a series of reasons showing why it was clearly wrong and why a legislator would be free to disagree with the Court and to act on a different view. A new law would go back to the Court eventually, but in the meantime it would be possible to influence the Court's ultimate decision by appointing new judges to replace those who died or resigned.[15]

Let me conclude this portion of my essay by pointing out that there are really two kinds of "interpretation," one being a strict or proper sense of the term, the other being a looser or more extended sense. The proper or strict sense is what I have been describing: the attempt to ascertain the meaning of the document. The form of judicial review that corresponds to this form of interpretation is the voiding of laws that are clearly incompatible with the Constitution. The other, more extended meaning of interpretation is the giving of meaning to the Constitution when it is ambiguous or unclear. Who, according to the Founders, should interpret the Constitution in those situations? The answer is that several institutions share responsibility.

First, the political branches of government, the legislature and/or the executive, have as much responsibility as judges to "uphold the Constitution" in their ordinary tasks. Second, the states can call to the attention of the American people possible violations of the Constitution, as Madison and Jefferson emphasized in the Virginia and Kentucky resolutions. And third, the American people share in this responsibility. Ultimately, the people have to make fundamental decisions about what the Constitution means and what it does not mean.

An example of how this shared responsibility was carried out in the Founding Era occurred in 1798, when the overwhelmingly Federalist Congress used its power to pass several laws, the Alien and Sedition Acts, which were directed largely against certain supporters of the opposition Republican (Jeffersonian) party. Not surprisingly, the Republicans were convinced that these laws were unconstitutional. The Sedition Act, in particular, they argued, was a flagrant violation of the First Amendment. That law had been passed by a Federalist Congress, signed by a Federalist president, and then put into effect in lower federal courts by Federalist judges. What could the Republicans do to rectify what they considered a serious violation of the Constitution? They fought it in the political process (in Congress). They went to state legislatures and in Kentucky and Virginia they succeeded in obtaining resolutions calling on the states to oppose this usurpation. Finally they took the issue to the people, making it one of the chief campaign issues in the election of 1800—and they won. One of the first things Jefferson did on entering office was to use the presidential pardoning power to release people who had been jailed under the Sedition Act. (Additionally, Congress voted to pay back fines that had been paid under the prosecutions.) All this was a way of enforcing the Constitution without judicial review.[16] The ordinary political process has the ultimate responsibility for enforcing the Constitution. (This does not mean that the judges should have no responsibility—the Republicans would have been happy to see judges strike down the law— but that was not where most of the Framers placed their primary reliance.)

WHY: THE RATIONALE FOR THE FOUNDERS' VIEWS

Why did the Framers have this more limited understanding of the nature of constitutional interpretation and the power of judicial review?[17] We can start by examining the nature of the arguments given for the broader form of judicial review. Two arguments are emphasized. One is a general, almost "nonpartisan" answer: time passes, and important changes inevitably occur. The Framers wrote the Constitution well before anybody could have envisioned jet planes, telephones, cars, nuclear weapons, television, and many other things that have since transformed the face of society. It is imperative, therefore, that somewhere in our government there exist the power to "update" the Constitution, to bring it in line with the needs of new times. What would that power be? Some people argue that it is precisely the judges, and especially the Supreme Court, who have the responsibility of keeping the Constitution up to date.

The second argument is that our democracy, like every other democracy, has a fundamental problem: how to deal with the always-present potential for tyranny of the majority. Democracy does a good job of preventing minorities from becoming oppressive, but the principle of majority rule may actually become a vehicle for majority tyranny. What we need, then, is some entity outside of majority control, independent of the majority, that can serve as an effective check to prevent majorities from enacting laws that deprive minorities of fundamental rights. Judges are particularly well placed to perform that function.

What grounds might the Founders have given for rejecting such arguments? First, on the question of the need to adapt the Constitution, I believe that they would have responded that adapting the Constitution undermines the whole point of having a written Constitution, which is to have fixed principles. A changeable Constitution creates enormous problems. If the Constitution changes over time, what is to prevent it from being changed to whatever today's prevailing views are? And if that occurs, how does the Constitution remain a genuine check? It must remain substantially fixed if it is to be a standard enabling the Court to resist some of the more unfortunate views that may emerge over time, some of the temptations to engage in oppressive action.

Let me give a more concrete example. In recent political history, who have been the great advocates of a very expansive judicial review? In general, since 1937, and especially since the early 1950s, those most enthusiastic about judicial review have been political liberals, and they were pleased with many of the decisions of the Warren Court. There was a near consensus among political scientists in the 1960s on the benefits of this expansive court power to defend rights that otherwise might have gone unprotected. But in the 1970s we entered a different world with the arrival of the Burger Court. This had a chilling effect on many people who in the 1960s had been so delighted with expansive judicial review. Since the early 1970s, the judges have sometimes acted as political conservatives and the Court's adaptation has looked much less attractive. Raoul Berger gives a wonderful example of this in his *Government by Judiciary,* in which he describes the evolving commentary of the well-known libertarian scholar Leonard Levy. In Levy's earlier writings, he was very much in favor of a broad power of judicial review, one that would allow judges to adapt things to the times. But in a later book on Burger Court criminal defendants' rights cases, he was very critical of the Court, arguing that it was distorting the Constitution.[18]

Let us consider a hypothetical example of an argument for the need to adapt the Constitution that a contemporary conservative might use. Generally, liberals have been comfortable with a broad form of judicial review to protect rights based on judicial "balancing" of different principles. In fact, in the modern era (since 1937), rights in the Constitution are usually treated as general presumptions in favor of a principle, with the Court having to balance these general principles against other values that might be at stake in a given case. What if a conservative made the following argument? "The privilege against self-incrimination in the Constitution seems very absolute. But there are no absolutes in the Constitution—its vague general principles must be balanced against other important social interests. One of our most pressing contemporary social interests is the present terrible crime problem. Something must be done about it. The prohibition against self-incrimination is a valuable right, but we cannot absolutize that any more than other important rights, such as free speech. We must recognize that there may be circumstances that require the police to use tactics that might not have been necessary in a less complicated age, as long as the core of the right (preventing the actual use of coercion, in particular) is respected."

It does not take much imagination to determine how a typical Warren Court liberal would react to that argument. But it is simply another form of many earlier (and contemporary) arguments that were used for liberal purposes (for example, with respect to the contract clause and property rights). And if that kind of balancing is legitimate for liberal purposes, it can be used for conservative purposes as well.

Indeed, this kind of case might not be simply hypothetical. In the early 1970s the Burger Court held that a jury trial need not consist of "twelve men good and true" who reach a unanimous verdict.[19] For about 180 years that had been the uncontested meaning of the federal constitutional right to trial by jury in criminal cases. In the 1960s the Warren Court had applied the federal right to the states via the Fourteenth Amendment's due process clause. Some of the states had jury trials by fewer than twelve people (e.g., six-man juries in Florida), and some allowed less than an unanimous verdict to convict (e.g., Oregon allowed a conviction with a ten-to-two vote by the jury). The Supreme Court upheld these variations, holding that the function of the jury is what counts and that this function does not require the specific historical forms of the jury. But at least part of what lay behind the Court's judgment here may have been a desire to give more leeway to the state criminal justice systems.

Justices like Douglas and Marshall dissented, complaining the "two centuries of American history are shunted aside." But these are the same men who had spent many years shunting aside American history for liberal purposes. It is hard not to be cynical about their protestations.[20] Consistency is essential for judicial review if it is not to become simply the judges' pursuit of their own policy preferences.

Nor should this requirement be imposed less on conservatives than upon liberals. Conservatives have long criticized liberal judicial activism. Now that the Court is somewhat more conservative, some conservatives are saying that there are additional phrases in the Constitution which could be used to protect property rights, that property rights have not been protected the way they should have been for a long time, and that perhaps it is time to start being more active in their protection. It seems to be a permanent danger that, given the power, one is tempted to use it for what one thinks are good purposes. Unless the Constitution is more substantially fixed, it is simply too easy to manipulate.

Is there any other mechanism besides judicial review to handle the problem of majority tyranny? Madison seems to take up that issue in *Federalist* No. 51. He says there are two ways to deal with the problem of a tyrannical majority: one way is to create a will in the community independent of the majority; the other way is to have an extended republic, one with so many different interests that a homogeneous majority cannot form. The only way to get a majority in such a country is to put together a coalition of different interests, and that process usually results in fairly moderate majorities.[21]

The second solution—the extended republic argument—is the one that Madison chose. This was the institutional characteristic of American government on which the Framers placed the greatest reliance in order to avoid tyranny of the majority. The first argument, the idea of setting up a will independent of society, sounds like judicial review. However, what Madison had in mind was not judicial review, but a monarch.[22] He rejected that approach because it was too dangerous, because it was "but a precarious security"; because "a power independent of the society may as well espouse the unjust views of the major as the rightful interests of the minor party, and may possibly be turned against both parties" (324). Even though Madison was talking about an hereditary monarchy, the argument seems to apply at least in a qualified way to judicial review as well—at least to a judicial review that is not tied to the Constitution in some fairly rigorous way. Is not expansive judicial review, like a hereditary monarchy, too precarious to rely on?

If modern judicial review is understood as a broad power to protect minority rights against majority tyranny, that poses some difficult questions. First, who *is* the minority? As it turns out, it is not so easy to say who the minority is in many different cases, if you look at the whole context. For example, consider the provisions of the Constitution dealing with criminal defendants' rights. What are the minority rights at stake in such cases? Is it the rights of criminal defendants, a good example of a minority that is politically powerless, since legislators usually do not seek their support assiduously, to say the least? Is it the rights of people who might have their rights violated even though they are not criminals? Illegal police searches and seizures, for example, may offend the rights not only of criminals, but also of other people who are illegally searched. There is another minority as well: the people who are going to be mugged or robbed or raped or killed by criminals who are free because of very broad versions of criminal defendants' rights. Criminal defendants' rights are, in general, intended to protect against innocent persons being convicted, while making it possible to convict the guilty.[23] They can fail not only by permitting the conviction of the innocent but also by freeing the guilty. Many people feel it is better that ninety-nine guilty people go free rather than one innocent person be convicted. But is that true? If it is true, would it be better that nine hundred ninety-nine guilty people go free rather than one innocent person be convicted? At some point we simply have to recognize the trade-offs involved and say, however unhappily, that sometimes innocent people will be convicted in any criminal justice system. The only way to be sure not to convict an innocent person is not to convict anybody.

Criminal justice systems do involve trade-offs, and we have to consider not only the rights of those who are charged with crimes, but also the future victims of criminals who are able to use the protections of the system to evade punishment. I do not mean to make any particular argument about where the line should be drawn, but merely to point out that a line does have to be drawn. In that sense, the "minority rights" involved in criminal defendants' rights case are not so clear.[24]

Other examples of questions about minorities should come readily to mind. What is the minority at stake with respect to questions about pornography? Is it the person who wants to read pornography, or sell it? Is it women who are raped by those for whom pornography has provided a stimulus of some sort (a "trigger" mechanism or a model) or, more often, who are subtly regarded as sex objects in a society that tolerates pornography? More indirectly, is it men and women that are deeply offended, not only by pornography, but also by less graphic sexual suggestion and innuendo that can appear now on television and in movies and magazines and advertisements because of the modification of social mores to which pornography has contributed? Or is it families attached to traditional morality who find it difficult to raise children in a society that is suffused with attitudes that pornography helps to shape? Which "minority rights" are at stake?

And finally, to give what is perhaps the most obvious example, who is the "minority" in the case of abortion? Is it the mother who wants the abortion, sometimes under very difficult circumstances? Is it the doctor who argues that he is engaged in an occupation providing a service for some who need it? Is it the unborn child, the fetus, or whatever you want to call it, whose existence is "terminated"? John Hart Ely, a liberal legal scholar, once wrote: "I'm not sure I'd know a discrete and insular minority if I saw one, but confronted with a multiple choice question requiring me to designate (a) women or (b) fetuses as one, I'd expect no credit for the former answer."[25] Pregnant women may not be very powerful politically, but they are much more powerful than fetuses, who have no votes at all.

In short, if it were simply a question of protecting obvious minority rights, expansive judicial review might be appropriate. But the proposition is actually quite different: judicial review based on the assumption of the general vagueness of the Constitution permits judges to define highly controversial issues in terms of their own policy preferences, vindicating some assertions of rights, but often at the expense of others. Why, in a representative democracy, should a group of unelected and relatively unaccountable figures be able to make their own judgments about "minority rights" law? It is possible that they will use it for good, and they have done so in some cases. But it is also possible that they will use it for ill, and there are good examples of that also. On the whole, Madison was right: a will independent of society, even one that is substantially but not completely so, is "but a precarious security" for our rights.

CONCLUSION

The occasion of the bicentennial of the Bill of Rights should be for Americans more than just an opportunity to utter comforting commonplaces about the desirability of liberty, the Founders' appreciation of that goal, and our triumphant realization of it (or stubborn refusal to realize it). It should be an opportunity for us to study what the Founders thought, because we can learn from it. In our time, this study and reflection will, in my opinion, teach us these particularly important lessons. First, it is possible to establish a Constitution with general (but not vague) principles that have a clear enough meaning to be understood and to set bounds on future political acts—a meaning that derives from the document itself and that is the goal of good interpretation. Second, the judicial branch has the appropriate authority to interpret the Constitution and to strike down laws or acts that clearly violate it, but only in cases of clear constitutional violations. The legislative and executive branches share the power of constitutional interpretation and development, it being especially their responsibility to deal with questions on which the Constitution is ambiguous or unclear. And third, an expansive form of judicial review according to which judges have broad legislative power to "balance" various constitutional principles and social interests, in order to permit constitutional adaptation and to protect (unspecified) minority rights, is a mistake. It is too "precarious" a security for our liberties. It may even end by jeopardizing them.

Notes

1. This description of the Founders' approach to constitutional interpretation is drawn largely from my book *The Rise of Modern Judicial Review: From Constitutional Interpretation to Judge-Made Law* (New York: Basic Books, 1986), esp. chaps. 1 and 2, which readers interested in more specific citations may consult.

2. Clinton Rossiter, ed., *The Federalist Papers* (New York: New American Library, 1961), 496. All references to the *Federalist* hereafter refer to this edition, and page numbers of quotations will appear in parentheses in the text.

3. 4 Wheaton 316, 414.

4. 32 U.S. (7 Pet.) 243, 250.

5. On Jefferson's attitude toward the judicial branch, see his letter to Ritchie, 25 December 1820, in Albert Bergh, ed., *The Writings of Thomas Jefferson* (Washington, D.C.: Thomas Jefferson Memorial Association, 1907), 15: 295. For his position on different branches' authority to interpret the Constitution, see his letter to W. H. Torrance, 11 June 1815, ibid., 14: 302.

For Antifederalist opposition to judicial review, see "Brutus" in Cecilia M. Kenyon, *The Antifederalists* (Indianapolis: Bobbs-Merrill, 1966), 334–57.

6. M. Farrand, ed., *The Records of the Federal Convention of 1787*, 3 vols., rev. ed. (New Haven, Conn.: Yale University Press, 1937), 2: 73.

7. 4 Wheaton 316, 430.

8. Gaillard Hunt, *The Writings of James Madison* (New York: G. P. Putnam's Sons, 1900–1910), 5: 271–75.

9. Bergh, *Writings of Thomas Jefferson,* 7: 309.

10. Jonathan Elliot, ed., *The Debates in the Several State Conventions on the Adoption of the Federal Constitution* (New York: Burt Franklin, 1974), 561.

11. This portion of the essay summarizes materials described at greater length, with citations, in Wolfe, *Rise of Judicial Review,* chap. 4.

12. 12 Serg. & Rawle (Pa.) 330.

13. 60 U.S. (19 How.) 393.

14. "First Inaugural Address," in Arthur Brooks Lapsley, ed., *The Writings of Abraham Lincoln,* National Ed., 8 vols. (New York: Lamb Publishing Co., 1905), 5: 262.

15. Ibid., 2: 291–93.

16. For a historical overview of the issues surrounding the Alien and Sedition Acts, see James Morton Smith, *Freedom's Fetters: The Alien and Sedition Laws and American Civil Liberties* (Ithaca, N.Y.: Cornell University Press, 1963). For a better view of the constitutional issues, however, see Walter Berns, *The First Amendment and the Future of American Democracy* (New York: Basic Books, 1976), chap. 3.

17. The arguments of this last section are given at much greater length, with citations, in my book *Judicial Activism: Bulwark of Liberty or Precarious Security?* (Pacific Grove, Calif.: Brooks/Cole, 1991).

18. Raoul Berger, *Government by Judiciary* (Cambridge, Mass.: Harvard University Press, 1977), chap. 17.

19. *Williams v. Florida,* 399 U.S. 78 (1970); *Apodaca v. Oregon,* 406 U.S. 404 (1972). The quotation is from Douglas, at 406 U.S. 383.

20. Even if one agrees with them in part. I think the Court was wrong to change the clear and settled understanding of the Sixth Amendment right to jury trial, which applies to the federal government. On the other hand, the states are limited by the "less specific contours" of the Fourteenth Amendment due process clause and therefore should be able to use different jury forms.

21. There are several reasons for this. First, the coalition process itself typically requires that groups drop their own more extreme demands in order to get support from others and that they recognize core interests of other groups. Second, when the process of coalition building is done not just once, but recurrently (as it is in Congress, on different pieces of legislation), then even the interests outside today's coalition cannot be treated so harshly that they would never consider joining future coalitions on different pieces of legislation where their votes may be crucial.

22. That sounds strange to us, since our democratic political culture—reinforced in our civic education by the attitude of the Declaration of Independence toward the British monarchy—rejects monarchy so completely. But, historically, centralizing monarchs from the thirteenth century on in many European countries were successful partly because they assumed the role of protector of popular liberties against the often-oppressive local nobility.

23. There are, of course, some provisions that are intended to protect even admittedly guilty people, such as the prohibition of cruel and unusual punishment; and the adversary system depends upon certain rights being available to all, regardless of innocence or guilt. Nonetheless, it is still fair to say that, in constructing a criminal justice system as a whole, legislators generally try to maximize the possibility of convicting the guilty while protecting the innocent.

24. To those who would argue that victims' rights versus criminals' rights actually represents a case of majority rights versus minority rights, I would give two responses. First, future victims are in fact a minority, and even those who think of themselves as very likely future victims are probably a minority. Second, and more importantly, even if victims' rights are "majority rights" in some sense, they are certainly individual rights that are at least as worthy of protection.

25. "The Wages of Crying Wolf: A Comment on Roe v. Wade," *Yale Law Journal* 82 (1973): 920.

IV

THE RELIGION CLAUSES: SOME BICENTENNIAL THOUGHTS ON AN IMPORTANT CORNER OF THE CONSTITUTION

★

Rex E. Lee

I want to address sixteen important words. They are the first sixteen words of the First Amendment to the United States Constitution:

> Congress shall make no law respecting an establishment of religion, or prohibiting the free exercise thereof.

There are two key phrases in those sixteen words, "establishment of religion" and "free exercise." Both deal with religion, but their concepts are quite different. The free exercise clause, like other First Amendment freedoms, contains a guarantee of individual liberty. And like other First Amendment guarantees, it deals specifically with a means of individual expression and conduct. But even more than the other First Amendment expression rights (freedom of speech, freedom of the press, and freedom of

Rex E. Lee is the president of Brigham Young University and formerly assistant attorney general and solicitor general for the United States.

association), the free exercise of religion also reaches matters of belief.

The establishment clause, by contrast, is the only First Amendment provision that does not deal directly with individual rights. On its face, it is a structural provision. Now, what does this mean? Structural provisions deal with the relationships among institutions, and the Constitution contains three of them. The establishment clause is the only one of the three that is explicitly mentioned in the Constitution. The first, the separation of powers principle, divides governmental authority horizontally among the three branches of the federal government: Congress, the president, and the judiciary. The second, which we refer to as federalism, divides powers vertically between the three branches of the federal government on the one hand and the various state governments on the other. The third and final of our Constitution's structural provisions—and indeed the only one that is explicitly mentioned in the Constitution—is the First Amendment's prohibition against establishments of religion, which is concerned with maintaining a certain degree of separateness, or nonentanglement, between government and churches.

The clearest example of an establishment of religion—and the one that the First Amendment draftsmen clearly intended to prohibit—would be the creation or maintenance by government of an official, exclusively recognized church, such as the Anglican church was in Virginia until the late eighteenth century. Indeed, the historical roots of both of the religion clauses can be traced to Virginia, and they result principally from the efforts of two Virginians, Thomas Jefferson and James Madison, with substantial contributions made by a third son of the Old Dominion, George Mason. To those of us who are so accustomed to taking their legacy for granted, it is difficult to realize that just a short two hundred years ago Virginians of equal stature, including Patrick Henry, George Washington, and James Monroe, were squarely opposed to something as basic as a prohibition against official state religions. During one of the Virginia debates, Jefferson, then in France, wrote to Madison this comment on Patrick Henry: "What we have to do, I think, is devotedly pray for his death."

Though they did not succeed in the more immediate and concrete issue of divine intervention to shorten Patrick Henry's life,

Jefferson and Madison did prevail over their fellow Virginians on the larger issue. On 16 January 1786, the Virginia General Assembly enacted the Virginia Statute for Religious Freedom, the predecessor of our First Amendment religious liberty clauses. We all recall that Jefferson's authorship of this statute (he actually wrote it seven years earlier, when the Revolutionary War was still going on) was one of three accomplishments for which the third president of the United States wished to be remembered. Probably not as well known, but equally important, is the fact that while this statute's author was in France, his friends Madison and Mason stayed at home and performed the difficult task of getting Jefferson's concepts enacted into law. Moreover, it was this same Madison, more than any other single person, whose dogged determination was ultimately responsible for the adoption of the Bill of Rights five years after the enactment of the Virginia Statute for Religious Freedom.

Today, the religion clauses are among the most fruitful sources of our constitutional litigation. They have been for several decades. But is was not always thus. As astonishing as it is to those who have been following the work of the Supreme Court over the last quarter of a century, it is nonetheless true that from the time of their adoption in 1791 until the 1940s—more than 150 years—the only religion cases that the Court considered were the Mormon polygamy cases.

Another significant historical note is this: the First Amendment says that *Congress* cannot establish a religion, nor prohibit its free exercise. Does this mean that Virginia could reestablish the Anglican church as the official state religion? Or that Maryland or Utah could do the same thing for the Catholics or the Mormons? For at least eight decades the answer to that question was yes, at least insofar as the federal Constitution was concerned. The United State Supreme Court held in 1834 that all of the provisions of the Bill of Rights—not just the First Amendment, but the first eight—are binding only on the federal government. The practical impact of this holding was blunted by the fact that provisions similar to the Bill of Rights were contained in most state constitutions, which were interpreted by state courts and enforced by state authorities. But insofar as the federal Constitution was concerned, for at least eight decades, our national Bill of Rights provided no protection against anything that the states did, related to religious practices or anything else. It was not until the adoption of the Fourteenth Amendment in 1868 that there was any basis in the federal Constitution for applying the religion clauses or any other provision of the Bill of Rights to the states. Over the intervening century and a quarter, the Fourteenth Amendment has been interpreted to mean that most of the Bill of Rights provisions—including the establishment and free exercise clauses—are binding on the states as well as the federal government.

There is an interesting irony peculiar to Mormon history that arises from this Bill of Rights issue. Most Latter-day Saints have grown up despising President Martin Van Buren for telling the Prophet Joseph Smith, in response to the violence aimed at Mormons in Missouri and elsewhere, "Your cause is just, but I can do nothing for you." Van Buren may well deserve disdain, because it is possible that his response was based on purely political considerations. But the irony is that from a technical legal standpoint he was right, because the wrongs of which Joseph Smith complained were committed by the state of Missouri, and in those pre–Fourteenth Amendment days there was no federal law to protect against that sort of thing.

After having been almost totally absent from our constitutional jurisprudence for a century and a half, the religion clauses have definitely made up for lost ground over the past four decades. In that relatively brief period there have been scores of Supreme Court decisions defining what is meant by establishment of religion and free exercise. The bodies of law applicable to each of these areas have developed largely independent of each other— though on occasion they converge—and the convergent areas are among the most interesting and the most difficult of our constitutional jurisprudence.

Let us look first at what the establishment clause means. Almost from the beginning we have attempted to describe what the establishment clause does with a metaphor that is (1) quite easy to remember, (2) useless at best, and (3) frequently quite mischievous. Writing to the Danbury Baptist Association in 1802, Jefferson described the religion clauses as "erecting a wall of separation between church and state." Is it really a wall? And does that metaphor help our understanding? The very first establishment clause case to come before the Supreme Court, *Everson v.*

Board of Education (1947)[1] involved a New Jersey Board of Education's practice of paying the bus fares for all children of certain ages who attended school, including those who attended parochial schools. As is the case with most establishment clause litigation, therefore, *Everson* involved a governmental program that benefitted some churches.

The *Everson* opinion is one of the truly astounding performances in the Supreme Court's history. The language of virtually the entire opinion talks of an absolute rule, a wall, an impregnable barrier which permits no breach. And then in a single sentence, the majority holds that the bus fare reimbursement program is constitutional. I believe it was former Utah Supreme Court Judge Dallin Oaks who said that it is not much of a wall if a bus can get through it but a prayer cannot.

Just looking at *Everson* on its facts, reimbursement for bus fares may not seem like a very important issue. But is was a landmark, because it was the first establishment clause case, and because it forced the Court to choose between an impenetrable wall and a rule which permitted at least some activities by government which affected religious institutions and religious values. The basic problem with an absolute rule—a high and impenetrable wall, as *Everson* said—is that our two hundred years of history are full of instances, which have become accepted aspects of our culture, in which official governmental acts acknowledge our religious heritage and constitute an official governmental identification on the side of things religious. One familiar example is the celebration of Christmas as an official governmental holiday. Even Scrooge in his early, unrepentant stage would not take that one on. Other examples include the reference to deity in our national anthem, the pledge of allegiance, the inscription on our coins, and the United States Supreme Court's own opening ceremony. These are the kinds of things that we take for granted, but the kinds of things that would not be permitted if the wall really were impenetrable.

The issue has rather large financial, and not just symbolic, significance. If the Supreme Court's 5–4 decision in *Everson* had gone the other way (as it would have with just one change of vote) it is hard to see how the provision of our income tax laws that permits a deduction for contributions to churches could have survived. And at that point the issue becomes very important, because it would make a difference of literally thousands of dollars every year to most income-earning people who pay tithes or other contributions to their respective churches.

Most of the establishment clause cases subsequent to *Everson* have arisen out of the same factual context: governmental programs which are helpful to religion. And most, though not all, of the cases have involved the same kind of effort that was involved in *Everson*—governmental aid to parochial schools. In 1972, in a parochial aid school case called *Lemon v. Kurtzman,*[2] the Court articulated a three-part test, which later cases have held is applicable not only to church-school aid cases, but all establishment clause challenges as well. The three prongs of the *Lemon* test inquiry require that (1) government act with a secular rather than a sectarian purpose, (2) the primary effect of what government has done neither advance nor inhibit religion, and (3) there be no undue entanglement between church and state. Though there had been instances in which the Court has decided establishment clause cases without applying the three-part test, it now appears to be rather firmly implanted as the basic constitutional requirement for establishment clause validity. The principal reason for its inadequacy is the rigidity with which the Supreme Court has applied the three prongs.

Beyond any dispute, inquiries such as the purpose and effect of a government program are relevant to its constitutionality, but the problem is that the Court has not only required that all three of the prongs be satisfied as a prerequisite to constitutionality, but it has also been quite inflexible in its application of some of those prongs. For example, it is not quite clear that any program which requires or permits governmental employees to go onto the premises of church-owned schools as part of their official duties violates the "effects" prong of the three-part test and for that reason alone renders the scheme unconstitutional as an establishment of religion.

This has led to some really quite absurd results. In 1985, in a case called *Aguilar v. Felton,*[3] the Supreme Court considered what is almost universally regarded as the most successful of the congressional efforts to provide equal opportunities for educationally deprived children. The program provided remedial reading and other services for children in economically deprived geographical areas, and Congress quite sensibly reached the conclusion that it wanted those services to be provided for all schoolchildren, including those who attended parochial schools. (And indeed, I submit that the more serious establishment clause issue would have arisen if Congress had made a determination to provide taxpayer funds for remedial assistance to only those children attending public schools.) After several years of working with the program, its public administrators found that the only effective way to provide these remedial services to the parochial student was at the place where those students went to school during their regular school hours. Experience showed that keeping them after school hours stigmatized them to an extent that adversely affected their ability to learn, and transporting them after hours to a public school was even worse. The virtually unanimous view of educators was that instruction on the parochial school premises was the only really effective way to provide these remedial services and that, using this approach, the program had been very successful. Moreover, it is quite difficult to perceive any great harm that comes from the bare fact of public employees stepping onto church property during school hours. The thought that the public teachers might thereby become religiously indoctrinated was not supported by experience and is nothing less than absurd. Nevertheless, applying the rigid three-part *Lemon v. Kurtzman* analysis, the Supreme Court held the scheme unconstitutional because the presence of nonchurch personnel in a parochial school failed the "effects" prong of the *Lemon* test.

What about the free exercise clause? Has the Court performed any better with respect to that provision? I believe that it has, both in theory and also in practical effect. As is the case with all constitutional guarantees dealing with individual rights or interests, the free exercise clause protects only against acts of government. The basic constitutional test appears to be well established. The starting point, which was announced about a hundred years ago in the polygamy cases, is that the First Amendment gives absolute protection to matters of belief. *United States v. Reynolds* (1878)[4] went on to say that conduct, unlike belief, can be regulated by government. Polygamy, of course, involved both belief and conduct, but the Court was able to resolve that particular case by holding that while the church's belief in polygamy was absolutely protected, its practice of polygamy was not.

This dichotomy between belief and conduct retains some viability, and certainly the first proposition—that belief is absolutely protected—remains good law. But it is no longer true that the First Amendment affords no protection to religious practices, which is where the constitutional protection really makes a difference. Even in the most totalitarian countries people can believe, so long as they do not do anything that reveals that belief.

In any event, the current governing constitutional standard for free exercise of religion is this: governmental acts which adversely affect the implementation of religious belief are constitutional only if the government can show that they are based on a compelling governmental interest not achievable through less intrusive means. The test has two parts and the government must satisfy both. First, government must show that its need to do what it did is compelling—not just substantial, but compelling. Second, even if the governmental need is compelling, the governmental infringement on individual liberty may be unconstitutional if there was some other way that government could have achieved its objective. This second part of the test is sometimes stated another way: the governmental effort must be narrowly tailored to the achievement of its objective.

Probably the leading free exercise case is a 1972 decision called *Wisconsin v. Yoder.*[5] It is also a case whose facts illustrate the competing considerations that the Court takes into account in deciding free exercise cases, and the tilt that the compelling state interest test gives to individual interests over governmental interests. At issue in *Yoder* was a Wisconsin law which required all students to attend public or private high school until they reached age sixteen. Jonas Yoder and others involved in the case were adherents of the Amish faith, which permitted formal schooling through the eighth grade. But beyond that, they believed in providing their own education in their own way. It was a classic case of conflicting governmental interests on the one hand and individual liberty interests on the other. Education is one of the most fundamental of government's activities, and an educated populace is certainly in society's interest. On the other hand, compulsory education beyond the eighth grade was conduct squarely at odds with Amish belief.

On both sides, the competing interests were legitimate and strong. The reason that Mr. Yoder and his Amish colleagues won and the state of Wisconsin lost is that the prevailing test for free exercise cases gives a decided advantage to the individual vis-à-vis his government. Though Wisconsin's interest in having an educated populace was strong, it was not compelling. Moreover, compulsory education was not the only means available to the state for achieving that objective. Thus, the Court's opinion notes that the Amish people not only accept the necessity for formal schooling through the eighth-grade level, but they also continue to provide effective vocational education for their children in the adolescent years.

As noted earlier, the establishment and the free exercise clauses deal, at least at the first level of analysis, with quite different and separate matters. One is a structural provision and the other an individual rights guarantee. Many of the Supreme Court cases, like *Everson, Felton,* and *Yoder,* have involved one or the other, but not both. Some of the most interesting and sophisticated religious liberty cases, however, are those whose fact situations necessarily involve both clauses, and the relationships between the two. I explore two of those below.

The first occurs where the values underlying the two clauses come squarely into conflict with each other. This happened, for example, in a 1981 Supreme Court case called *Widmar v. Vincent,*[6] which held that the University of Missouri's practice of excluding religious groups, and only religious groups, from the extracurricular use of its Kansas City classrooms was a violation of the religious groups' free exercise rights. The free exercise values were obvious, because the religious clubs had been singled out and discriminated against solely on the basis of the fact that they were religious clubs. But the reason that the University of Missouri at Kansas City had adopted this particular policy was not due to any antipathy toward religion. Rather, those who adopted the policy thought that they were required to do so because of establishment clause concerns. If they permitted church groups to use government property for church purposes, they feared that the prohibition against entangling church and state would be violated.

Probably the best-known case involving tension between the two clauses is a 1963 decision, *Sherbert v. Verner.*[7] Adele Sherbert was a devout Seventh-day Adventist. She was also unemployed. The unemployment compensation laws of the state of South Carolina, where she lived, provided that she would be ineligible for unemployment compensation if she refused employment for which she was eligible. The only work that she had been able to find was in a textile mill, which would have required her to work on Saturdays. The infringement on her free exercise rights was different from that involved in *Yoder.* The Wisconsin compulsory attendance law in *Yoder* gave the Amish no option. South Carolina's workman's compensation law, by contrast, imposed no affirmative obligation on Ms. Sherbert. It simply set conditions for her eligibility for unemployment compensation. And it was the compliance with one of those conditions that would have put her into conflict with her religious belief.

Nevertheless, the free exercise considerations prevailed, and Ms. Sherbert won her case. And in a consistent line of cases since that time the Court has held that the free exercise clause prohibits government from conditioning eligibility for otherwise available government benefits on the individual's doing things that would offend his or her religious beliefs. If you look at the issue solely from the standpoint of free exercise values, the result seems quite clearly correct. But the fact of the matter is that free exercise values are not the only relevant constitutional concern. The state of South Carolina, as a condition for unemployment compensation eligibility, has set that the applicant be "available for work," and the South Carolina courts had consistently applied that to mean that unavailability for personal reasons, no matter how compelling, did not satisfy the statutory condition. This means that the United States Supreme Court's holding in *Sherbert v. Verner* carved out one exception from the otherwise consistently applicable state law, and that single exception depended on religious belief. Clearly, in some contexts, the establishment clause would be violated if otherwise applicable government regulation were made inapplicable only to persons with certain religious beliefs. In any event, the tension between the two clauses is readily apparent, and in *Sherbert v. Verner,* as in *Widmar v. Vincent,* it was the free exercise values that prevailed.

Then came the bombshell, *Employment Division, Department of Human Resources of Oregon v. Smith,* in 1990.[8] It involved a set of facts that the Supreme Court—and all constitutional scholars—had been long awaiting. Two employees of a private drug rehabilitation organization were fired because they ingested peyote, a hallucinogenic that was illegal in Oregon. They were using it for sacramental purposes as a ceremony of the Native American church. There was no dispute in the case that this was a legitimate religious belief, and that they were apparently sincere in holding that belief, but the state of Oregon refused to give them unemployment benefits because they were fired on account of their use of this drug. The two employees argued, of course, that the sacramental use of peyote was a sacred part of their religion and for that reason they should have been exempted from the generally applied state law that made use of peyote a crime. In my opinion, if the traditional compelling state interest test had been applied, Smith and his companion would have lost and the state of Oregon would have won. It is much more compelling for the state of Oregon to be able to control drugs than it is to be able to force people to go to school beyond the eighth grade. Indeed, that is the way Justice O'Connor wrote her concurring opinion. It is a compelling state interest test, narrowly achieved, and it is a very difficult hurdle to get over, but Oregon meets it in this instance because of the enormous problem that Oregon and other governments face in controlling drugs. However, that is not the ground on which the majority ruled in Oregon's favor; they took a very different approach. Instead of using the traditional analysis of balancing the individual's free exercise interest against the state's regulatory interest, and then asking whether it was or was not a compelling state interest, the Court, in an opinion written by Justice Scalia, held that the right of free exercise of religion does not relieve an individual of the obligation to comply with what the court called generally applicable criminal laws. Now, what does that mean? It means that so long as the state of Oregon has not deliberately attempted to regulate religion but has attempted to regulate something else (in that instance, drugs), then the fact that there is an incidental effect on religion does not bring the First Amendment into play at all. It is a very different approach from the traditional compelling state interest test and gives a much-lessened level of protection to religious liberty and to individual exercise of religion. Moreover, serious questions can be raised as to whether this new test provides much protection at all, because virtually all laws which in fact impinge on religious exercise were enacted for some purpose other than the impingement.

Wisconsin v. Yoder itself is a good example. The purpose of the state of Wisconsin in that case was not to infringe on the Amish religion. It was something quite different. It was to see to it that there was a uniform level of education that all Wisconsin residents had. The lower court cases are taking the Smith case seriously, and I worry about that. I worry because the compelling state interest test, particularly insofar as it applies to First Amendment rights, has been a great protection and specifically will be a great protection for the constitutional rights of many, if and when they ever need it.

The final category of cases that I will discuss involving the interrelationships between the First Amendment's two religion clauses includes the so-called accommodation issues. These involve cases that challenge the constitutionality of laws whose purpose is to remove barriers to the free exercise of religion, or otherwise to facilitate free exercise. They are like the parochial school aid cases in that they involve government efforts which benefit religion and therefore raise establishment clause concerns. But the parochial school aid cases are different in that they involve direct financial benefits, and they are not directly aimed at facilitating free exercise.

The most recent accommodation case—and perhaps the leading case—arose out of what I think was The Church of Jesus Christ of Latter-day Saints' first appearance in the Supreme Court since polygamy days.[9] *Corporation of the Presiding Bishop of the Church of Jesus Christ of Latter-day Saints v. Amos* (1987) involved the constitutionality of a key provision of Title VII, the federal statute that prohibits employment discrimination on the basis of race, sex, religion, or national origin. Section 702 of that statute exempts religious employers from the prohibition against employment discrimination based on religion. That is, it permits churches as employers to hire only members of their own faith if they choose to do so. When originally enacted in 1964, there was such an exception for religious employers, but it was limited to "work connected with the carrying on . . . of . . . religious activities." In 1972 the exemption was broadened to eliminate the "religious activities" qualification. The net upshot of this was that, as of 1972, churches were free to hire their own members without regard to whether the work for which they were employed was religious in nature or not.

The constitutionality of this statute was attacked by an employee who was threatened with dismissal from a maintenance position at the Deseret Gym because he did not hold a current temple recommend. He contended that exempting churches from discriminating in employment on the basis of religion was a violation of the establishment clause because it gave to church employers an exemption that no other employers enjoyed. Relying on the traditional three-pronged establishment clause test, he argued that the exemption ran afoul of the "effects" prong, because it gave religious employers a privilege that no other employers enjoyed. The district court ruled in his favor, holding that the maximum permitted by the establishment clause was the 1964 congressional exception, which was keyed to work connected with religious activities. Thus, in the district court's view the congressional exception would be constitutional only if limited to "work connected with the carrying on . . . of . . . religious activities." Since the 1972 amendment—which was the provision at issue in the case—permitted churches to restrict their hiring to members of their own faith in areas not directly connected with religious activities, it was, in the district court's view, unconstitutional.

The United States Supreme Court reversed, with all nine justices agreeing that the statute was constitutional at least insofar as churches' nonprofit activities (such as Deseret Gym) are concerned. It is a significant opinion for several reasons. First, the Court reasserts that Congress (as in the *Amos* case) or the state legislatures have some room within which they may permissibly legislate in order to accommodate religion between the constitutional floor provided by the free exercise clause and the ceiling provided by the establishment clause. For this reason, the Court found it unnecessary to pass on whether Section 702 was constitutionally required by the free exercise clause.

One of the most interesting opinions is that of Justice Brennan, with whom Justice Marshall joined. That opinion is the clearest articulation thus far of the First Amendment–based rights of religious organizations. It is sometimes referred to as a constitutional right of church autonomy. As stated by Justice Brennan:

> Religious organizations have an interest in autonomy in ordering their internal affairs so that they may be free to: "select their own

97

leaders, define their own doctrines, resolve their own disputes, and run their own institutions."[10]

He further reasoned that it lay within the churches' constitutionally protected prerogative to determine that

> certain activities are in furtherance of an organization's religious mission, and that only those committed to that mission should conduct them. . . . Solicitude for a church's ability to do so reflects the idea that furtherance of the autonomy of religious organizations often furthers individual religious freedom as well.[11]

Finally, given the recognition by both the majority opinion and also Justice Brennan's concurrence that churches also have First Amendment–protected rights, *Amos* presents the clearest example in Supreme Court history of a confrontation between the free exercise rights of individuals and the free exercise rights of religious organizations. The burden on the individual, frankly, was very similar to the burden on Ms. Sherbert: in order to keep his job at Deseret Gym, Mr. Mayson had to conform to religious practices with which he did not agree. On the other hand, both the majority and Justice Brennan agreed that the church has a constitutionally based right to determine what its religious objectives are, and also to determine that these objectives can best be achieved by persons who agree that they are good objectives. As I read the opinions, the church's interests prevailed because in this particular case they were more weighty than those of the individual. The principal free exercise significance of the case is its implicit recognition that there is something on the church's side of the balance scale, because churches also have free exercise rights.

Two other issues deserve mention, both having to do with those instances in which you have the free exercise clause and the establishment clause. There are at least a couple of contexts in which the two actually overlap. Indeed, they cut in opposite directions. In most instances where that has happened, interestingly enough, it is the free exercise clause that has prevailed. It is unclear whether the *Smith* decision will affect this matter in the future.

What are likely to be the large freedom of religion issues over the next few decades? My guess is that we can expect more assaults on the three-pronged establishment of religion test, even though recent assaults on that test have not been successful. The three-part test in its present rigidity, quite simply, gives results (such as *Felton*) that are so far out of harmony with sound principles and common sense that some change has to be made. I think it is virtually certain that the three-pronged test will eventually be replaced or at least made much more flexible. I also think that in the wake of the *Amos* case, we may see a new round of cases that will further develop the accommodation principles and specifically, I would hope, further define the free exercise rights of religious institutions. But the safest prediction of all is that the religion clauses will continue to be a fruitful and fascinating source of Supreme Court litigation, and that the basic provisions will continue to guarantee that this country will enjoy religious liberty of a quality that is unmatched in most parts of the world and unexcelled in any.

Notes

1. 330 U.S. 1.
2. 403 U.S. 602.
3. 473 U.S. 402.
4. 98 U.S. 145.
5. 406 U.S. 205.
6. 454 U.S. 263.
7. 374 U.S. 398.
8. 494 U.S. 872.
9. 483 U.S. 327.
10. Ibid.
11. Ibid.

V

ABORTION, ETHICS, AND CONSTITUTIONAL INTERPRETATION

★

Leslie P. Francis

I write this paper from three perspectives: woman and mother, moral theorist, and legal theorist. It is unusual for me to link the personal and the academic in this way. I do so for several reasons. First, the issue of abortion joins the personal and the theoretical with particular intensity. Politicians struggle to link together the personal and the political on the abortion issue. Governor Cuomo, a devout Catholic who opposes restrictive abortion legislation, is a highly visible example. Many Americans hold incompatible, absolutist, and deeply felt personal views about abortion that do not permit easy compromise on the political level—if they permit any compromise at all. Others are unsure about how to provide a principled justification for a compromise—or whether any principled account of a compromise is possible.[1]

Second, with the Supreme Court's decision in the Pennsylvania abortion case of *Planned Parenthood of Southeastern Pennsylvania v. Casey* (1992), we have entered into a period in which the right to reproductive liberty before fetal viability remains constitutionally fundamental, yet complex state regulation is also permissible

Leslie P. Francis is a professor of law and associate professor of philosophy at the University of Utah.

so long as it does not unduly burden that right.[2] Questions about state regulation of abortion remain at the forefront of the political process. So do discussions about the political and intellectual viability of compromise. As abortion is debated in state legislatures and Congress, these struggles with linkages between policy and personal morality are acutely apparent. This essay, then, is as much about moral and political theory and abortion as it is about current constitutional law or predictions about how constitutional law may evolve over the next few years.

Third, I believe that understanding the moral structure of important arguments in opposition to abortion is helpful to constitutional theory. I argue that the moral structure of one major view in opposition to abortion is fundamentally theological. If opposition to abortion is theologically based, I then argue, the constitutional line for prohibition of abortion is rightly drawn at viability; at viability, but not before, consensus about the wrongness of abortion is such that the state's interest in protecting potential life becomes compelling.

As Woman and Mother

I am the mother of three children. I have thought a great deal about whether, emotionally, I could ever have an abortion. I believe there are only two circumstances in which I could: if the child were not the result of a voluntary union with my husband, or if the child were so damaged as to be incapable of meaningful interaction with myself and my family. I am less certain about whether I could bring myself to have an abortion in cases of serious physical risk to myself, largely because of the enormous disappointment the decision would involve but also because of the feeling that the decision to abort to protect myself would be undeniably selfish.

The common factor in these emotional observations is my understanding of relationality. I would not feel—or want to try to feel, or think I ought to feel—related to a child who was the result of rape. Nor would I feel any of these relational connections to a child with whom I could not interact in minimal human fashion. And for me the most powerful reason for terminating a pregnancy that threatened my own life or capacities would be the ways in which it would threaten ongoing relationships with my husband, my existing children, my friends, and my work.

It is common in feminist moral theory to emphasize the relational element in morality, to ground moral analysis and moral claims in underlying relationships and caring.[3] Some legal theorists have also approached the issue of abortion in this way.[4] In this view, an understanding of the ethical issues posed by abortion begins by seeing both mother and fetus as embedded in relationships. In general, relationships may be central to moral theory, an issue I largely leave to the side here.[5] Several observations about relationality and abortion, however, are important to my argument.

Most centrally, the relationality I described in my thinking about abortion is subjective, dependent on my own feelings and perceptions. There are, of course, objective ways in which any woman pregnant as a result of rape is related to the child she bears: she is its genetic and gestational mother. Nonetheless, her feelings toward the child may not coincide with any of the objective categorizations. Theories that take relationality to be central to morality often do not focus on whether it is subjective or objective relationality that is meant. Yet theories of subjective and objective relationality lead in quite different directions on the abortion issue.

Subjective relationality links what is said morally about abortions to feelings of the individuals involved.[6] This link may be drawn quite directly: abortions are wrong when the mother has strong feelings toward the fetus, or abortions are permissible when the mother lacks these relational ties. Or it may be indirect: the feelings of the mother for the fetus are grounds for protecting the mother's power to choose whether to continue the pregnancy. In assessing the moral significance of the mother's feelings, it is important to remember that women have widely varying reactions to pregnancies. Many women feel deeply attached to the children they bear. Others resent the stranger within. In a wide range of cases beyond rape, the woman may have little or no feelings of relationship to the fetus; these include involuntary sexual relationships that are not legally chargeable as rape and voluntary sexual relations that result in unwanted and rejected pregnancies. It seems reasonable to assume that the pregnancies in which the woman has weak emotional bonds with the fetus are many of those in which abortion is most likely to be considered.[7] But it does not follow that these are the cases in which decisions to have abortions are morally permissible, or that abortion is more problematic morally in cases in which subjective relational ties are stronger. We would need further argument to show that abortion is more problematic morally when the woman is struggling emotionally with the decision because of her feelings toward the fetus and less problematic when the mother has no feelings whatsoever. Nel Noddings, for example, contends that an abortion chosen by a mother who is struggling emotionally is more problematic than an abortion chosen by a mother who has no feelings toward the fetus, precisely because of the feelings the first abortion would deny. Nonetheless, Noddings also holds that there comes a point in an infant's development at which responsive caring is demanded and the mother's lack of feeling is itself morally problematic.[8]

Indeed, there is a general difficulty with relying on subjective relationality to provide exclusive guidance about how entities on either side of the relationship should be treated: it ignores features of the entities that are independent of their relationship. Noddings, as I have just noted, finds abortions after viability, like infanticide, morally problematic because the infant calls forth caring responses. Or consider the homeless or the friendless: their unconnectedness does not mean that others may treat them miserably or that they lack moral claims or moral status. On the moral agent's side, a generalized emphasis on subjective relationality as the source of moral claims would yield the—perhaps problematic—conclusion that those who care about others would bear a greater burden of moral claims than those who lack fellow feeling.[9]

The relevance of subjective relationality to morality may also be found in the importance of protecting certain valuable relationships—for example, by developing institutions that allow these relationships to flourish. Perhaps the link between subjective relationality and a moral theory of abortion is indirect: that because some women have very strong positive feelings about pregnancy and others have very strong negative feelings, we ought to design legal institutions to protect women's choices. This argument for the "pro-choice" position will not seem plausible, however, to those who believe that abortion is wrong for reasons that are independent of the fetus's relational situation. And there are general problems in relying on the strength of felt relationships for drawing conclusions about the allocation of decision-making authority. Consider medical decision making as an analogy. The strength of parents' feelings for their children is surely relevant to whether we should let parents make medical decisions on their children's behalf. But it is not always decisive—for instance, in situations in which parents choose nontraditional therapies such as laetrile for relatively treatable childhood cancers. Or consider adoption. The strength of relational feelings is a reason for supporting a birth mother's claim to search for a child given up long ago, or a child's claim to search for birth parents. But it is not the only morally relevant consideration. The point of these examples is not that subjective relationality is morally irrelevant, but that these situations are morally complex. The protection of subjectively valued parent-child relationships is surely an important issue in the allocation of decision-making authority to parents, including pregnant women. Indeed, this protection is a very important, principled reason why some people who believe personally that abortion is wrong at the same time defend legal protection for procreative liberty. But it seems that factors other than the protection of subjectively valued parent-child relationships are also relevant to a full moral theory of abortion.

Objective relationality, by contrast with subjective relationality, can be the basis for moral claims that transcend feelings. There are certainly a number of objective relationships that hold between the fetus and the pregnant woman, as well as between the fetus and other people. The fetus is related gestationally and (usually) genetically to the pregnant mother.[10] Cultural and legal categorizations may link the fetus to the gestational mother. But a central difficulty in arguing from objective relationality to a general theory about abortion lies in singling out which relationships matter and arguing why they do make a difference. With subjective relationality, the felt urgency of the relationship can be the basis of an argument for its moral significance and the desirability of protecting it. With objective relationality, the import of the relationship must be given some other grounding. For example, suppose we were to explore the moral significance of genetic connections between parents and child—an objective relationship. We would then need an account of why genetic relationships generate moral claims independently of the feelings of those who are genetically related. Should a sperm donor, for example, be called upon for a bone marrow transplant for his genetic offspring, even though he gave the sperm with the understanding that it was solely in order to enable someone else to become a father?[11] Apart from attributing intrinsic value to genetic relationships—a position with potentially racist implications—perhaps the most likely account would be that genetic relationships uniquely equip the parties to contribute to each other. This unique ability, for example, might be regarded as a moral reason for requiring the genetic father to donate bone marrow for his offspring. A similar account based on unique ability has been given of the importance of gestational relationships: until we develop the technical ability to allow fetuses to develop outside the womb, gestational mothers are uniquely placed and, so the account goes, uniquely obligated to carry their pregnancies to term. Nonetheless, these accounts based in uniqueness are not in themselves enough to establish moral claims on the part of the fetus. Arguments from the standpoint of uniqueness identify the relevant source of aid, if aid is morally required, but they do not create a moral basis for the aid itself. That is, arguments founded on the unique capacities of the mother show why it is the *mother* who should aid the fetus, if the fetus has claims to aid in the first place.

Thus, relationality does not provide a full account of the morality or immorality of abortion. Subjective relationality may be part of an argument for protecting relationships when they are taken to be important by the parties to them, but not for imposing relations on people who would choose not to be engaged. Objective relationality may establish direction when the fetus has moral claims to aid, a separate issue to which I will turn in a moment. So although my mothering emotions explain why I would not choose to have an abortion, they are not enough for a full moral theory of abortion.

But perhaps there is a deeper moral point about relationships. Feminist theories of virtue turn our attention to the attitudes we have toward relationships. Perhaps what is wrong with the discussion so far is that it looks at relationships in a vacuum. Rosalind Hursthouse, for example, explores those attitudes that are morally appropriate for women to have toward pregnancies in different life circumstances.[12] Noddings's position is that we should view decisions about abortion in different circumstances in terms of what they reveal about caring.[13] The possibility of developing a theory of virtue without moral presuppositions about moral rights, duties, or claims is controversial. With respect to abortion, the controversy centers on whether we can develop an account of the attitudes which are morally appropriate toward pregnancy without a theory about the moral status of the fetus. Although I shall not argue for this view here, I think that discussion of the moral status of the fetus is at least *relevant* to attitudes about pregnancy in different circumstances, as Noddings indicates,[14] although it may not be the whole story about these attitudes either. So it is to the fetus itself, rather than its relational situation, that I now turn.

AS MORAL THEORIST

Suppose we approach the issue of the moral status of the fetus by outlining the moral conclusions of one familiar right-to-life position. We can then work backwards to moral theories that would justify these conclusions. Central to opposition to abortion is the view that abortion of a human fetus[15] is a serious moral wrong—a wrong serious enough to be outweighed only in very special circumstances, if at all.[16]

Although the seriousness of the moral wrong of abortion takes center stage, there are as well some other conclusions that should be included in the reconstruction of familiar right-to-life views. While abortion opponents certainly disagree about contraception, at least some foes of abortion believe that abortion is a serious wrong in a way that the use of contraceptives to prevent the union of sperm and egg is not (leaving aside for the moment the use of those contraceptives that function as abortifacients). Indeed, some antiabortionists regard contraception as a highly desirable means for avoiding pregnancy in the first place. Second, while our treatment of nonhuman species is surely also a subject for debate, it has not taken center stage with abortion in the activities of many abortion foes. So for at least some opponents of abortion, human abortion is a special and different kind of moral wrong from killing of members of nonhuman species.

These additional propositions—the moral differentiation of abortion from contraception and of human abortion from the killing of nonhuman species—are not required by a commitment to the moral rights of the human fetus. Indeed, there are life-centered views that would see a natural link between respect for nonhuman species and opposition to abortion. And there are many who would extend opposition to abortion to opposition to contraception. Moreover, the views that link opposition to abortion with concerns about contraception, or concerns about treatment of nonhuman species, may very well be theoretically more plausible than the distinctions between abortion and contraception and between humans and nonhumans. But they are not the views I explore here, because I think it is fair to say that they are not the most familiar right-to-life views. Studies of the political values of antiabortion activists, for example, do not reveal frequent linkages to animal rights activists.[17] State efforts to limit abortion have not been coupled with efforts to limit contraception,[18] although it is certainly true that some groups that oppose abortion—such as the Catholic church—officially oppose contraception as well. Nor have state antiabortion statutes been introduced in tandem with animal protection statutes. At the federal level, efforts to limit abortion have been human-centered;[19] and opposition to the experimental use of human fetal tissue has not gone hand in hand with opposition to the use of animals in medical research. So I take as my starting place the right-to-life view that regards abortion of a human fetus as a serious moral wrong but does not regard contraception or killing of a nonhuman fetus in the same light. I then ask what moral framework or frameworks will get us the conclusions of this right-to-life position.

The language frequently invoked to explain the moral uniqueness of the human fetus is that conception is the moment "when life begins." But this language is misleading.[20] "Life" in the sense of mere vitalism is too broad to yield the conclusion that abortion of a human fetus is a special moral wrong. Other animal and plant species are alive. So the appeal to conception as the dividing line must be crucially qualified as the moment "when human life begins." This qualification would capture the moral uniqueness of the human fetus. Nonetheless, it may not yield a moral conclusion, for "when human life begins" is a crucially ambiguous phrase. Does it express a moral judgment, that conception is the moment at which a being of moral significance comes into existence? Or does it express a scientific judgment, that conception is the moment after cells start to divide in a particular way? Or does "when human life begins" straddle both the moral and the scientific claims? In other words, does "when human life begins" refer to the underlying biology, the moral conclusion, or an argument from the biology to the moral conclusion?

The biological description alone cannot be what is meant by "when human life begins," if the description is to be the basis for the right-to-life position. In reconstructing the right-to-life position, our concern is an account of when the fetus becomes morally considerable, when it is a source of moral claims, when it has the right to life. Moving from the biological description to the normative account, then, requires an explanation of why the biological process has the moral significance that it does, an account that goes beyond physiological description. On the other hand, the understanding of "when human life begins" as a moral claim about the status of the fetus simply restates the moral conclusion; it does not provide an argument for it. We need to know what it is about the biologically developing entity that matters morally, and why. There are a number of suggested characteristics of the developing fetus that could lend it moral significance. I will begin with the characteristics that are least successful as bases for the moral argument and move to the better ones.

One suggested feature that is often invoked to differentiate the human fetus from the young of other species is that it has human form. The human fetus begins to look remarkably infant-like quite early in pregnancy.[21] This resemblance is what gives such emotional power to legislation that would require pregnant women to view pictures or ultrasound images of the children they carry. But it is difficult to explain the moral importance of "human form"—why its human form is the characteristic that gives the fetus moral significance. To equate "human form" with the simple "it looks like us"—the appeal of pictures—opens the way to deeply problematic moral differentiation: acceptance of those who resemble us (whites, males, the able-bodied) and rejection of those who do not (blacks, females, the disabled). If, instead, the physical resemblance is taken to reveal other characteristics—as the physical resemblance in the pro-life film *The Silent Scream*[22] is taken to reveal the capacity to suffer—then it is those other characteristics and not the similarity of form that bear the real weight in attributing special moral significance to the human fetus.

Historically, perhaps the most frequently invoked basis for the moral or legal status of the human fetus was "quickening," the moment at which the mother can feel fetal movement. According to English common law, abortion was permitted up until quickening. Abortion before quickening was prohibited by statute in Britain in 1803. Connecticut, in 1821, was the first American state to prohibit abortion before quickening.[23] One reason for the legal reliance on quickening was that it was thought to provide evidence of the fetus's capacity for eventual survival outside the womb.[24] But quickening is at best an imperfect measure of fetal development—albeit perhaps the best available in the days before modern science. Quickening requires the mother's perception of movement, which may vary for reasons other than fetal vitality. In any event, the capacity for movement is surely not the basis for the special moral significance of the fetus; it is a characteristic widely shared by other animal species. Instead, quickening in the human species may be regarded as a sign that some other morally significant process—for example, ensoulment—has taken place; this was the view of some early Catholic theologians.[25]

Another candidate for a characteristic that gives the fetus moral status, suggested by *The Silent Scream,* is the capacity to feel pain or experience pleasure. There are two difficulties in regarding the capacity to feel pain as foundational to the right to life. First, while the capacity to feel pain may give rise to some moral claims, it is unclear that it gives rise to moral claims to *continued* existence.[26] The connection between a being's capacity to feel and the moral wrongness of causing it present pain is direct. If it is morally wrong to cause suffering, it is morally wrong to cause pain to a sentient being. The connection is surely grounds for objecting to methods and timing of abortions that cause the fetus physical pain. If the capacity to feel pain develops incrementally in later stages of pregnancy, this criterion would provide grounds for objecting to later abortions if they are performed in ways that cause pain.[27] On the other hand, the connection between current sentience and rights to continued existence is indirect at best. When an individual lacks the capacity to understand the significance of future pleasure or pain, Michael Tooley has contended, there is no basis for arguing that future pleasure or pain is a good to the individual.[28]

A second difficulty with using sentience as the moral basis for the right-to-life position under consideration is that it does not draw distinctions between humans and many nonhuman species. The capacity to feel pain is not unique to human beings. If sentience grounds moral claims to continued existence, it does so for members of many other species in addition to preborn human infants. This argument has been the basis for objections to animal experimentation, as well as for defenses of vegetarianism.[29] But it links objections to abortion to objections to our treatment of all sentient creatures, rather than providing an account of the special wrongfulness of human abortions.

A third suggested basis for the moral status of the fetus is the capacity to reason. This criterion, if interpreted to mean the capacity for reasoning of abstract or logical significance, is clearly too strong to serve as a reconstruction of the standard right-to-life position. As Michael Tooley has pointed out, even newborn human infants do not have capacities to reason of any very sophisticated sort.[30] On the other hand, if some very minimal neural activity is what is meant by the capacity to reason in the right-to-life argument, that begins to appear at about eight to ten weeks' gestation. Diminishing the rationality criterion, therefore, would not establish the right-to-life view that abortions are wrong from conception. Moreover, many nonhuman creatures share the minimal neural capacity of fetuses in the earlier developmental stages. This weaker rationality criterion, therefore, is also too broad to establish the special wrongfulness of human abortions.

Thus, actualized biological characteristics do not serve very well to make the theoretical distinctions that are the basis for the right-to-life view under examination. The most plausible biological candidates either include too much or occur too late in pregnancy to give us the conclusion that abortion from the time of conception is a serious moral wrong. There are better ways to try to reconstruct the right-to-life view. The best accounts of the special status of the human fetus rest either on its potential to acquire characteristics such as sentience or reason or on a nonbiological explanation of the value of human life.

Let us try potentiality. Can the suggestion that the fetus has the potential to develop characteristics such as reason or sentience explain the special moral status of the human fetus from conception? If abortion is to be distinguished from contraception—and, as I have said above, this distinction is a plausible one but certainly not always linked with right-to-life views—we need to understand the kind of potentiality claim that is made about the postconception fetus in a way that distinguishes it from the kinds of potentiality claims that might be made about a not-yet-united sperm and egg. "Potential" just in the sense of being part of a biological process that may ultimately result in a human being does not clearly distinguish abortion from contraception. The formation of egg and sperm are earlier stages in the biological process that can yield fertilization under appropriate circumstances. That the appropriate circumstances include human voluntary actions does not distinguish fertilization from subsequent stages in the human reproductive process, which also require various forms of human cooperation. To be sure, the probabilities of any particular fertilization are very slim, but so are the probabilities of continuation for some pregnancies. Moreover, do the lower chances of fertilization demonstrate that there is a difference in principle between the sperm and egg before fertilization and the zygote afterwards, or do they simply give us more reason to try to increase the probabilities of fertilization? Potentiality in the sense of a biological process that will ultimately result in a human being unless interrupted by human action likewise does not distinguish postconception fetuses and the not-yet-united sperm and egg; human interventions occur both before and after conception to interrupt the process.[31]

Nonetheless, it may seem that there are crucial differences between the biological process before conception and the process after conception. First of all, before conception the entity (or entities) that will result has not as yet been identified. At a point relatively soon after conception, the entity (or entities) will be identifiable.[32] Whether unique identifiability is necessary to the moral status of a creature, however, is problematic. To take an analogy, we may not know who are the likely victims of an explosion in a nuclear power plant, or even whether they are all in existence at the present moment; but it does not follow from their nonidentifiability that there are no moral claims to be made with respect to them. Certainly, there is a difference between an actual entity that we cannot identify and an entity that we cannot identify because it is not yet actual: we owe the nonidentified actual being whatever duties we owe actual beings. But actuality is not the issue here; we are comparing potentiality before and after conception. The question is whether identifiability makes the moral difference between two different kinds of potential creatures, and I have argued that it does not. The lingering sense that what has just been said is unsatisfactory, I think, should be attributed to the sense that the postconception fetus is somehow different from the not-yet-united sperm and egg in that the fetus has some actual characteristics yet to be explained.

As mentioned above, another suggested difference between the not-yet-united sperm and egg and the postconception fetus lies in degrees of probability. The likelihood of a given sperm and egg uniting to form a conceptus is far less than the likelihood of that conceptus developing into a live-born infant, although in the early stages of its development that too is relatively unlikely. And the probability continues to be low for the postconception fetus during the early stages of development. Moreover, the general statistics about miscarriage rates and their decline as pregnancy advances do not tell us the probability that a particular pregnancy will be successful. Some pregnancies of sixteen weeks' gestation may have very low chances of resulting in live births, depending on the conditions of the fetus and the mother. Some fetuses are thus highly potential in the sense that they are quite likely to be live-born if they are not aborted; others are not so highly potential, at all different stages of pregnancy. One possible conclusion to draw from these differences is that the more probable fetuses have a greater claim to life and the less probable fetuses have a lesser claim. But this conclusion would be unsettling to those who think that fetal rights are based on characteristics intrinsic to the fetus and that all fetuses are of similar moral value. Those who value the fetus in its own right, moreover, might take the difference in probable outcomes to suggest that we should work to increase the probability of fetal success, for example, by medical efforts to avert miscarriages. So another possible conclusion to draw is that all potential entities have claims and that we should work to increase their potentiality where possible.[33] This position, however, once again extends right-to-life claims to entities before conception.

These persistent difficulties with reliance on biological characteristics or potentiality to ground right-to-life claims suggest the hypothesis that these kinds of characteristics are not really what is central to the right-to-life view. Rather, the crucial point is that the fetus, from conception, is "human" in some special sense. It has an actualized characteristic—"humanity"—that the preconception sperm and egg do not. This hypothesis explains the persistent appeal in the abortion debate of the language that "human life begins" at conception. But we as yet lack an explanation of the moral significance of the conceptual moment. Let us try one final theory: that from conception the embryo is "human" because it has a God-given spark of life, a soul. Conception is special because it is the moment when what might be called "ensoulment" occurs.[34]

This doctrine of ensoulment captures the language and scope of the right-to-life position we are examining: that human embryos are special, from conception, in a way nonhuman embryos are not. Nevertheless, our religious traditions have disagreed about the occurrence of ensoulment. Some have put ensoulment at conception. The Septuagint, an early Greek version of the Old Testament, located ensoulment at the moment when the fetus became fully formed. Aristotle and some of his followers within the Catholic tradition put it at motion, supposedly at forty days for the male fetus and ninety days for the female.[35] Theological controversy within the Catholic church continues to this day, both about the timing of ensoulment and about whether ensoulment and the status of the fetus or a more general commitment to procreation explains the moral wrongfulness of abortion.[36] Even the LDS church, a contemporary staunch religious opponent of abortion, has apparently held different doctrines about the timing of ensoulment.[37]

There are clearly disagreements here, within and among religious faiths. At least among faiths, we lack an epistemological method for adjudicating doctrinal disagreements. Different faiths make different kinds of claims about the justification for essentially religious doctrines such as when ensoulment occurs. Moreover, whether or not we can settle these disputes on religious grounds, use of a religious criterion for deciding "when life begins" places us face to face with the role of religious judgments in public policy and law. Perhaps this dilemma helps to explain the persistent dissatisfaction with Justice Blackmun's statement in *Roe v. Wade* (1973): "We need not resolve the difficult question of when life begins."[38]

AS LEGAL THEORIST

Roe v. Wade held that women have an interest in reproductive liberty, constitutionally protected under the Fourteenth Amendment and overrideable only by a compelling state interest.[39] According to *Roe,* both the woman's rights and the state's interests are limited. *Roe* fit these limits into the trimester framework, with the woman's interest paramount during the first trimester, the state's interest in protecting the woman's health permitting regulation during the second trimester, and the state's interest in protecting potential life becoming compelling during the third trimester.[40]

The fit between protected interests and the trimester framework, never entirely comfortable, became increasingly stretched as innovations in medical care moved viability back from the final third of pregnancy to twenty-four or twenty-five weeks' gestation. The trimester framework was brought into serious doubt in the *Webster v. Reproductive Health Services* decision in 1989. The question posed in *Webster* was the constitutional permissibility of a state statute, designed to protect viable fetuses, that required testing for possible fetal viability from twenty weeks of gestational age. In *Webster,* Chief Justice Rehnquist, joined by Justices White and Kennedy, wrote that the *Roe* trimester framework should be overruled.[41]

Webster also reopened more general speculation about the central holding of *Roe* that the woman has the right to reproductive liberty. In *Webster,* Justice Scalia stated explicitly that *Roe* should be overruled.[42] Chief Justice Rehnquist, joined by Justices Kennedy and White, urged that the state has a compelling interest in protecting potential human life throughout pregnancy and not simply at viability.[43]

The speculation opened by *Webster* was laid to rest nearly three years later. In *Planned Parenthood of Southeastern Pennsylvania v. Casey,*[44] the Court reaffirmed the woman's right to reproductive liberty. Justice O'Connor's opinion for the Court emphasized both the constitutional importance of liberty and the value of *stare decisis*. The Court's endorsement of what it characterized as the central holding of *Roe* has, for the present, put to rest arguments that the Court was prepared to approve of state efforts to prohibit abortion.[45] At the same time, six justices voted in *Casey* to overrule the trimester framework of *Roe*.[46] Despite ending speculation about whether *Roe* would be overruled, the Court in *Casey* left other questions significantly open. In reaffirming *Roe*, the *Casey* court characterized its earlier holding as having three essential parts. First, the woman has the right "to have an abortion before viability and to obtain it without undue interference from the state." Second, after viability the state has the power to restrict abortions, provided it makes exceptions for pregnancies endangering the woman's life or health. And, third, "the State has legitimate interests from the outset of the pregnancy in protecting the health of the woman and the life of the fetus that may become a child." The Court concluded this reconstruction of *Roe* by observing that "these principles do not contradict one another."[47]

Nonetheless, there are obvious tensions between the three principles extracted by the Court from *Roe*. As states contemplate what they may and may not regulate in the wake of *Casey*, one of the most significant tensions lies between the state's interest in protecting the life of the fetus and the woman's right not to have her reproductive liberty unduly burdened. A powerful source of this tension is that the Court characterized the state's interest in potential life as lying in "the life of the fetus that may become a child" rather than in "the child that the fetus may become, if it is born alive." The latter characterization focuses on the state's interest in ensuring health to the future child, if the pregnancy is continued. It would apply, for example, to state efforts to reduce drug abuse during pregnancy—itself a controversial issue of maternal-fetal conflict. But the Court's actual characterization suggests a state interest in fetal life itself, and thus in whether pregnancies are continued. It is state efforts to promote this interest, such as by enforcing waiting periods for women seeking abortions or by requiring that women be given information about fetal development and alternatives to abortion, that have generated continued controversy about what the Court really means by an "undue burden" on reproductive liberty, and that will continue to be litigated in states such as Pennsylvania, Utah, and Louisiana. Yet if I am right that there is significant disagreement about the moral status of the fetus before viability and that the most plausible reasons for according the fetus full moral status before viability are religious, the Court's characterization of the state's interest in protecting fetal life before viability is problematic. Moreover, it is at odds with the Court's discussion in *Casey* of the importance of protecting women's liberty interests. Underlying the woman's liberty interest, the Court said, is the utterly personal nature of the decision to have an abortion:

> The destiny of the woman must be shaped to a large extent on her own conception of her spiritual imperatives and her place in society. . . . Reasonable people will have differences of opinion about these matters. One view is based on such reverence for the wonder of creation that any pregnancy ought to be welcomed and carried to full term no matter how difficult it will be to provide for the child and ensure its well-being. Another is that the inability to provide for the nurture and care of the infant is a cruelty to the child and an anguish to the parent. These are intimate views with infinite variations, and their deep, personal character underlay our decisions in Griswold, Eisenstadt, and Casey.[48]

Suppose, then, that at this juncture we reach more deeply into constitutional theory, to ask what kinds of considerations the Court should invoke in deciding whether to reevaluate the permissibility of states' asserting powerful interests in protecting fetal life before viability.

Some early commentators on *Roe* suggested that Justice Blackmun had appropriately avoided the issue of "when life begins" because of the religious linkages it suggested. Laurence Tribe, for example, suggested that because of the religious controversy involved in the discussion of "when life begins" *Roe* had appropriately allocated the abortion decision to private judgment rather than to the state.[49] This line of analysis has long since been abandoned, perhaps because of increasing confusion about what separation of church and state should itself mean. Tribe himself now rejects his earlier view, because he believes it is constitutionally and politically important for religious groups to be involved in political debate.[50] Nonetheless, I think that Tribe's original line of argument is one that we should revisit as the essentially religious nature of the controversy about abortion persists.

Certainly, reasons based in religious judgment shape and influence and support our law in all sorts of ways, from the prohibition of murder to the recognition of advance directives for health care. To say that it is theoretically problematic for legislatures or courts to take religiously based reasons into account would surely remove an important dimension from our public life, as Kent Greenawalt has recently pointed out.[51] So it would be too strong to say that we should never let legislators or the public act on the basis of religious judgment.

On the other hand, we can look at the nature of the consensus within which religious judgments play a part. Some consensus is what we might call "thick": many different perspectives and lines of argument, secular and religious, converge on the same conclusion.[52] Other consensus is "thinner": some religious or secular traditions point in one direction while other traditions point in other directions. Consider, for example, whether adult Jehovah's Witnesses should be required to receive blood transfusions in life-threatening situations. Both the Jehovah's Witnesses' injunction against transfusions and the secular view that competent adults should be able to determine their own fates lead to the same conclusion: that transfusions should not be compelled. This is a "thick" consensus. By contrast, consider whether adult Witnesses should be allowed to refuse transfusions on behalf of their minor children. Here, both religious traditions and secular arguments that would protect children line up against allowing parents to refuse transfusions on behalf of their children. The consensus that children *should* be treated is therefore relatively thick, despite religious dissent. Thus, my point is not that we should limit the role of churches in American public debate. It is rather about when the nature of political controversy permits state intervention with liberty. When the controversy tends to divide along religious lines, with a solidly religious explanation for one side's position and a more secular consensus on the other side, we do not have the kind of thick consensus that permits state intervention.

About the status of the fetus before viability, moreover, we do not have anything like a thick consensus. We are deeply divided about whether "life" begins at conception. Some religious traditions place ensoulment at that point; other traditions place it later or earlier. Secular arguments largely support protection of the fetus at a later point in time. On the other hand, we do have a far thicker consensus that supports protecting fetuses that have reached viability. A variety of arguments, both religious and non-religious, support asserting state interests after the point of viability. If the presence of thick consensus can support the assertion of compelling state interests, it would therefore be appropriate to assert state interests in protecting the life of a viable fetus.

I am thus suggesting that there is an interface between moral analysis and constitutional theory of the following sort: When moral analysis reveals thin consensus, it is inappropriate for the state to assert one side in the dispute as a compelling interest. It is especially inappropriate for the state to support an essentially religious point of view. But this is exactly what the Court will allow states to do, if it allows states to regulate abortions by invoking compelling interests in protecting potential life before viability.

Notes

1. See, for example, Richard Epstein, "Rights and 'Rights Talk'" (Review of Mary Ann Glendon, *Rights Talk: The Impoverishment of Political Discourse*), *Harvard Law Review* 105 (1992): 1106, 1122. ("The difficulty with abortion lies in the enduring split in basic value structures in the United States. The secular left and the religious right bring to this debate fundamental differences in philosophy.")

2. 112 S.Ct. 2791.

3. See, for example, Nel Noddings, *Caring: A Feminine Approach to Ethics and Moral Education* (Berkeley and Los Angeles: University of California Press, 1984); Carol Gilligan, *In a Different Voice: Psychological Theory and Women's Development* (Cambridge, Mass.: Harvard University Press, 1982).

4. See, for example, Robert Goldstein, *Mother Love and Abortion* (Berkeley and Los Angeles: University of California Press, 1988).

5. See, for example, Sarah Lucia Hoagland, "Some Thoughts about 'Caring,'" in *Feminist Ethics,* ed. Claudia Card (Lawrence: University of Kansas Press, 1991).

6. Nel Noddings holds that early abortions do not diminish caring if the woman lacks relational responses to the child. On the other hand, there comes a point in pregnancy at which the fetus is so much like a child that caring responses are called forth. *Caring,* 87–88.

7. For some examples that support this hypothesis, see Gilligan, *In a Different Voice,* chap. 3.

8. Noddings, *Caring,* 88.

9. For the suggestion that women have a more relational understanding of self, and as a result may be at a disadvantage in mediation of child custody disputes, see Trina Grillo, "The Mediation Alternative," *Yale Law Journal* 100 (1991): 1545, 1550.

10. Is the moral permissibility of abortion affected if the pregnant woman is related to the fetus gestationally but not genetically? If not, does the gestational mother have stronger claims to parenthood of a child carried to term than its genetic parents have? These questions, raised now by some surrogate pregnancies, force us to confront which objective relationships we think matter to which decisions, in what contexts, and why.

11. Typical statutes authorizing artificial insemination by donor absolve the donor/genetic father of paternal responsibilities for the child. See, for example, Uniform Parentage Act 5(b), 9B *Uniform Laws Annotated* 301 (1987).

12. See Rosalind Hursthouse, "Virtue Theory and Abortion," *Philosophy and Public Affairs* 20 (1991): 223–46; *Beginning Lives* (Oxford, Engl.: Basil Blackwell's, 1987).

13. Noddings, *Caring,* 87–88.

14. "Since the infant, even the near-natal fetus, is capable of relation—of the sweetest and most unselfconscious reciprocity—one who encounters the infant is obligated to meet it as one-caring." Ibid., 89.

15. A note about language is important at this point. Opponents of abortion prefer to refer to the fetus as an "unborn child" or a "preborn child"; pro-choice advocates prefer the term "fetus." These terms convey unarticulated but obvious moral analogies. I have struggled to find a neutral descriptive term, because these analogies of language beg the moral issue to be argued. But no neutral term seemed readily available ("descriptum" as in "thing to be described" is too ugly), so I have settled for using "fetus" and "child" interchangeably, with this reminder that nothing moral hinges on my choice of words.

16. Several different accounts have been offered of what these special circumstances might be, accounts that can be traced to different theoretical foundations. Danger to the mother's life or health may be regarded as outweighing the wrong of abortion by analogy to self-defense. Severe fetal malformation may be regarded as an outweighing factor on the theory that continuation of the pregnancy would be fruitless in protecting the fetus. Other circumstances frequently mentioned as outweighing the wrong of abortion single out pregnancies that are unlikely to be voluntary, such as pregnancies resulting from rape or incest. Those holding a less strong view of the fetus's rights may argue that the wrong of abortion is outweighed when continuing the pregnancy would be very burdensome to the mother; in this category might fall proposed exceptions for fetal abnormalities, for risks to the mother's physical health, or for risks to the mother's mental health.

17. See, for example, Kristin Luker, *Abortion and the Politics of Motherhood* (Berkeley and Los Angeles: University of California Press, 1984), chap. 7 (describing pro-life activists as holding strong family values, as differentiating the roles of men and women, and as rejecting many forms of contraception in favor of the rhythm method of family planning); Raymond Tatalovich and Byron W. Daynes, *The Politics of Abortion: A Study of Community Conflict in Public Policymaking* (New York: Praeger, 1981), 161. ("One reason the Right-to-Life committees are so politically interesting is that they represent, more than any other group in either movement, the pristine, hard-core single-issue group.")

18. Indeed, Utah's recent statute specifically defines "abortion" to exclude both methods of contraception that prevent fertilization and methods of contraception that prevent implantation: "'Abortion' means the intentional termination or attempted termination of human pregnancy after implantation of a fertilized ovum . . . ." *Utah Code Annotated* 76–7–301(1) (Supp. 1991).

19. For example, in the early 1980s, the two pro-life proposals that dominated debate in the United States Senate were Senator Helms's "Human Life Statute" and Senator Hatch's "Human Life Federalism Amendment." See Laurence H. Tribe, *Abortion: The Clash of Absolutes* (New York: W. W. Norton, 1990), 161–62.

20. The points in this paragraph have become standard in the philosophical literature. See, for example, L. W. Sumner, *Abortion and Moral Theory* (Princeton, N.J.: Princeton University Press, 1981), 92–93.

21. It is, however, worth noting that an extensive process of cell division is needed before the fetus begins to assume human form; abortifacient contraceptives such as the IUD or some forms of the pill function before the fetus assumes human form; and RU–486 certainly can be used before human shape appears.

22. Bernard Nathanson, *The Silent Scream* (Anaheim, Calif.: American Portrait Films, 1985), film.

23. "Special Project: Survey of Abortion Law," *Arizona State Law Journal* 1980: 67, 93.

24. See James W. Knight and Joan C. Callahan, *Preventing Birth: Contemporary Methods and Related Moral Controversies* (Salt Lake City: University of Utah Press, 1989), 210–11.

25. Ibid., 211.

26. For a defense of animal rights based not on welfare but on a view of animals as moral agents, see Tom Regan, *The Case for Animal Rights* (Berkeley and Los Angeles: University of California Press, 1983).

27. Early in pregnancy, fetal neural development is rudimentary. The fetal spinal cord does not emerge until the third week of pregnancy; and the major divisions between the forebrain, midbrain, and brainstem appear about the eighth week. EEG activity is detectable at the end of the first trimester of pregnancy; by the beginning of the third trimester the fetal brain resembles the brain of a newborn infant. The best estimates are that the ability to feel pain emerges somewhere in the second trimester of pregnancy (see Knight and Callahan, *Preventing Birth,* 217; Sumner, *Abortion and Moral Theory,* 146–51).

28. Michael Tooley, *Abortion and Infanticide* (Oxford, Engl.: Clarendon Press, 1983), 120.

29. Peter Singer, *Animal Liberation* (New York: Random House, 1975).

30. Tooley, *Abortion and Infanticide,* 360–62.

31. See, for example, ibid., 167–68. Tooley also draws a useful distinction between logical possibility and potentiality in the sense under discussion here; potentiality occurs when there are factors in the world that are causally sufficient, or nearly causally sufficient, or causally sufficient without interruption, to bring about the existence of a person.

32. For a discussion of the early development of the conceptus and the point at which it becomes uniquely identifiable, see Knight and Callahan, *Preventing Birth,* esp. 99–102.

33. Sumner suggests a consequentialist argument for this view: that if the existence of rational, or sentient, or some other kind of creature is a good, we should work to produce as much as possible of these goods (*Abortion and Moral Theory,* 101).

34. See, for example, ibid., 88. Sumner dismisses beliefs about ensoulment as too personal to ground either moral theory or public policy.

35. For fascinating discussions of the Catholic theological tradition, see John Connery, *Abortion: The Development of the Roman Catholic Perspective* (Chicago: Loyola University Press, 1977); Knight and Callahan, *Preventing Birth,* 210–11.

36. See "Catholic Scholars, Citing New Data, Widen Debate on When Life Begins," *The New York Times,* 13 January 1991; James J. McCartney, "Some Roman Catholic Concepts of Person and Their Implications for the Ontological Satus of the Unborn," in *Abortion and the Status of the Fetus,* ed. William B. Bondeson, H. Tristram Englehardt, Jr., Stuart F. Spicker, and Daniel H. Winship (Dordrecht: D. H. Reidel, 1983), 313–23.

37. For example, Bruce R. McConkie, in *Mormon Doctrine* (Salt Lake City: Bookcraft, 1958), states that the eternal spirit enters the body at an appreciable time prior to normal birth and cites as his authority President Brigham Young, who taught that "when the mother feels life come to her infant, it is the spirit entering the body preparatory to the immortal existence." Brigham Young et al., *Journal of Discourses . . . ,* 26 vols. (London: Latter-day Saints' Book Depot, 1875), 17: 143.

38. 410 U.S. 113, 159.

39. Ibid., 154.

40. Ibid., 163.

41. 492 U.S. 490, 513–17.

42. Ibid., 532 (Scalia, J., concurring in part and concurring in the judgment).

43. Ibid., 519.

44. 112 S.Ct. 2791.

45. *Sojourner T. v. Edwards,* 974 F.2d 27 (1992).

46. The section of Justice O'Connor's opinion rejecting the trimester framework (*Casey,* 112 S.Ct. 2791, 2860) was joined by Justice Kennedy and Justice Souter. Chief Justice Rehnquist's dissent, urging that *Roe* be overruled in its entirety (2873), was joined by Justice Scalia and Justice Thomas.

47. Ibid., 2804.

48. Ibid., 2807.

49. Laurence H. Tribe, "Foreword: Toward a Model of Roles in the Due Process of Life and Law," *Harvard Law Review* 87 (1973): 1, 23.

50. Tribe, *Abortion,* 116.

51. Kent Greenawalt, *Religious Convictions and Political Choice* (New York: Oxford University Press, 1988).

52. The idea of "thick" or "thin" consensus, as I am developing it, refers to the extent to which different lines of argument converge on the same conclusion, not to the quality of any of the arguments themselves. A "thick" consensus thus differs from the notion, explored by Greenawalt, that liberal democracies should limit themselves to consideration of publicly accessible reasons. Ibid., esp. chap. 4.

VI

ABORTION AND EQUALITY UNDER THE LAW

★

Camille S. Williams

rior to 1973 there was no constitutional right to an abortion;
it was then that abortion activists, tired of coaxing individual states to liberalize their laws, took to the courts to argue that
the First, Fourth, Fifth, Ninth, Thirteenth, and Fourteenth
Amendments provide a basis for the liberty to abort.[1] In effect,
individual rights arguments used federal law to trump state
laws.[2] Basing much of his historiography of abortion on the dis-
putable work of counsel to the National Abortion Rights Action
League, Justice Blackmun concluded in *Roe v. Wade* (1973) that
nineteenth-century abortion restrictions were designed to protect
maternal health, not the unborn child.[3] In addition to his concern for the "medically diagnosable" "specific and direct harm"
that a woman might suffer from pregnancy, he was cognizant
that "maternity, or additional offspring, may force upon the
woman a distressful life and future."[4] He concluded that maternal health and privacy outweigh the "State's interest and general
obligation to protect life" before the unborn are viable.[5] Mindful
of "the wide divergence of thinking" about when life begins,[6]
Justice Blackmun grounded this private right to choose abortion

*Camille S. Williams is an instructor of philosophy at Brigham Young University and is
in her third year of law studies at the university's J. Reuben Clark Law School.*

on his analysis of the medical aspects of abortion and birth and upon the view that the law considered the unborn to be not quite "persons" entitled to protection.[7]

Roe's articulation of our duty to the unborn has proven unsatisfactory and has launched a nationwide discussion about the reach and purpose of law for the individual and the community. Abortion, as a penumbral right, is likely to remain legally accessible under the "Fourteenth Amendment's concept of personal liberty and restrictions upon state action."[8] However, in a society which prizes equality and individual autonomy, *Roe's* "privacy" claim may never be less than disquieting. "How can any activity that involves the consent of one individual, requires the professional assistance of a second, and results in the destruction of a third be called a matter of privacy?" asks legal scholar Lynn D. Wardle.[9] Imaging the unborn as not fully human or not fully alive requires specious reasoning unworthy of us. According to Professor Daniel N. Robinson, "the root question" is "the extent to which human fetal life qualifie[s] for the protections otherwise available to human postnatal life and the extent to which the protections unarguably available to a citizen (e.g., a pregnant woman) can be diminished or withdrawn in favor of human fetal life."[10]

Citizens are not accurately described as merely rights-bearing "self-interested, presocial, unconnected individuals," as Professor Linda C. McClain and other feminist scholars point out. Each of us has "duties arising from personhood, citizenship, and fraternity or sorority," responsibilities derived from the life of the community and the family.[11] Fulfillment of these duties, even when they were unchosen, does not diminish individual agency— rather, it is part of what it means to belong to family or community. Because "it is the law that illuminates the complex and daunting world of the morally free," and which creates a "community fully compatible with the reasonable aspirations of rational beings,"[12] abortion law will not only reflect but also shape our view of ourselves and others.

Each unborn child is sustainable only by his or her own mother.[13] Is it better for an individual woman to determine whether this relationship is one she will continue, or may the community influence her decision by limiting her access to legal abortion? Equal protection arguments assert that it is unfair to *require* mothers to do something that neither fathers nor the larger community *can* do: directly sustain the unborn. Following from *Roe*'s emphasis on abortion as a medical procedure, one line of thought is that women are denied equal protection under the law because only mothers, but not fathers, have been required to bear the weight of children prior to their birth. Because fathers' bodies are not housing the unborn child, fathers can abandon their children more easily than can mothers; mothers should, therefore, be allowed to abort their unborn children as a means of equalizing their status with potentially irresponsible fathers.

Another argument focuses on the social aspects of mothering, asserting that the work of motherhood "entangle[s] women in relations of emotional and economic dependency—to men, extended family, or the state," and is the "principal cause of [women's] secondary status."[14] When pregnant women choose abortion or childbirth, they are choosing their futures. If their educational and social lives, like men's, are to be relatively uninterrupted by the biological and social roles of parent (i.e., motherhood as now constituted), it is argued that women must have the legal right to abort the unplanned, untimely, or too-burdensome child.

I argue that although both equal protection approaches have a powerful emotive appeal to those with the contemporary preference for individuality, neither accurately represents legal and social practices which have traditionally subordinated the individual rights of men and women to their respective familial duties. Equal protection arguments are representative of what Mary Parthun calls "a strongly-voiced belief . . . that legal abortion is a civil right of women and that progress of women's rights can be charted by the ease of access to abortion." This view interprets "opposition to complete access to abortion as opposition to the full liberation of women."[15] Such a position, however, "fails to take account of the humanity of the unborn child"[16] and substitutes a short-sighted notion of what is in the parents' best interest for the best interest of the child, the standard so prevalent throughout family law.[17] Making the decision to protect human young on criteria such as "meaningful life," "ability to exist outside the womb," or "viability" is "dangerously subjective because they could be equally applied to question the humanity of any vulnerable minority."[18] I agree with those who "hold that the parents' right to decide on the life or death of a child is socially regressive."[19] Reducing parental obligations to the unborn child is beneficial neither to parents, nor to their children, nor to society at large.

I am a partisan in this discussion; as the fifth child of a seventh child and granddaughter of a sixteenth child, I belong to a class of those most likely to be considered excess and abortable. I am acquainted with some of the costs and benefits of motherhood.[20] My concern both for women with problem pregnancies and for their unborn children is a response to the generous care given me by my husband and family and to the lessons learned in caring for my own children. Because of the birth of my children, my respect for each individual human being has increased significantly.[21] The distress that women with unwanted pregnancies suffer is real and substantial; but I am convinced that in seeking to help women we must not "deploy base methods in order to be effective."[22]

We must not continue to pit the interests of women against the interests of their own children.[23] "In the end," Daniel N. Robinson states, "it must come down to the weighing of two different but to some extent interdependent sets of interests, though the life interest is the fundamental one. If wisdom prevails—even in a climate hostile to it—life will be affirmed over death, and the *polis* will marshal its moral and material resources in such a way as to make the burdens of this affirmation not fall entirely on one citizen."[24] Such an approach, so fundamental to family law, is entirely within the spirit and the letter of the equal protection clause.

FAMILY LAW AND CONSTITUTIONAL LAW IN TENSION

Much of the Constitution was designed to protect states from federal domination. The Bill of Rights, appended soon after the Constitution's ratification, protected the rights of the individual in the face of federal government power. Still later, ratification of the Fourteenth Amendment with its due process clause provided a way of requiring that state laws yield to the guarantees promised by the Bill of Rights. But despite these guarantees of individual liberty, family law has traditionally imposed obligations such as support and consent that stand in some tension with the notion of unrestrained personal liberty.

Family law—where interdependent interests are played out—
was once the province of the church, then of state governments.
Each state created its own version of domestic law, reflecting the
culture and beliefs of its settlers. Though varying in detail, state
laws require that individuals exhibit minimal levels of responsibility—that is, family members must refrain from killing each
other and are obligated to provide each other with the necessities
of life. Originally, abortion law was wholly a matter of state law;
there was no link between the Bill of Rights and abortion, nor
between the equal protection clause of the Fourteenth
Amendment and abortion. Historically, all of the states discouraged abortion and its damaging effects upon the unborn and
upon mothers by punishing abortionists and, sometimes, the
women who sought abortion.[25]

For well over a century, the Supreme Court deferred to the
power of the states to determine matters ranging from family law
to employment and voting rights. During this century, assertions
of individual fundamental rights were used to preserve *within
families* the right to make decisions regarding the education of
one's children, contraception, and procreation itself.[26] Liberty-
based arguments can encourage or discourage responsible familial
interaction; currently, appeals to the fundamental individual liberty to abort are being used to curtail legal obligations within
the family. Supreme Court decisions striking down laws restricting abortion have had the effect of weakening the obligations an
individual woman has to her unborn child, along with limiting
the legal ability of other family members or the state to influence
her decision about abortion or to protect the unborn child.

The legal and moral traditions of the West—and most of the
world—have consistently assumed that the fulfillment of family
responsibilities is not antithetical to the interests of individuals
themselves. Dysfunctional behaviors within families—acts such
as adultery, bigamy, spouse abuse, incest, and nonsupport—violate prior commitments which were either voluntarily assumed
or imposed by the larger community. The state protects the family[27] as an institution from grossly dysfunctional or criminal acts
for reasons other than merely protecting the individual rights of
family members, important as that may be. An individual
human life is relatively short; the family is more long-lived, with
several generations involved in caring for the aged members

while simultaneously reproducing and nurturing dependent young. Handicapped or sick individuals often receive a quality of care from family members that public or private agencies find impossible to duplicate. In both favorable and adverse conditions, familial bonds are encouraged and sometimes compelled, not simply because one individual is in need, nor even because the state by comparison is inept, but because of the underlying belief that it is in the interests of *all* members of the family that those obligations of care be kept—or, if broken, broken only for the most serious reasons. At some level, we view fulfilling our familial obligations as part of what it means to be a member of the human family, not as a quirky punishment of fate.

While contemporary theories dispute the naturalness of biological and social relationships, much family law still rests on traditional notions that through the asymmetrical, sometimes nonreciprocal obligations of family life we find individual fulfillment.[28] The law has recognized the family as encompassing both physiological and social relationships and has, with varying degrees of success, discouraged the abuse or neglect of dependent family members. The history and critique of family law is too long and complex to examine here;[29] the aspect of these laws important to this discussion is the idea that women and men who engage in consensual sexual activity must refrain from hurting or exploiting each other and that they jointly bear minimal responsibility to care for the children they conceive: they should not be able to kill those children at will.

Fathers, as well as mothers, are required by law *to take affirmative action* to promote the welfare of their children. State paternity statutes may authorize blood or DNA tests to establish paternity and fathers reluctant to support their children may have their wages garnished or may be jailed for nonsupport. Because the pregnant woman must seek third-party aid for abortion, she is particularly easy to identify as a parent whose actions could negatively affect her unborn child; but state regulation of abortion was intended to protect both mother and child, not merely to control women or their sexuality. In fact, some aspects of laws related to sexual activity (e.g., prostitution, indecent exposure, notification of sexual partners of patients with sexually transmitted diseases), marriage, family support, and inheritance may be seen as regulating, channeling, or even "punishing" the sexual activity of both women and men. While historically such laws have at times been related to concerns about morality, they have also related to utilitarian concerns about the state's inability to adequately address the problems attendant upon unrestricted sexuality, such as the abandonment of children, persons without a means of support, care of persons disabled or dying from sexually transmitted diseases, and disputes over the succession of property.

Central to equal protection arguments justifying abortion is the view that both nature and society have burdened parents unequally, with women bearing far heavier burdens of reproductive and child care labors. It is asserted that only by freeing women from the biological and social burden of gestating and caring for untimely or unwanted children can women be free to create for themselves the family and social interaction they desire. Abortion or the choice to abort is viewed as beneficial or, at least, less harmful than pregnancy and childbirth. The strains of pregnancy and child care are considerable, and they should not be dismissed as trivial or irrelevant to the abortion debate. Granting that the burden of maternity may be great, however, does not in itself prove that abortion is better or "easier," or that elective abortion is a justifiable or even effective means to achieve equality for women. Unwanted pregnancies may be trying in the extreme, but they are not dissimilar to other family crises, such as providing care for a severely physically or mentally handicapped child or parent. The difficulty of familial obligation does not erase the humanity of dependent family members nor justify active efforts to bring about their deaths in order to be relieved of the hardship of caring for them.

Current abortion law is incompatible with the purposes of family law. Family law seeks to protect the vulnerable; *Roe* stripped the most vulnerable members of the human family of legal protection. Family law restrains the powerful from exploiting the weak; *Roe* increased the ability of mothers to *legally* harm their unborn children. Family law requires parental involvement in and consent to a minor child's decisions; as a consequence of *Roe* and its progeny, parental actions in regard to their minor child's abortion are limited. The unborn are the smallest members of the human family, the weakest members of individual families. In giving some family members the liberty to cause the death of their vulnerable dependents, the Court may open the way to state-sanctioned, lightly regulated euthanasia,[30] just as it has paved the way for state-funded, lightly regulated abortion.[31] We can anticipate Court decisions to come: How dependent and how burdensome to caretakers must a human be before a family member may cause or a judge may accede to his or her death? Who is qualified to decide whether a being has achieved, retained, or lost the right to have his or her life protected by the state?

If an unborn child is, as Dianne Irving explains and as science and tradition have long indicated, "an already existing human being with the power or potency to continue its own development"[32]—though powerless to control such lethal external circumstances as an incompetent cervix, abruption of the placenta, or a mother's decision to abort—legalized elective abortion is a great breach in our system of individual human rights. We cannot fully resolve the moral and legal problems associated with abortion by declaring the unborn "not persons in the fullest sense."[33]

The definition of "person" under the law has varied over time. In 1800, slaves, children, and women were "not persons in the fullest sense" of the law. In our present social climate, we would view the failure to protect these living beings as reprehensible. Arguing that state protection extends only to "persons" is a facile and futile exercise, for

> if it is meant to be applied only to rational and social beings in possession of some threshold level of intellectual prowess, clearly some nonhuman animals qualify (e.g., cats, dogs, monkeys, elephants, dolphins)—or, at least, are not obviously disqualified—though many fellow citizens fail the test; for example, all infants, many late-term Alzheimer sufferers, some stroke victims.[34]

The law distinguishes between rights, duties, and protection in that a high standard for personhood applies when rights and duties are considered, but minimal protection is offered living beings unable to meet such qualifications. For example,

> the profoundly retarded are not permitted to serve in the military or to enter into binding contractual relations, but they are fully protected against assaults, libels, fraud, and theft. Nonhuman animals are not permitted to vote or to avail themselves of public accommodations, but the law forbids their torture.[35]

The law is most protective of humans, and family law protects both the most vulnerable humans and fundamental human relationships. Life, of course, is prerequisite to any right or duty. Even after twenty years of abortion on demand, many people and their state governments persist in viewing the unborn child as worthy of *some* protection, as manifest in statutes which define the killing of an unborn child as a form of homicide.[36] These homicide statutes attest to the "humanness" and the "aliveness" of the unborn child, realities obvious to the mother of the near-term child. While birth clearly marks a major developmental stage in a child's life, it is certainly not the beginning point, biologically or legally.

> The Court in *Roe* did no service to clear thinking or intelligible discourse when it suggested that the question of when life begins is at the root of the abortion issue. No one seriously (or at least competently) doubted that fetuses are alive, nor was there ever a statute that prohibited the aborting of dead fetuses. Matters were made no clearer by rephrasing the question in terms of the commencement of *human* life, for fetuses carried by human beings can only be human. A biological entity is human if and only if its genetic composition is drawn from the gene pool *Homo sapiens*. All fetuses carried by human mothers are human in this biologically informed sense.[37]

The liberty to terminate another living being—especially one's own flesh and blood—goes against the weight of lived familial experience and contradicts the best in our collective history. The constitutional right to elective abortion cheapens the rule of law that values human life because it fails to adequately protect the most defenseless human beings; it undercuts family law and family relationships because it fails to encourage mothers and fathers to protect their unborn children.

EQUAL PROTECTION FOR MOTHERS AS CONSCRIPTED SAMARITANS

Donald Regan's equal protection justification of abortion rests on "'the law of samaritanism,' that is, the law concerning obligations imposed on certain individuals to give aid to others."[38] He argues that a pregnant woman—unlike the mother of a postnatal child—bears no *special* responsibility to her unborn daughter or son merely by virtue of her conceiving the child through consensual sexual activity.[39] The potential physical and psychic burdens of carrying an unwanted child to term, he reasons, are far more "physically invasive" than the "burdens of parenthood,"[40] and "there is no escape from the burdens of pregnancy save abortion."[41] He invokes the equal protection clause with an eye to the biological differences between the sexes: "Since pregnancy happens only to women, and since no one has any choice about whether to be a woman, susceptibility to pregnancy (and to being in the position of wanting an abortion) is a nonchosen characteristic." Professor Regan concludes that restrictions on abortion coerce pregnancy, conscript a woman's body as an "incubator," and humiliate her in a manner not unlike rape.[42] I argue that, rather than providing a reasonable justification for abortion, such reasoning undermines family relationships, family law, and the community's obligation to help women with problem pregnancies.

Professor Regan contends that it is unreasonable to expect women either to refrain from sex or to carry to term unwanted children.[43] However, all human interaction, especially within the family, requires of us a significant degree of restraint in sexual matters and entails for us serious legal and social responsibilities—even toward people we do not know or do not like or would not choose to serve if that choice were unilaterally ours. Not every social or familial tie is freely and explicitly chosen; according to Maura Ryan, parental responsibility has generally entailed an acceptance of "inequities in benefits and burdens." She cautions that a contractural model of human reproduction may distort the parent-child bond, displacing "indissoluble and predefined obligations" and threatening the "transcendent commitment" so necessary to the family. "The involuntary quality of kinship," notes Ryan, "can also teach us how to accept others as intimately connected to us, even when they fail to live up to our standards or when they do not possess the physical or personal qualities most attractive to us." She predicts that seeking individual or familial autonomy in the rhetoric of reproductive rights may not "encourage more respectful and cooperative parenting styles but may further facilitate the abuse of parental power." Because a rights model assumes proprietary interests, it may not facilitate intimacy or more humane parenting. She warns that "it may not be enough simply for feminists to argue for equality between women and men in the holding of these [reproductive] rights. Rather, the very language of rights, implying as it does some exclusive access to property, must be seen as inappropriate when describing the structure of the family."[44]

With relatively inexpensive contraceptives widely available, today's potential parents can more readily choose to delay or prevent conception than could previous generations.[45] Children, however, are in the same position as previous generations of children vis-à-vis their parents—completely dependent upon parental care and compassion. Normal postnatal children have more legal protection now than in previous generations. Though prenatal care is better and more widely available than in our mothers' generation, today's unborn child may be more at risk than we were as unborn children.[46]

Admitting that a woman who voluntarily engages in sexual intercourse is in some sense responsible for bringing into existence an unwanted entity, Regan nevertheless claims that the resultant fetus has, in effect, "physically invaded" the woman.[47] Describing pregnancy as physical invasion by the fetus and physical subordination to the needs of the fetus[48] reconceptualizes abortion as an act of self-defense to preserve the life, health, or autonomy of the pregnant woman. Pride in medical technology, perhaps, leads us to believe that we are in control of conception (or at least in control of preventing it) and tempts us to label our failure to contracept as an invasive action on the part of the growing child. Such logic seems perversely self-interested and wholly ungenerous. Called into being by the actions of her parents, the unborn child within the mother is, even if unwanted, precisely where she should be at that stage of her development. As Stephen D. Schwarz notes, "That a woman looks upon her own child as . . . an intruder is already an evil, even if she then refrains from killing her. Imagine the mother of a born child looking upon her as an intruder in her house, being in the way, restricting her freedom. We would perceive this as a terrible selfishness. It is the same thing when the child is smaller, and in 'her house' in another, more intimate sense, [in the mother's] . . . own body."[49] Even if the born or unborn child is perceived as an intruder, we commonly accept the law that intruders may not be killed simply because they are intruding; our response to them must still endeavor to be reasonable and humane.[50]

Children frequently "invade" parental time, space, and economy; the law expects parents to care for their children, even when parents are themselves victims of unfair social practices or the criminal acts of others.[51] Parents who fail to provide minimal care for their children, or who actively abuse their children, are prosecuted. Only in the case of the mother and her unborn child is a parent given the legal right to destroy "invasive" offspring. In a very real sense, parents' bodies *are* conscripted for the support of their children in that the law expects parents to work on a round-the-clock basis to provide for the child's basic needs.

Much of the impact of Professor Regan's bodily invasion argument is carried by his assumption that pregnancy causes women significant bodily harm that the reasonable woman would try to avoid. He believes such potential harm should not be suffered by women who want sexual activity but who do not want to be pregnant, give birth, or care for a child. His list of physical maladies a pregnant woman may suffer is formidable,[52] but it is not unlike the list of potential side effects from oral contraceptives. His argument about potential physical harm could also be extended to some sexual activity itself, since sex can produce immediate physical pain and transmission of various diseases, including increased susceptibility to cancer or AIDS. Moreover, his focus on physical harms of pregnancy as a reason to abort is contradicted by the reasons women actually give for aborting. Few women (less than 10 percent) cite health reasons as their motivation for aborting. Most give social reasons: having a baby would interfere with work, school, or other responsibilities; they cannot afford to have a child; they do not want to be single parents; or they have relationship problems.[53]

It may be that the bodily invasion argument reduces to a social argument: the notion that women have the constitutional right to separate themselves from some of the consequences of their sexual activity. If this is valid in reference to mothers during pregnancy before viability, might it not at some time be expanded to include parents who discover that their five-year-old son has an incurable disease or that their teenage daughter is criminally insane, to the extent that they are free to abandon the child or dispose of him or her in some other way? Or—more to the immediate point—might it be claimed that men also have a constitutional right to evade consequences of their sexual activity, such as child-support payments, if the children were unplanned or unwanted? Marriage ordinarily suggests a willingness to procreate, and even unwed fathers are held accountable for child support, whether their children were wanted or unwanted (and it is fair to assume that the overwhelming majority of unwed fathers do not want the child conceived). The New York Court of Appeals decided that a father was liable for child support for his out-of-wedlock child even though he engaged in sexual intercourse with the mother only after she had falsely assured him that she was using a contraceptive. According to the court,

> the interest asserted by the father . . . is not, strictly speaking, his freedom to choose to avoid procreation, because the mother's conduct in no way limited his right to use contraception. Rather, he seeks to have his choice regarding procreation fully respected by other individuals and effectuated to the extent that he should be relieved of his obligation to support a child that he did not voluntarily choose to have. But respondent's constitutional entitlement to avoid procreation does not encompass a right to avoid a child support obligation simply because another private person has not fully respected his desires in this regard.[54]

Aborting is not an avoidance of procreation—the vulnerable life is already *in utero*—but a termination of maternal support for the child. Just as reluctant fathers are obligated to support children they did not intend to engender, reluctant mothers are morally obligated to support children they did not intend to conceive, and should be encouraged by law to do so except in the gravest circumstances.[55]

The focus on the right of choice of the pregnant woman is not manifestly more logical than discussion of her choices before intercourse or after the birth of her baby. A woman—or man—cannot control in advance all the possible consequences of a particular instance of sexual intercourse any more than a parent can control all the consequences of taking a newborn home to raise. Taking birth, rather than, say, implantation as the starting point for parental responsibility makes it easier to identify the child involved, but can the state reasonably suppose that taking a child home from the hospital (even when abandonment is punishable by law) means a willingness to accept responsibility for damage or deviance in offspring? The state routinely *does* expect parents to assume responsibility for their children or to make alternative provisions for them, even when the parents are in a state of duress. If women and society want fathers to provide adequate support for their children and the mothers of their children, it is a wiser practice to make the legal assumption that, by engaging in voluntary sexual intercourse, *both* men and women are assuming the risks and rewards of pregnancy and parenthood.

Restrictions on abortion are, in Regan's view, a way of conscripting women's bodies for state purposes. This argument is unpersuasive, for the state neither compels women to have intercourse, nor forcibly inseminates them, nor routinely confines women during the gestation of their children. State refusal to facilitate abortion falls short of the coercion implied by Regan's use of the term *conscription.* He underscores the "coercive" nature of an unplanned pregnancy by equating it with rape. "Is it clearly worse," he asks, "to be treated as an object by one deviant individual [the rapist] than to be relegated to the status of a broodmare (for this is how the pregnant woman may well view the matter) by society at large?"[56] His emotionally charged language may accurately replicate the initial response of some pregnant women, but it obscures a simple reality outlined by Daniel N. Robinson:

> No one denies the injustice of laws that would make a pregnancy compulsory: that is, that would require nonconsenting women to become pregnant. But the pregnancies reached by *Roe* were neither commanded nor rewarded by the state. They appear now as social facts to be dealt with according to canons of justice and not with slogans.[57]

Referring to "both the woman's feelings of being used during the pregnancy and her dismay at the consequent choice between actually raising the child and giving it up for adoption," Professor Regan asserts that, to a woman with an unwanted pregnancy, the fact that the fetus, unlike the rapist, is not "a full-sized, visible, malevolent, *active* attacker" does little to reduce her "intrinsic horror."[58] While rape involves an attacker using the woman's body, "laws forbidding abortion involve the requisitioning of the woman's body by the state," insists Professor Regan.

A central concept of *Roe,* and of Professor Regan's equal protection argument, is that we are not individually or collectively required to protect some dependent humans, though we may *choose* to do so. In short, an individual has obligations toward "viable" life, but none toward "non-viable" life. In the case of a dying patient, it is quite understandable why useless or unhelpful treatments are unnecessary, but in the case of the growing unborn child, it seems directly in conflict with principles of family law that hold parents responsible for the protection of their children and the state responsible for minimally protecting each of us.

It matters where we as a community draw the line requiring parents to protect their children. If we view parenthood as beginning at the birth of a child, then it is reasonable not to hold parents responsible for the care of their children until after the child is born. But if parenthood begins earlier—before intercourse,[59] or at conception, or implantation, or during gestation, it is fair to require parents to take reasonable measures to protect their child long before birth. Traditionally, the time for choosing whether to bear or beget a child was before intercourse or before marriage. Regan, the *Roe* Court, and abortion activists generally deny that the biological dependency of the unborn child creates for the mother the moral obligation to carry the child to term. By placing choice after intercourse, after conception, sometime during pregnancy before the time of viability, they allot the unborn child legal protection only at the point in his or her physical development at which protection is, in some sense, less necessary— the point at which, if born and given adequate care, the child could probably survive. The idea of extending *less* protection to an individual at a point when *more* is needed is generally antithetical to the purposes of the law, and particularly so in terms of family law.

> If a common thread runs through developed law as it pertains to the gamut of psychobiological beings, it is the thread that identifies *interests* and *vulnerabilities*. The rationale behind laws that protect the nonthreatening being from the assaults of others includes

centrally the potential victim's capacity for pain. This is not the only consideration, but it is the one that is nearly identically applied to cases involving manifestly different potential victims: infants, children, animals, the aged, the insane, prisoners, etc. What the law forbids are actions reasonably expected to cause pain or distress to those who do not in any morally meaningful sense deserve it but who are capable of experiencing it.[60]

It may be regarded as unfair that maternal duties in some sense begin earlier and are more personal than paternal duties; but it can also be said that society has sought to give support to women through equitable remedies: the state will support (minimally at least) indigent pregnant women and will help them obtain support for their children from the fathers of the children. Discussions of abortion sometimes reduce to whether the unborn "deserve" protected status; more interesting, in my view, is the discussion of whether we are willing to treat with respect and compassion our sexual partners and our unborn children. In my opinion, the protection we accord them is a measure of our own humanity, not a measure of the humanity of the unborn child.[61]

Family law has traditionally encouraged parents to provide for and protect their children by intervening in the family when it appears that parental behavior is manifestly inadequate. From the perspective of family law that recognizes the unborn as family member, an unwanted pregnancy is a special case of a child's dependence on one parent, but it is not wholly different from the care required by dependent children in general. If an obligation not to kill the unborn is viewed as inherently unfair to women, any parental obligation to a postnatal child may, in time, be viewed as an inequitable encroachment upon parental liberty. Further, the needs of the unborn for compassion and support are not unlike the needs of the unwillingly pregnant woman. If the needy unborn is defined out of existence, unprotected, or attacked as parasitic, we should not be surprised if the community as a whole ignores the plight of pregnant women, is slow to police abortion providers who damage women,[62] or sees such women with crisis pregnancies as an undue burden on an already strained welfare system. In the end, the liberty to abort could work against equitable treatment for women by weakening the sense of obligation felt toward women with unwanted pregnancies.[63]

EQUAL PROTECTION FOR THE SOCIALLY CONSTRAINED MOTHER

A second equal protection argument, articulated by Professor Reva Siegel, sees "deep commonalities between fetal-protective regulation of the present and the antiabortion laws of the past that are obscured by habits of physiological reasoning the [earlier] campaign engendered."[64] She holds that abortion law doctrine has been "inordinately preoccupied" with the physiology of motherhood and "correspondingly inattentive to the social logic of its regulation."[65] As she analyzes abortion regulation of the past hundred and fifty years, Professor Siegel charges that "in crafting equal protection and due process doctrine concerning reproductive regulation" the Court has been dominated by physiological naturalism.[66] Rather than focusing on the potential physiological harms of pregnancy, Professor Siegel argues that abortion legislation is "state action compelling motherhood [which] injures women" economically and socially.[67] What society imposes on mothers, according to Professor Siegel, is "deeply distorted by a long history of denigrating, controlling, and using women as mothers."[68] She concludes that before the nation judges the conduct of women toward the unborn, "it ought to reflect upon its own conduct toward women."[69]

Professor Siegel contends that in the last century and in our own, "the objective of abortion-restrictive regulation is to force women to assume the role and perform the work that has traditionally defined their secondary social status."[70] Without access to abortion, Professor Siegel believes that women will be deprived of "some rudimentary control over the sex-role constraints this society imposes" on mothers.[71] In this equal protection approach, "claims about women's bodies" are seen to be "judgments about women's roles."[72] Abortion laws of the nineteenth century grew out of views that women were legally obligated to perform "the physical and social work of reproducing family life."[73] These attitudes toward proper roles for women, it is claimed, still permeate efforts to restrict access to abortion by reasoning in "'scientific' ways that ignore women's role in gestating human life"[74] and by focusing public attention on the unborn as an autonomous individual.[75]

Historically, a pronatalist, pro-motherhood attitude contributed to the states' willingness to restrict abortion; but the nineteenth century's new scientific approach to the unborn as a separate individual deserving of protection was of primary importance. Professor Siegel's view of the history of abortion law is similar to that articulated by the "Historians' Briefs" in *Webster v. Reproductive Health Services* (1989), which one critic describes as "advocacy pieces with a highly selective examination of the evidence to support a partisan and distorted history of abortion."[76] Viewing the "law of abortion as a story of oppressors and oppressed," with a focus shifting from "the increasingly clear history of the law of abortion to less determinate questions of the 'true' social attitudes toward abortion in our history," these historians assert, as does Professor Siegel, that abortion restrictions were part of a pattern of subordinating women.[77] As feminist philosopher Andrea Nye explicates, those who view gender roles as oppressive believe that "submission and domination are not contingent features of particular kinds of economic relations; they are the only possible attitudes human beings can have towards each other."[78]

Social analysis is a job better suited to legislatures than to courts; approaches to abortion mirror competing social models reflected in the Constitution and current challenges by legal theorists seeking change. Equal protection theories presume a number of conditions that American law does not accept. Our law assumes that citizens are rational agents capable of responsibility and restraint; equal protection abortion advocates assert a form of cultural determinism that locks individuals and groups into patterns of conflict.[79] Nineteenth-century social prescriptions for women have given way to affirmative efforts to destroy stereotyped thinking about women. Compared to their great-grandmothers, women of today suffer few legal disabilities. We are left to decide the floor issue: will we kill our unborn in the hope that the social status of women will thereby be improved or will we find nonviolent methods for enhancing women's status?

Even if it were accurate to characterize the antiabortion movement of the nineteenth century as interested in circumscribing women's roles by law, it is not accurate to claim that the pro-life movement of the past two decades is based on such a view of women.[80] According to former abortionist Bernard N. Nathanson, it is the study of the unborn child that has prompted increasing knowledge and respect for human life before birth.[81] In this century, advances in medical science have further confirmed that the unborn child is a genetically unique individual,[82] whose sex and blood type may differ from that of the woman whose body houses that child. Current practice allows physicians to treat and cure some medical problems suffered by unborn children. Accumulating scientific study does not demonstrate that the unborn child is anything less than the individual life whom physicians of the last century were seeking to save.

That mothers had and have legal obligations to their children is not in itself sufficient proof that mothers are accorded secondary social status. Implicit in Professor Siegel's view of the history of motherhood are what a marxist or socialist might see as the brute "facts" of the family in a capitalist economy:

> No modern legislature interested in adopting restrictions on abortion has, to my knowledge, offered to compensate women for this work; to protect women's employment and education opportunities while they perform the work of motherhood; or to provide women adequate childcare so that they are not pushed into dependency upon men or the state. Nor has a legislature required that men fathering the children women are forced to bear assume primary responsibility for the work of nurturance and maintenance women typically provide. Thus, when the state enacts restrictions on abortion, it coerces women to perform the work of motherhood without altering the conditions that continue to make such work a principal cause of their secondary social status.[83]

It is true that the work women do in bearing and rearing children has not been adequately recognized and rewarded; neither does the state recognize or reward the work of fathers in the family. That parenting is not monetarily rewarded by the state is an objection to a capitalist economy, not proof that mothers are second-class citizens. Failure of the state to compensate women and men for family work is the result of a complex web of beliefs about the public and private spheres within our managed free market structure, not simply the result of discriminatory attitudes toward women.

In this economy, as well as in socialist countries which profess comparable value across occupations, social value does not necessarily correspond to economic reward or public recognition; consider the relative need for and economic status of mothers, plumbers, elementary school teachers, and doctors. Social status is dependent upon more factors than gender alone. Previous generations saw families as private arrangements which placed the woman's role primarily within the private sphere, but it does not follow that the private sphere was less valued, particularly when production of the necessities of life was centered in the home and the welfare state had not yet arisen.[84] It also does not necessarily follow that current economic policies are designed to maintain women in an inferior status due to their role in reproduction.[85] It is more likely that abortion laws, like other aspects of Anglo-American law, assume that women are rational and autonomous in their sexual and economic lives.[86]

Roe v. Wade granted abortion, in part, to alleviate the distressful conditions faced by unwed mothers and unwanted children. However, *Roe* struck down no laws directly barring mothers from participating in the work force or from seeking education.[87] "Before and after *Roe,* the Supreme Court has shown a sensitivity to sex discrimination claims, but there is no evidence that *Roe* itself enhanced that sensitivity," points out Paige Comstock Cunningham. "*No* decision of the Supreme Court on gender-based discrimination relies upon *Roe v. Wade. Roe* has been cited in less than a dozen lower court cases involving sex-discrimination and was dispositive in none."[88]

In *Planned Parenthood v. Casey* (1992), the plurality opinion,[89] written by Justices O'Connor, Souter, and Kennedy, held that a woman's desire not to be pregnant outweighs her unborn child's right to live.[90] Apparently applying a form of equal protection analysis to parental roles, the plurality held that because fathers are not burdened by pregnancy, mothers should not be unduly burdened either.[91] The Court appears to have interpreted abortion as "a variation on the theme of a 'parental' right," a stance Bruce C. Hafen criticized as "a complete perversion of the liberty of parenthood."[92] Hafen points out the self-contradictory nature of such an approach:

> If the fetus she carries is significant enough to give rise to such a lofty claim, it is significant enough to bar an abortion as the earliest form of child abuse. . . . If the direct effects of pregnancy are

the source of her interest, it is difficult to see how those effects— except in the case of a therapeutic abortion—could outweigh the traditional interest of the Constitution in family relationships and childrearing, an interest the father has and will continue to have if the child is born and raised—no matter which parent then carries the heavier physical burdens of childrearing.[93]

Apparently echoing the sentiment that the burdens of motherhood necessarily preclude activity outside the home,[94] the plurality declared that "an entire generation has come of age free to assume *Roe*'s concept of liberty in defining the capacity of women to act in society."[95] Implicit in this statement is the view that without access to abortion women lack the "capacity . . . to act in society" and that progress for women has been directly attributable to the Court's legalization of abortion, "rather than as a result of [women's] determination to obtain higher education and compete with men in the job market, and of society's increasing recognition of their ability to fill positions that were previously thought to be reserved only for men."[96]

The Court, not unlike Professor Siegel, seems to view the activities of caring for home and family as nonparticipation in society. Many of us who care for our children and our homes see our work in our families as the first and most important contribution we make to a humane and caring community. In our mobile, urbanized society, with pervasive networks of electronic communications systems, the notion that a woman in her home is isolated from society is archaic and, to many, offensive.[97] While bearing children presents specific practical and social problems for women, by 1973 women's access to education and employment was already well established,[98] and women's participation in the workforce was steadily increasing prior to *Roe*. The *Casey* plurality distanced itself from stereotyped views of woman as mother, declaring that the state is barred from insisting "upon its own vision of the woman's role, however dominant that vision has been in the course of our history and our culture."[99] In contrast, family law has always insisted that parents are obligated to care for their offspring in specified economic and interpersonal ways; parents have not been allowed to decide for themselves which obligations they will keep and which they will reject.[100]

145

The *Casey* plurality alludes to the potentially negative economic impact of pregnancy, childbirth, and childrearing on women, rehearsing the "fact" that prosperity and progress are attributable to *Roe* because "for two decades of economic and social developments, people have organized intimate relationships and made choices that define their views of themselves and their places in society, in reliance on the availability of abortion in the event that contraception should fail."[101] The Court misjudges abortion's place in our society. According to Paige Comstock Cunningham, "the implication that women organize their lives around 'abortion availability' would come as a great surprise to many women."[102] In fact, a July 1989 *New York Times* poll showed that most women are more concerned about job discrimination, child care, and balancing work and family than about abortion.[103] Mrs. Cunningham contends that the equal protection argument for abortion is actually a concession that "an abortion right is not rooted in the Constitution."[104]

The Court's focus on the potentially negative impact of parental responsibilities ignores the affiliative nature of family life and the high value that people place on belonging to a family.[105] "Apart from judicial considerations, an autonomy/equal protection approach to the abortion question contradicts many of the core values of feminism, values which are shared by millions of American women," Mrs. Cunningham states. These are the values of care, nurturance, compassion, nonviolence, and inclusion. These values include care for those who are less fortunate, less able to speak for themselves. For many of us, it requires no great leap to include the preborn child within the circle of care and protection. Out of the natural biological connection between the intrauterine child and mother arises recognition of that dependent relationship which deserves heightened protection, both in law and in society.[106]

The abortion restrictions that were struck down by *Roe* merely required women to bring their children to term; they did not require women to personally raise every child conceived. Affluent women have generally hired poorer women to care for their children, leaving themselves relatively unencumbered; women unable to care for their children have had the option of applying for private or public aid or of relinquishing their parental rights and placing their children for adoption. In describing abortion restrictions as coercing motherhood, Professor Siegel asserts that adoption as an alternative to abortion is an illusory solution:

> Hypothetically, a woman compelled to bear a child she does not want could give it up for adoption, abandon it, or pay someone to care for the child until maturity. In this society, however, these are not options that women avail themselves of with great frequency for the simple reason that few women are able to abandon a child born of their body. . . . Once compelled to bear a child against their wishes, most women will feel obligated to raise it.[107]

Professor Siegel grants that mothers may derive "meaning, value, pleasure, and purpose from work that this society all too frequently disparages" but concludes that to restrict abortion is to "coerce" motherhood and is "an act of violence against women, one that devalues what women give, and give up, in parenting and who they might be apart from that work."[108] That a woman may find it easier to abort than to relinquish the child says much about the nature of the maternal bond and its development during pregnancy. If it is likely that the mother will love the child by the time the child is born, perhaps laws restricting abortion actually facilitate mother-child relationships by underscoring the importance of that relationship. Though Professor Siegel is acutely aware of what a woman may "give up" to care for her children, she does not explore what fathers sacrifice for their families, nor even what women give up when they abort rather than interrupt work or schooling with child care. To interrupt schooling or employment to care for children can be hard economically and emotionally; to abort offspring rather than interrupt education and employment is to deny the humanity of the unborn and destroy the possibility of what could, despite its difficult beginning, become a mutually beneficial and loving relationship with a child.

The humanity of the unborn child is understood to be a matter of individual opinion in Professor Siegel's analysis—"that society as a whole, or some women in particular, may judge it morally preferable to give a child up to adoption rather than abort a pregnancy is beside the point."[109] Her point is that pregnant women become mothers, mothers take care of their children, and "childcare remains status work, organized and valued in ways that limit the life prospects of those who perform it."[110]

Most laws limit our life prospects in one way or another, and those laws affirm that some actions *are* morally preferable to others; abandoning a child is less reprehensible than killing the child outright, as may be inferred from the punishments meted out to parents who fail their children in these ways. Our law does embody our common morality and does acknowledge our duties to others. Feminist theorist Elizabeth Fox-Genovese maintains "that important moral issues must be recognized as public matters. Do we leave murder, after all, to the disposition of private conscience?" Such radical individualism is antithetical to notions of family, just as anarchy is antithetical to notions of community. Fox-Genovese continues, "To recognize the fetus as 'some form of person' . . . and then leave the termination of a pregnancy to the disposition of the individual conscience is effectively to endow individuals with the right to terminate life for personal convenience. And no amount of moral anguish on the part of the individual who makes the decision changes the outcome one bit."[111]

Choices about childbearing, as Professor Siegel points out, are "both deeply personal *and* profoundly social: When a pregnant woman decides whether to become a mother, she faces dilemmas in which the community itself is inextricably complicit."[112] She argues that "this society has 'unclean hands' in matters respecting motherhood. While it may possess the power, it sorely lacks the moral grounds to 'balance' the rights of women and the unborn as if it were a disinterested bystander to the conflict thrust upon women by nature."[113] Until the state has more consistently promoted the welfare of women, it has no right, in her view, to restrict their access to abortion. Even if the state has unclean hands in that U.S. economic support of mothers is meager compared to that of countries such as Sweden, we must still ask whether abortion is the best, or even an adequate, solution for mothers lacking social and economic support. Widespread use of elective abortion to "solve" such problems could have the opposite effect of reducing people's willingness to help women with problem pregnancies—in effect, abandoning those women.

Both equal protection arguments, whether stressing potential physical duress or asserting oppressive social conditions, view the woman as an individual with a privacy claim against all others—even her own dependent child. This sort of privacy claim is not legal for a man to make in regard to his dependent children or spouse; desertion, refusal to support, and infanticide are crimes, as is treatment of a pregnant woman that brings on miscarriage. It is the view of the woman as an individual with private needs and goals that fueled the *Roe* and *Casey* decisions. In this same vein, Regan and Siegel use the failure of family and society to support women with problem pregnancies adequately as evidence that access to elective abortion is necessary for women to receive equal treatment. If women are disadvantaged by nature or society in that they cannot escape the consequences of their sexual activity (or the sexual activity of men), then they are in a position to demand equity, not merely an equal treatment that takes little account of their unique position. Justifying abortion on the basis that women must be treated as "equal" to irresponsible fathers who are already in defiance of the law seems a giant step backward in legal logic as well as in our view of the family. Such a policy is likely to encourage more family failure, rather than less, and may heavily disadvantage women unwilling to exercise their "right" to abandon (abort) their children.

There is little virtue in abortion as a private right. Fox-Genovese contends that "we must finally agree that reproduction is *not* exclusively a private matter, that it cannot be completely accounted for in the language of individual rights." Instead, she cautions, "any social vision of reproduction must begin with an acknowledgment of the sanctity with which society endows human life and, accordingly, of the social commitment to support that life in all its diversity."[114] The worst aspect of our national policies on abortion, birth, families, and children is that abortion may have become the "first resort."[115] Explication of abortion narratives by researchers Kate Maloy and Maggie Jones Patterson suggests that "a great many unwanted pregnancies— perhaps even the majority of them—can be traced to women's fears, poor self-esteem, victimization or insecurity, all of which interfere with safe, careful sexual behavior."[116] Up to 60 percent of those unintended pregnancies resulted from "birth control misuse or neglect on the part of one or both partners."[117] Unlike Siegel's conclusion that this situation justifies abortion on demand, Maloy and Patterson view choosing abortion under such circumstances as a symptom of abandonment which can be addressed only when families are supported by all social institutions, so that "members begin to feel valued in ways that might

gradually diminish the forces that lead to high rates of unplanned and out-of-wedlock pregnancies. These forces can include family breakdown, dysfunction, violence, or neglect of
children."[118]

While acknowledging the suffering Siegel details, it may be
that neither the woman nor her unborn child "*can* be valued—by
the law, the individual, or society—at the price of disregarding
the other."[119] Suffering cannot provide ready justification for in-
flicting suffering on others. Arguing that elective abortion should
not be restricted until mothers and families are adequately supported may have initial appeal, but this same line of reasoning
would also support the view that until poverty is eradicated there
should be no laws against stealing because neediness justifies violating the rights of other people. Siegel asserts that laws such as
Utah's abortion statute "punish pregnant [women] who have
'voluntarily' engaged in sex by making them bear children, yet it
has . . . impos[ed] no similar duties, burdens, or sanctions on the
men who were co-participants in the act of conception."[120] This
is not true; in fact, Utah and other states have enacted laws holding male parents responsible for their children.[121] The fact that
state efforts to collect child support may sometimes be ineffectu-
al does not mean that efforts to hold both parents responsible for
the welfare of their children are essentially misguided. Fathers
have no legal right, no liberty interest, in abandoning their children. Failure to support a child is disfavored socially and is punishable by law. Equal protection does not require that women be
given more opportunity to engage in disfavored or illegal behavior simply because men may find it easier to disobey the law.[122]
David M. Smolin calls this argument a way of abstracting about
abortion as "nonfeasance" toward the fetus.

> The abstraction allows one to say: men and women are really the
> same in relation to the fetus, therefore women are as free as are
> men to abandon them. It becomes a kind of syllogism. One begins
> with the image of woman as man and fetus as stranger or artificial-
> ly attached appendage. One ends by declaring that any other ver-
> sion is sexism.[123]

Holding women responsible for reasonable care of their unborn children is neither sexist, nor an undue burden, nor a deval-

uation of women's contribution to the life of the unborn child. In fact, unless women are considered capable of weathering an unplanned pregnancy, they may not be taken seriously as competent workers in stressful jobs or as moral agents in society. Given the knowledge we now have of the unborn child, it takes a willful disregard of contemporary medical science to support the belief that the unborn deserve no protection whatsoever before viability. But abortion debate in this century has hinged less on scientific facts than on their interpretation. Many women hear the shoosh—shoosh of the unborn heart at the first prenatal exam and see the face of their moving, growing unborn child in an ultrasound image early in the second trimester. Some give permission for surgery to save the life of the unborn child. Perhaps the previous century was too rigid in its interpretation of the demands of motherhood; perhaps we are too interested in asserting ourselves as individuals.[124] It was as evident to our forebears that the unborn person was an individual worthy of protection as it was evident that a minor child required parental permission in major life decisions; to the contemporary pro-choice mind, it is evident neither that the unborn deserves our protection nor that a minor child should be required to seek parental consent in order to obtain an abortion. Changing attitudes toward individual rights and family obligations support elective abortion; abortion rights did not grow out of the simple accumulation of biological or sociological data. Viewing abortion as a benefit which has few physical or emotional costs is as unrealistic as the belief that giving birth and caring for a child is necessarily or primarily an oppressive experience.

The *Casey* plurality disregarded the casualties of laissez-faire sexuality:[125] in extraordinary numbers we are maiming and killing ourselves with sexually transmitted diseases[126] and we are aborting almost a third of our own offspring. If our social and legal systems are judged by the way in which we care for others, particularly dependents, these statistics suggest that for our own survival and for the well-being of others we must discourage uncommitted sexual activity, which so often leads to abortion.[127] Smolin states that "abortion rights are a type of disassociation right. Abortion itself constitutes a forceful separation of mother and child. Under the regime of autonomy we are supposed to view disassociation rights as protective of rich associations." This does, indeed, represent an "impoverished view of human related-ness," which reduces the human family and each individual fami-ly within it to "a collection of self-interested individuals."[128]

CONCLUSION

Seeking to ground a right to an abortion on the equal protec-tion clause is no more satisfactory than attempting to ground the right on the First, Fourth, Fifth, Ninth, or Thirteenth Amendments. Because abortion may significantly impact all family relationships, good abortion policy will encourage both men and women to plan their sexual activities so that they do not harm others, rather than invoking constitutional rights to absolve individuals from the responsibilities of treating their sex partners and their own children with respect and care. We all pay for our individual and collective mistakes; laws which encourage us to abandon our sex partners and kill our unborn children may help convince us that we are capable of caring for no one but our-selves, or that we may destroy those we do not choose to love. Though the law cannot compel people to love each other, it may discourage them from lightly abandoning or killing each other.[129]

If we may, without good cause, terminate our responsibilities to an unborn child, what argument will persuade us to fulfill our obligations to the initially wanted child who has grown tire-some, or to the marital partner who has developed irritating habits? Unless we see ourselves as *having* responsibilities to oth-ers, we may not try hard enough to develop our capacity to meet those responsibilities. If we are to understand the problem of abortion and the possibilities for helping women with unplanned pregnancies, we must give up the simplistic framework of indi-vidual rights arguments—including equal protection claims—and consider the abortion decision in the context of the family.

Mary Ann Glendon notes that we "are producing too many in-dividuals who are capable neither of effective participation in civic life nor of sustaining personal relationships," though she ac-knowledges that "the tale currently being told by the law about marriage and family life is probably more starkly individualistic than the ideas and practices that prevail." Despite the fact that "individuals have been emancipated in fact, law, and imagination from group and family ties to a historically unprecedented degree," Glendon maintains that "it is also the case that most men and women still spend most of their lives in emotionally and economically interdependent family units."[130]

The good of the individual and the good of the family usually converge over time, and only in unusual circumstances should individuals need to sever family ties in order to thrive or survive. Families

> remain, for most of us, the only theater in which we can realize our full capacity for good or evil, joy or suffering. By attaching us to beings and feelings that are perishable, families expose us to conflict, pain, and loss. They give rise to tension between love and duty, reason and passion, immediate and long-range objectives, egoism and altruism. But relationships between husbands and wives, parents and children, can also provide frameworks for resolving such tensions.[131]

This nation does need to "promote the welfare of future generations by means that respect and support women in their work as mothers."[132] But respect and support for the work of "mak[ing] infants into adults"[133] cannot spring from an analysis that repudiates the humanity of any member of the human family.

Notes

1. Although states were passing less restrictive abortion laws, many of them based on the Model Penal Code of the American Law Institute, abortion rights activists found the courts more sympathetic to change than were state legislatures. See Marian Faux, *Roe v. Wade: The Untold Story of the Landmark Supreme Court Decision That Made Abortion Legal* (New York: Macmillan, 1988), 70–78. See "Brief for Appellants," No. 70–18, in Philip B. Kurland and Gerhard Casper, eds., *Roe v. Wade (1973),* Landmark Briefs and Arguments of the Supreme Court of the United States: Constitutional Law (Frederick, Md.: University Publications of America, 1990), 91. State legislatures are still bypassed by those seeking a national abortion right under the proposed Freedom of Choice Act, and it is anticipated that the government's basic health package for all citizens will include funding for abortion.

2. Their success has been more pronounced in the courts than in society at large, where abortion law remains far wide of public opinion. Despite twenty years of almost unregulated abortion on demand, there is still strong support for protecting the unborn. Generally, the public agrees that abortion should be legal in the hard cases involving rape, incest, fetal deformity, or risk to the mother's health but disapproves of legalized abortion for social problems such as low income, unwed parenthood, or birth control. Compare Austin C. Wehrwein, "Abortion Reform Supported in Poll," *New York Times,* 24 April 1966, 8 (reporting a poll conducted by the National Opinion Research Center), with Eloise Salholz et al., "Pro-Choice: 'A Sleeping Giant' Awakes," *Newsweek,* 24 April 1989, 39.

3. 410 U.S. 113, 153. See John Keown's analysis of Justice Blackmun's reasoning, "*Roe v. Wade*: A Historic," *World & I* 7 (May 1992): 472–75.

4. *Roe,* 727.

5. Ibid., 724–26.

6. Ibid., 730.

7. "In short, the unborn have never been recognized in the law as persons in the whole sense" (ibid., 731).

8. Ibid., 727. See the analysis of past and present abortion law by Lynn D. Wardle, "Back to the Ban: Abortion Law after the Demise of *Roe v. Wade,*" *World & I* 7 (May 1992): 465.

9. Wardle, "Back to the Ban," 463.

10. See Daniel N. Robinson, "The Standing of the Fetus," *World & I* 7 (May 1992): 522.

11. Linda C. McClain, "'Atomistic Man' Revisited: Liberalism, Connection, and Feminist Jurisprudence," *Southern California Law Review* 65 (1992): 1171, 1263.

12. Daniel N. Robinson, "Races and Persons," *World & I* 7 (February 1992): 498–99.

13. McClain, "'Atomistic Man' Revisited," 1261–62.

14. Reva Siegel, "Reasoning from the Body: A Historical Perspective on Abortion Regulation and Questions of Equal Protection," *Stanford Law Review* 44 (1992): 261, 377–78.

15. Mary Parthun et al., *Abortion's Aftermath: Psychological Effects of Induced Abortion, Physical Complications of Abortion,* 2d ed. rev., Human Life Research Institute Reports No. 2 (Toronto: Human Life Research Institute, 1987), 7.

16. Ibid.

17. Or, worse, it argues that it is in the best interest of the child to destroy him or her before birth. Another standard in family law, of course, protects parents' rights to be with and care for their children. Sometimes the rights of the parents seem to conflict with the best interests of the child. See the discussion of the conflicts between contractual and biological rights of parents and children in Earl M. Maltz, "The State, the Family, and the Constitution: A Case Study in Flawed Bipolar Analysis," *Brigham Young University Law Review* 1991, no. 1: 489, 497–505.

18. Parthun, *Abortion's Aftermath,* 7.

19. Ibid.

20. My husband and I are the parents of two daughters and three sons; since my marriage I have been employed part-time (fifteen to thirty hours per week) outside the home; our first two children were born while I completed an M.A. in English; I am currently a third-year law student. Since 1977 I have worked with pro-life organizations who seek to help women with problem pregnancies and the children they carry.

21. Camille S. Williams, "Sparrows and Lilies," *First Things,* no. 35 (Aug./Sept. 1993), 12–13.

22. Jean Bethke Elshtain, *Power Trips and Other Journeys: Essays in Feminism as Civic Discourse* (Madison: University of Wisconsin Press, 1990), 145. Elshtain used this phrase in reference to women working for peace throughout the world; finding her phrasing to be well expressed and well advised in its substance, I have borrowed and applied it to abortion. However, as I am not sure that *she* would apply it to abortion, I caution the reader that the application is mine.

23. Richard G. Wilkins, Richard Sherlock, and Steven Clark, "Mediating the Polar Extremes: A Guide to Post-*Webster* Abortion Policy," *Brigham Young University Law Review* 1991, no. 1: 403.

24. Robinson, "The Standing of the Fetus," 529.

25. Frequently the abortion attempt was discovered only because the mother died. The abortionist was then charged with the death of the mother and her child. Joseph W. Dellapenna, "Brief of the American Academy of Medical Ethics as Amicus Curiae in Support of Respondents and Cross-Petitioners Robert P. Casey et al.," nos. 91–744 and 91–902, *Planned Parenthood of Southeastern Pennsylvania v. Casey,* 112 S.Ct. 2791, 2807 (1992).

26. *Meyer v. Nebraska,* 262 U.S. 390 (1923); *Pierce v. Society of Sisters,* 268 U.S. 510 (1925) (upheld parents' rights to decide aspects of their children's education); *Griswold v. Connecticut,* 381 U.S. 479 (1965) and *Eisenstadt v. Baird,* 405 U.S. 438 (1972) (upheld the notion that there are zones of privacy related to individual sexual activity inside and outside marriage); and *Skinner v. Oklahoma,* 316 U.S. 535 (1942) (struck down mandatory sterilization of some categories of habitual criminals).

27. The law recognizes several kinds of familial ties: biological (as between birth mother and child), legal (as between husband and wife), and social (as between stepparent and stepchild). We ordinarily think of "the family" as consisting of all three; but specific facts may bring a case before a court where one of the familial ties must be recognized legally and others excluded—as in the case of an abandoned infant girl, whose birth parents' rights may be terminated through due process to allow the child to be adopted by adults willing to assume responsibility for her and treat her as their own.

28. See the final paragraph of *Griswold v. Connecticut,* in which Justice Douglas describes marriage as "a coming together for better or for worse, hopefully enduring, and intimate to the degree of being sacred. It is an association that promotes a way of life, not causes; a

harmony in living, not political faiths; a bilateral loyalty, not commercial or social projects" (381 U.S. 479, 486). Similarly, the *Casey* plurality describes motherhood as requiring "sacrifices [which] have from the beginning of the human race been endured by woman with a pride that ennobles her in the eyes of others and gives to the infant a bond of love" (112 S.Ct. 2791, 2807).

29. See, for example, Susan Moller Okin, *Justice, Gender, and the Family* (New York: Basic Books, 1989); see also Mary Joe Frug, *Postmodern Legal Feminism* (New York: Routledge, 1992).

30. The practice of voluntary euthanasia, assisted suicide, and the administration of massive overdoses of opiates with the intent of causing death to patients who have not requested euthanasia has made the Netherlands the test site for observing how light regulation of euthanasia slips toward eugenics. See R. Fenigsen, "The Report of the Dutch Governmental Committee on Euthanasia," *Issues in Law & Medicine* 7 (1991): 339–44, reported in "The Truth about Euthanasia in the Netherlands," *Pro Vita* 3 (May 1993): 4.

31. With Justice Ginsburg on the Court and a national health plan which will likely fund abortion, the funding ban will be challenged and probably struck down. Justice Ginsburg wrote in 1985 that after finding abortion to be a "fundamental right" it was incongruent for the Court not to uphold government funding of abortions. Ruth Bader Ginsburg, "Some Thoughts on Autonomy and Equality in Relation to *Roe v. Wade*," *North Carolina Law Review* 63 (1985): 375, 386.

32. Dianne Irving, "Abortion: For and Against," excerpts reprinted in *Pro Vita* 3, no. 3 (May 1993): 3.

33. *Roe v. Wade,* 410 U.S. 113, 162.

34. "If the term is confined to entities that are rights-bearing (or duties-bound), then it not only refers to what is finally a creation of legislatures but to entities that surface and disappear right before one's eyes! (Consider convicted felons or those judged insane or mentally defective.)" Robinson, "The Standing of the Fetus," 523.

35. Ibid.

36. Nine states define the killing of an unborn child as a form of homicide, regardless of the stage of pregnancy; six states define the killing of an unborn child after quickening as a form of homicide; three states define the killing of an unborn child after viability as a form of homicide, and one state defines the killing of an unborn child after the twenty-fourth week of pregnancy as a form of homicide. Two other states, without the benefit of a fetal homicide statute, have held the killing of a viable unborn child a form of homicide. Paige Comstock Cunningham, "Testimony . . . [Submitted to the Senate Judiciary Committee] Concerning the Nomination of Ruth Bader Ginsburg to Be an Associate Justice of the United States Supreme Court," n. 55, pp. 37–38. Typescript; copy in the possession of the author.

37. Robinson, "The Standing of the Fetus," 522.

38. Donald H. Regan, "Rewriting *Roe v. Wade*," *Michigan Law Review* 77 (August 1979): 1569. He believed this "the most promising argument in support of the result of *Roe*" and offered it as a suggestion for the rewriting of that opinion (ibid). In *Casey,* the latest rewriting of *Roe,* the plurality echoed the good samaritan argument in finding that "the mother who carries a child to full term is subject to anxieties, to physical constraints, to pain that only she must bear. That these sacrifices have from the beginning of the human race been endured by woman with a pride that ennobles her in the eyes of others and gives to the infant a bond of love cannot alone be grounds for the State to insist she make the sacrifice. Her suffering is too intimate and personal for the State to insist, without more, upon its own vision of the woman's role, however dominant that vision has been in the course of our history and our culture." 112 S.Ct. 2791, 2807.

39. Regan, "Rewriting *Roe v. Wade*," 1599.

40. Note that this definition could *exclude* conceiving and carrying a child as part of parental service or duty. Ibid., 1598.

41. Ibid., 1612. Professor Regan's argument is more sophisticated than it may appear from this brief treatment.

42. Ibid., 1616–17.

43. Ibid., 1596–97, 1630–35.

44. Maura A. Ryan, "The Argument for Unlimited Procreative Liberty: A Feminist Critique," *Hastings Center Report*, 20, no. 4 (July/August 1990): 6–12. Ryan's argument is in the context of access to reproductive technology. I am applying her argument to the problem of abortion; I am not certain that she would.

45. In fiscal year 1990, federal and state governments spent "$504 million to provide contraceptive services and supplies, according to results of a survey of state health, social services and Medicaid agencies. . . . Medicaid accounted for 38 percent of all public funds spent on contraceptive services, Title X provided 22 percent, and two federal block-grant programs—Social Services and Maternal and Child Health—together were responsible for 12 percent of public expenditures. State governments accounted for the remaining 28 percent of public funding." "In 1980, only 25 states and the District of Columbia used their own funds for family planning services; in 1990, 44 states and the District did so." The major source of funding subsidizing sterilization, federal and state governments spent $95 million; *providing less than 1 percent of abortion funding*, state and federal governments provided $65 million. Rachel Benson Gold and Daniel Daley, *Family Planning Perspectives*, 23, no. 5 (September/October 1991): 204; emphasis added.

46. The law's treatment of children and childrearing practices have changed over time and across cultures. We now have more laws protecting children from parental abuse than were extant in our nation at the turn of the century; medical care for the child *in utero,* at birth, and during childhood is much improved, though not universally accessible. Fetal mortality could be reduced further with better prenatal care, but the single most preventable cause of fetal mortality is elective abortion.

47. Regan, "Rewriting *Roe v. Wade,"* 1569, 1619.

48. An early advocate of this approach was Judith Jarvis Thomson, "A Defense of Abortion," *Philosophy and Public Affairs* 1 (1971): 47–66. See also McClain, "'Atomistic Man' Revisited," 1259–69.

49. Stephen D. Schwarz, *The Moral Question of Abortion* (Chicago: Loyola University Press, 1990), 122–23.

50. We would also recognize it an evil for the teenager to resent her concerned mother as an expendable intruder or the middle-aged child to view her aged mother, dependent upon the daughter because of ill health, as an intruder whose life deserves no protection. Just as a woman cannot be "a little pregnant," no human being is only partially "human." A human being can be incapacitated, dependent, ill, disabled, asleep, or comatose, but none of these states of being makes the individual less than fully "human," though the individual may not be able to develop or express himself or herself fully. Even dead human beings are accorded particular kinds of care and respect.

51. For example, battered women are still responsible in the eyes of the law for protecting their children. A father who was beaten as a child or who is discriminated against at work is still considered responsible for the affirmative support and protection of his children.

52. Regan, "Rewriting *Roe v. Wade,"* 1579.

53. Aida Torres and Jacqueline Darroch Forrest, "Why Do Women Have Abortions?" *Family Planning Perspectives* 20 (1988): 169.

54. *Pamela P. v. Frank S.,* 59 N.Y.2d 1, 6–7 (1983).

55. Exceptions for rape, incest, fatal fetal deformity, and significant risk to the health or life of the mother have commonly been recognized as circumstances in which abortion may be sought with the sympathy and support of most of the community.

56. Regan, "Rewriting *Roe v. Wade*," 1617.

57. Robinson, "The Standing of the Fetus," 529.

58. Regan, "Rewriting *Roe v. Wade*," 1617.

59. As, for example, in the case of a woman who takes prenatal vitamins before conception to reduce the risk of spinal or neural defects in the child she expects to conceive, or in the case of women and men who act to reduce their exposure to sexually transmitted diseases or to lead or other toxic substances in an effort to improve their chances of producing healthy children.

60. Robinson, "The Standing of the Fetus," 523.

61. For a detailed examination of arguments about when life begins, the moral status of the unborn, whether abortion equals "killing," and so on, see Stephen D. Schwarz, *The Moral Question of Abortion* (Chicago: Loyola University Press, 1990).

62. While discipline of any doctor may not be rapid, recent cases in Los Angeles and New York suggest that abortion doctors may continue to harm women for several years after authorities receive the first complaints of dirty facilities or of malpractice resulting in the injury or death of patients. A seven-year investigation of one Los Angeles abortion clinic resulted in no formal charges for five years; after the deaths of three women and serious injury to several others, one doctor lost his license for failure to treat respiratory distress that resulted in a patient's death during the abortion and for failure to administer examinations, take medical histories, and administer standard tests prior to performing abortions. See Pamela Warrick, "State Slow to Discipline Physicians: Many Doctors Remain in Practice Despite Accusations," *Los Angeles Times,* 18 March 1993; Warrick, "Despite Criminal Records and Malpractice Judgments, Some Doctors Remain in Practice for Years; Critics Blame the Besieged State Medical Board: Watching a Watchdog," *Los Angeles Times,* 31 January 1993; Claire Spiegel, *Los Angeles Times,* 17 June 1991.

Thirty women, mostly poor immigrants "who did not know that better, cheaper care was available" accused New York doctor Abu Hayat of botching their abortions. He was convicted of performing an illegal third-trimester abortion and of assaulting a patient by stopping midway through the abortion to demand an additional sum of money for his services. He was also charged with assault for severing the arm of a thirty-two-week-old fetus who survived the abortion attempt. (Pro-choice activists argued that, because *Roe* declared the fetus not a person under the law, the latter assault charge would not be upheld.) In addition, one seventeen-year-old patient apparently died due to Dr. Hayat's negligence. See Richard Perez-Pena, "Doctor in Abortion Case to Appeal Assault Count," *New York Times,* 7 March 1993; Perez-Pena, "East Village Doctor Convicted of Performing Illegal Abortion," *New York Times,* 23 February 1993.

63. See Camille S. Williams, "Thoughts of a Pro-Life Feminist," *World & I* 6 (October 1991): 569–85.

64. Siegel, "Reasoning from the Body," 324.

65. Ibid., 268.

66. Ibid., 267.

67. "Considered in cold dollar terms, it is the institution of motherhood that gives a gendered structure to the economics of family life, and a gendered face to poverty in the nation's life." Motherhood—"both the work of childbearing and the work of childrearing compromise women's opportunities in education and employment; neither the work of childbearing nor the work of childrearing produces any material compensation for women; [and] most often . . . entangle women in relations of emotional and economic dependency—to men, extended family, or the state." Ibid., 377–78.

68. Ibid., 380.

69. In her view, the state must see "that women's lives are required to make potential life recognizable as a person, and recognize that because women are equal citizens too, their

labor in bearing life is a gift with which they can endow the community, not a resource the community can expropriate to its use." Ibid., 380–81.

70. Ibid., 261, 390.

71. Ibid., 378.

72. Ibid., 281. Most law deals with bodily actions of some sort; but the fact that physical action is an inherent focus of the law does not by itself show that laws dealing with women's bodies are discriminatory.

73. Ibid., 321.

74. Ibid., 325.

75. Ibid., 324–27.

76. Dellapenna, "Brief of the American Academy of Medical Ethics," 710. Full citation for the case is *Webster v. Reproductive Health Services,* 492 U.S. 490 (1989).

77. Compare Dellapenna's discussion of the historians' veracity—"Sylvia Law, Counsel of Record on the Webster Brief, candidly lamented the authors' 'serious deficiencies as truth-tellers'" ("Brief of the American Academy of Medical Ethics," 710)—with Siegel's discussion of the AMA's involvement with abortion legislation in Ohio ("Reasoning from the Body," 314–18).

78. Andrea Nye, *Feminist Theories and the Philosophies of Man* (London: Croom Helm, 1988), 82.

79. For a critique of the alienation justification for abortion, see Camille [S.] Williams, "Abortion and the Insatiable Self," *World & I,* 7 (May 1992): 554–55.

80. Pro-life attorney Paige Comstock Cunningham contends that the majority of the leaders and members of the pro-life movement include 1.8 million women who view abortion as a violent act against women and their unborn children. Cunningham, "Testimony Concerning Ruth Bader Ginsburg," 28.

81. See Bernard N. Nathanson, *The Abortion Papers: Inside the Abortion Mentality* (New York: Frederick Fell Publishers 1983), 111–75.

82. With increasingly sophisticated methods of *in vitro* fertilization and embryo transfer, the unborn child may even be the offspring of more than two "parents," as in the case of a child resulting from donated egg and sperm gestated by a surrogate mother contracted by an infertile couple. While the methods of conception may be more numerous and more expensive than sexual intercourse, the result is the same: pregnancy leading to the birth of a child.

83. Siegel, "Reasoning from the Body," 377.

84. See "The Body and the Earth," in Wendell Berry, *The Unsettling of America: Culture and Agriculture* (San Francisco: Sierra Club Books, 1977), 97–140.

85. Siegel, "Reasoning from the Body," 270. Rather than being evidence of "social relations of reproduction which define motherhood as a condition of economic dependency," laws denying pregnant women unemployment insurance or access to elective abortion may reflect a view of women today as having adequate personal autonomy to choose whether and when to engage in sexual intercourse and sufficient access to effective methods of contraception to choose generally when to be pregnant or to avoid conception altogether. Because pregnancy is considered an option to be chosen, it is assumed that women who choose to be pregnant also have the resources to significantly affect the timing and circumstances of the pregnancy so that it does not unduly impact their planned education, job, or economic status.

86. Siegel and others deny this view of female autonomy and assert a "dominance feminist" view of male-female interaction in which women have much less control over their sexual and reproductive lives. These are alternative readings of our past and contemporary practices. I do not find the "dominance feminist" interpretation persuasive. It is inconsistent to hold that women are coerced sexually while simultaneously supporting abortion as an individual liberty for women; the same people or influences which would circumscribe

the woman's sexual activity would likely dominate her "choice" for abortion. Thus, abortion would be simply another kind of injustice borne by the already oppressed woman, not a constitutional liberty freely exercised. Recognition of women as moral agents capable of making and implementing their choices is crucial to any discussion of abortion except those which would represent women as incapable, either in theory or practice, of giving consent either to sexual activity or to abortion. For a discussion of dominance feminism and other feminisms in legal theory, see "Feminist Perspectives and Constitutional Theory," in Michael J. Gerhardt and Thomas D. Rowe, Jr., *Constitutional Theory: Arguments and Perspectives* (Charlottesville, Va.: Michie, 1993), 271–72.

87. This is not to say that mothers were not discriminated against; pregnant high school girls often had to drop out of school and some employers arbitrarily laid off workers who were in the last trimester of pregnancy. Such discriminatory practices still exist.

88. Cunningham, "Testimony Concerning Ruth Bader Ginsburg," 17; emphasis in original.

89. The plurality consisted of three members of the Court: Justices O'Connor, Kennedy, and Souter. Other Justices concurred in part and dissented in part. Laudatory and acrimonious dissents to various portions of the plurality opinion were filed by Justice Stevens; Justice Blackmun; Chief Justice Rehnquist, joined by Justices White, Scalia, and Thomas; and Justice Scalia. For a discussion of the fractured *Casey* Court, see Lynn D. Wardle, *Whither Abortion? Whither the Court? Reflections on Casey and on Its Consequences,* Essays on Our Times, no. 24 (Washington, D.C.: Free Congress Research and Education Foundation, 1992), 1–8.

90. The Court's respect for the life of the unborn increases at the point of viability; prior to that "the urgent claims of the woman to retain ultimate control over her destiny and her body" require the Court to grant abortion rights to the woman. 112 S.Ct. 2791, 2816.

91. "It is an inescapable biological fact that state regulation with respect to the child a woman is carrying will have far greater impact on the mother's liberty than on the father's." Ibid., 2830. This is true, however, not because the state imposes upon the woman but because the woman is able to do something the man cannot: physically support the child prior to birth.

92. Bruce C. Hafen, "The Constitutional Status of Marriage, Kinship, and Sexual Privacy—Balancing the Individual and Social Interests," *Michigan Law Review* 81 (1983): 464, 535.

93. Ibid., 535–36.

94. An assumption true neither in our own time nor as applied to the past: Elizabeth Cady Stanton, mother of seven, had a significant public life as well as a busy private one.

95. 112 S.Ct. 2791, 2812.

96. Ibid., 2862 (dissenting opinion of Chief Justice Rehnquist, joined by Justices White, Scalia, and Thomas).

97. Many women and men work full- or part-time at home either as owners of their own businesses or as valued employees. Women "at home" also serve in their communities as volunteers in directing youth groups and working in hospitals and schools. For a discussion of professional women returning to the home, see Linda Burton, Janet Dittmer, and Cheri Loveless, *What's a Smart Woman Like You Doing at Home?* rev. ed. (Vienna, Va.: Mothers at Home, 1992); Arlene Cardozo, *Sequencing* (New York: Atheneum, 1986); but see also Alecia Swasy, "Status Symbols," *Wall Street Journal,* 23 July 1993, discussing the re-emergence of the stay-at-home mother as a status symbol.

98. For a concise and generally balanced discussion of the changing status of women in the United States, see Rita J. Simon and Gloria Danziger, *Women's Movements in America: Their Successes, Disappointments, and Aspirations* (New York: Praeger, 1991).

99. 112 S.Ct. 2791, 2807.

100. In practical terms individuals do choose which obligations they fulfill; the law "catches" a minuscule amount of abuse or neglect but may still function as a societal standard against which behavior can be judged and sometimes compelled.

101. 112 S.Ct. 2791, 2809.

102. Cunningham, "Testimony Concerning Ruth Bader Ginsburg," 28.

103. E. J. Dionne, Jr., "Struggle for Work and Family Fueling Women's Movement," *New York Times,* 22 August 1989. Women ranking the importance of personal issues ranked abortion behind equal pay, day care, rape, maternity leave, and job discrimination. Claudia Wallis, "Onward, Women!" *Time,* 4 December 1989, 80, 82.

104. Cunningham, "Testimony Concerning Ruth Bader Ginsburg," 20.

105. See Bruce C. Hafen, "Individualism and Autonomy in Family Law: The Waning of Belonging," *Brigham Young University Law Review,* 1991, no. 1: 1–42.

106. Cunningham, "Testimony Concerning Ruth Bader Ginsburg," 21.

107. Siegel, "Reasoning from the Body," 371–72.

108. Ibid., 378–79.

109. Ibid., 371.

110. Ibid., 376.

111. Elizabeth Fox-Genovese, "Society's Child," *The New Republic,* 18 May 1992, 39. The article is a review of Roger Rosenblatt's *Life Itself: Abortion in the American Mind* (New York: Random House, 1992).

112. Siegel, "Reasoning from the Body," 380.

113. Ibid., 379.

114. Fox-Genovese, "Society's Child," 43; emphasis in original.

115. Kate Maloy and Maggie Jones Patterson, *Birth or Abortion? Private Struggles in a Political World* (New York: Plenum Press, 1992), 127–28.

116. Ibid., 324.

117. Ibid.

118. Ibid., 128.

119. Ibid., 3.

120. Siegel, "Reasoning from the Body," 364.

121. At least nineteen states hold fathers liable for the expenses relating to the child's birth and the mother's lost wages and expenses due to pregnancy. See Lynn D. Wardle, Christopher L. Blakesley, and Jacqueline Y. Parker, *Contemporary Family Law: Principles, Policy, and Practice,* vol. 2 (Deerfield, Ill.; Callaghan and Co., 1989), 47, 50–51 (§9:06). It is true that reasonable costs associated with pregnancy are usually not available to unmarried women until after the birth of the child. This may be an area where the law has not sufficiently adapted to social practices and could be improved. Calling restrictions on abortions "punishment" or "sanctions" on women's sexual activity is conclusory and not supported in Professor Siegel's essay, nor by what I witnessed of the legislative history of that particular piece of legislation.

122. It could be argued that since men tend to have greater body mass and are socialized to be tough, they can commit assault more easily than can women (and they do); men's capacity for assault, however, does not provide a basis for decriminalizing assault by women.

123. David Smolin, "Why Abortion Rights Are Not Justified by Reference to Gender Equality: A Response to Professor Tribe," *John Marshall Law Review* 23 (1990): 621, 645. While physiological naturalism may make some women feel that they are relegated to the status of wombs working for society, some fathers have lost their bodies altogether—only their wallets remain connected to their children.

124. See Williams, "Abortion and the Insatiable Self."

125. Richard A. Posner explains that "the Court is not immune to the *Zeitgeist.* How else to explain the reversal of constitutional values between the late nineteenth century and

Roe, from laissez-faire in the economic sphere and laissez-faire in the sexual? . . . If permitting nonmarital intercourse is a method of regulating sex, then equally is deregulating the economy and allowing the free market to order our economic affairs a method of regulating the economy." *Sex and Reason* (Cambridge, Mass.: Harvard University Press, 1992), 338–39.

126. In addition to the growing thousands with HIV or AIDS, 12 million sexually transmitted infections occur yearly; 56 million people (more than one in five) have incurable viral STDs such as genital herpes or hepatitis B; and 1 million women suffer pelvic inflammatory disease yearly (usually the result of an undiagnosed STD). Because of STDs, as many as 150,000 women may become infertile and 45,000 may experience an ectopic pregnancy (a life-threatening condition); in addition, STDs are strongly linked to the development of cervical cancer. These figures were compiled in a study made by the Alan Guttmacher Institute and reported by AP in the *Deseret News,* 1–2 April 1993. Abortions hover around 1.5 million a year. "A 1989 survey by the Alan Guttmacher Institute shows that 1.6 million abortions were performed in the U.S. in 1988, a number that has remained relatively unchanged since 1980." *Family Planning Perspectives* 22 (May/June 1990): 102.

127. Since sexual practices are integrally related to abortion practices, it is time for us to reevaluate the notion that an individual's sexual activity is of no concern to anyone but the individual himself or herself.

128. Smolin, "Why Abortion Rights Are Not Justified," 635.

129. This appears to be at least one purpose of laws prohibiting child and spouse abuse and mandating support for dependent family members.

130. Mary Ann Glendon, *The Transformation of Family Law: State, Law, and Family in the United States and Western Europe* (Chicago: University of Chicago Press, 1989), 312.

131. Ibid., 313.

132. Siegel, "Reasoning from the Body," 381.

133. Ibid., 375.

VII

TOWARD A FEMINIST REGROUNDING OF CONSTITUTIONAL LAW

★

Gayle Binion

In her pathbreaking book *In a Different Voice,* Carol Gilligan (1982) documented differences between men and women (indeed, even between boys and girls) in the ways in which they conceptualize moral dilemmas and seek their resolution.[1] In rebutting the conventional wisdom suggested by Kohlberg and others about the lesser state of the moral development of women, Gilligan offered a very different appraisal of the moral *voices* of men and women. Whereas men are hierarchical, women are contextual. Whereas men see themselves in opposition to others, women speak of the web of connectedness among people. To the extent that moral reasoning is assumed to be measured by the ability to see values in a hierarchy, men are deemed to be morally more developed. The *different voice,* the voice of women, the *voice* of context of values has received less attention, implicitly less respect. To the extent that Gilligan has invited a thorough reevaluation of the assumptions of male-centered research and male-based definitions of moral development, her book has already become a classic and has encouraged stimulating reassessments not only in psychology but as well in the other social sciences

Gayle Binion is a professor of political science and chair of the Law and Society Program at the University of California at Santa Barbara.

and in the study of law. Gilligan has shown the significance of gender in one's sense of the social fabric; she has suggested the importance of integrating *women's experience* into social theories and ethos. With respect to the study of law and legal institutions, her work demands that we ask basic questions about how law would be different if women's experience were systematically incorporated into it.[2]

Gilligan's work appeared at a very propitious time for feminist research in law. By the early 1980s legal scholars were already steeped in controversy about how best to operationalize the concept of equality within the equal protection and due process clauses of the U.S. Constitution. Debate was similarly strong with respect to framing and interpreting statutory provisions designed to effect equality for women. In either context the concern was thought to be whether the law is most sexually egalitarian when it is facially neutral as to gender or whether some recognition of gender difference may be necessary for sexual equality to be furthered in actuality. The core of the difference in approach is generally described by the somewhat cliché dichotomy between equality of treatment and equality of impact.

STAGES OF FEMINIST JURISPRUDENCE

In the analysis which follows,[3] I suggest that first-stage feminism is characterized by reliance on the *equality of treatment model* and second-stage feminism, alternatively, suggests a concern with the *equality of impact* of public policy. The movement from first- to second-stage feminist jurisprudence reflects a broadening of perspective, and a tension over the power and responsibility of the judiciary to scrutinize not just the content of law but as well the effects of legislation. It is best seen as a disagreement between *conservative* and *liberal* feminist theorists, wherein the former, as conservatives, oppose an active role for the judiciary in equal protection cases beyond reviewing the facial content of statutory law.

The substantive schism within feminist jurisprudence is, however, far more pronounced in the third stage,[4] and it is at this point that the significance of Gilligan's findings about gender difference emerges fully. What Gilligan's work invites us to ask, and what third-stage feminist jurisprudence questions, is whether law is not in general modeled on only male experience, and, therefore, whether the questions about the substance and interpretation of law are far more fundamental than had been previously suggested by an equality-of-treatment–equality-of-impact dichotomy.

First-Stage Feminist Jurisprudence

In its *first stage*, a *conservative* stage, American feminist jurisprudence argued for only the constitutional *identity* of women with men. *Reed v. Reed* (1971), *Frontiero v. Richardson* (1973), *Taylor v. Louisiana* (1975), *Stanton v. Stanton* (1975), *Califano v. Westcott* (1979), and *Orr v. Orr* (1979) are but a few of the most prominent examples of the victories for gender *blindness* that were accomplished before the U.S. Supreme Court.[5] The controlling philosophy behind this litigation was that *official* distinctions *on the basis of gender* required at least an intermediate (if not a compelling state interest) level of scrutiny by the judiciary. Based on the model of *Loving v. Virginia* (1968),[6] that distinctions on the basis of race were *constitutionally suspect* and, therefore, must be subjected to the strictest scrutiny, the agenda for *stage-one* feminist litigation was to expose sex-based criteria in public policy as equally pernicious. This support for "equality of treatment" was as much about the equality of men as it was about women. This is apparent in the fact that a majority of the cases on sex discrimination decided by the U.S. Supreme Court during the 1970s and 1980s were brought by male plaintiffs alleging that laws governing alimony, child custody, insurance benefits, and military conscription were discriminatory toward *them. First-stage* feminist jurisprudence was, thus, not fundamentally about women's experience and the sociolegal values engendered by this experience. Nor was *first-stage* feminist jurisprudence especially sensitive to the possibility that public policy, neutral on its face with respect to gender, could, in its impact, discriminate against women and undermine the legal interests of women as a class. In its most prominent and effective voice it demanded only that women be treated by the system as indistinguishable from men, a demand common in industrialized societies during the past two decades.[7]

Second-Stage Feminist Jurisprudence

In contrast, second-stage or liberal feminist jurisprudence is posited on the demand for application of stricter scrutiny to those public policies which, despite their *facial neutrality,* in their effects serve to discriminate against women as a group. Cases such as *Personnel Administrator v. Feeney* (1979) challenged the assumption that apparent gender blindness in policy necessarily reflects or furthers sexual equality in impact. In *Feeney* the U.S. Supreme Court upheld a Massachusetts policy of granting lifetime employment preference to military veterans, despite the fact that a major impact of the policy was, and continues to be, the disqualification of all but 2 percent of women from virtually all governmental employment other than secretarial jobs. The *facial neutrality* of the law on the basis of gender masked the differential experience of men and women with respect to the military's substantial recruitment of only the former. In sum, by incorporating veteran status into its employment scheme, the state of Massachusetts had adopted the overt discrimination of the armed services. Because the Supreme Court saw no evidence of nefarious *motive* in the state's policy, it chose to define as *gender neutral* a statute that was only superficially such. Thus, what the second stage brought to the fore is the principle that the use in public policy of variables highly correlated with gender, such as veteran status or height and weight standards, which, in their impact, serve to limit options for women, particularly with respect to employment, are as discriminatory and as unconstitutional as is the use of gender per se. A majority of the U.S. Supreme Court has continued to disagree with this proposition.[8]

Third-Stage Feminist Jurisprudence

Third-stage or *progressive* feminist jurisprudence contrasts sharply with the first and second stages in that it is philosophically proactive, and, while it is fundamentally concerned with women's rights, it is more broadly committed to integrating women into law generally. It is argued that women's experience, women's values, and women's needs, to the extent that they differ from those of men, must also be incorporated into the ethos of public and private institutions including the legal system. Perhaps no constitutional litigation has made this claim more directly than *California Federal Savings and Loan v. Guerra* (1987).[9] *Cal. Fed.* raised the question of whether a state law protecting women's jobs during childbearing leaves violates the federal Pregnancy Discrimination Act of 1978 which prohibits "discrimination on the basis of pregnancy." The California law requires employers either to hold a woman's job for up to four months of unpaid medically necessary childbearing leave or to provide her with a similar position when she returns to work. While the statute covers no other causes of temporary "disability," it also does not prevent employers from granting such leaves to other temporarily disabled workers. It should also be noted that, as is common in antidiscrimination legislation, the employer is relieved of its obligation to provide childbearing leave if able to demonstrate a "business necessity" for doing so.

The *Cal. Fed.* case highlighted a schism within the feminist community, politically and intellectually. First-stage feminists, treasuring gender blindness in the terms of the law, saw the California statute as constitutionally invalid because they view pregnancy as a surrogate variable for sex, a variable that should never be used in public policy. Their concern was that allowing governments to use pregnancy in a so-called *benign* manner simply reinforces the power of governments to use the classification in the manner traditionally used, that is, to disadvantage women. The precedents of *Geduldig v. Aiello* (1974) and *General Electric v. Gilbert* (1976), the former still good constitutional law, were very recent evidence in support of this concern.[10]

In contrast with the concern that pregnancy is itself a sex-based classification, *third-stage* feminists, supportive of the California statute, assessed the law in terms of its incorporation of women's experience. The workplace, they noted, is organized around the male reproductive model; if women's reproductive experience were integrated, pregnancy leave would be considered "natural," and not "special treatment." While they too were severe critics of *Geduldig* and *Gilbert*, it was not because of their legitimation of pregnancy as a consideration in public policy; it was because of the use of pregnancy in a gender-biased manner which deprived pregnant women of the benefits of employment enjoyed by other workers.

In sum, third-stage American feminist jurisprudence, stressing that women's experience be integrated into law, was furthered in *Cal. Fed.* In upholding the statute, the high court advanced sexual equality by specifically validating women's experience and by lessening a barrier to the full integration of women into the labor force. *Cal. Fed.* aside, what has been taken for granted in western industrialized societies—that women as workers and mothers may legitimately demand both jobs and the time necessary for childbearing—has been considered largely alien to American constitutional jurisprudence.[11]

In addition to arguing for incorporating into our laws, including our constitutional exegesis, the experience, the rights, and the needs of women as a group, third-stage feminist jurisprudence also provides a framework of values and principles from women's experience that may transform our thinking about constitutional law more generally. This potential transformation would extend well beyond the jurisprudence of sexual equality per se to many other kinds of constitutional rights issues and cases, directly affecting both men and women.

THE CONTOURS OF A FEMINIST CONSTITUTIONAL ANALYSIS

While there is a debate about whether feminist principles can simply be incorporated into or grafted onto the constitutional system,[12] a developing school of thought suggests that our approach to and understanding of constitutional principles might be quite different if women's experience and feminist values were a part of the interpretive enterprise.[13]

The civil and criminal law have already been challenged by scholarship suggesting how the integration of the experience and values of women's lives would alter, indeed in some areas revolutionize, American law. West, in her provocative "Jurisprudence and Gender," argued effectively that the harm of invasion (in rape or unwanted pregnancy), unrecognized as *itself* a harm in American civil or criminal law, would be given in a woman-based legal system.[14] Similarly, Elizabeth Schneider has suggested how the law of self-defense, which limits one's use of force to that which is "equal to" the force of the assailant, ignores women's subjective experience.[15] In recounting her experience in a

successful appeal in *State v. Wanrow* (1977), Schneider demonstrated the importance of integrating into the legal system the
experience of women, in this case the fear, for herself and her
children, on the part of a Native American woman five feet four
inches tall, with a cast on her leg, when accosted by an inebriated
white man six feet two inches tall, who had allegedly tried to
molest one of her children on a previous occasion.[16] Wanrow's
conviction for murder was overturned on appeal by the supreme
court of the state of Washington because of the restrictive nature
of the instructions to the jury in this regard.[17] Indeed, but well beyond the scope of this essay, it may be argued that these feminist
critiques of American law are exceptionally restrained in that
they do not maintain that law, as an institution, is itself unre-
formably male and thus not possible to transform. The proponents of this more radical view cite the hierarchical and adversarial quality of American law as itself inimical to women's
experience which values context and connectedness.

RECASTING RIGHTS ANALYSIS

The more limited focus of this essay is, however, on how constitutional jurisprudence would be altered by the integration of
women's experience. It is suggestive rather than comprehensive
and is limited to constitutional rights analysis. Despite the limitations of hierarchy and adversarial process there are several observations that may be made about the effects of integrating
women's experience in constitutional analysis. This undertaking
might well entail a recasting of rights analysis to (1) reassess the
origins of rights, (2) redefine liberty as more than an immunity
from government, (3) reconsider the "state action" and "intent"
requirements in defining abridgements of constitutional rights,
and (4) reconceptualize the nature of "community."

There has been the suggestion that feminists eschew *rights*
analysis.[18] The skepticism tends to reflect the dichotomous quality of rights analysis: individual versus state, rights versus power.
It also reflects the static quality of such analyses as well as the essential statism which promotes the notion that only government
can protect us.[19] More empirical and less philosophical is the observation that perhaps women are more inclined to this view of
rights analysis, than are men, because women tend to think in

terms of "responsibilities" rather than "rights,"[20] "rights" are generally operationalized in adversarial or male terms,[21] and rights speak to separateness, not connectedness. Nevertheless, I would suggest that feminist jurisprudence directs us not to a rejection of rights analysis but rather a recasting of our understanding of constitutional rights. The challenge for feminist thought is thus to reground concepts of law and of rights to empower women's experience and to integrate feminist values: connectedness, caring, and responsibility for the social fabric.

Origins of Rights

Feminist jurisprudence, like feminist theory more generally, looks to concrete experience, and *not* abstract theory, as the source of values. In a substantial sense feminism is more anthropological than it is philosophical. In this vein, a constitutional rights analysis from a feminist perspective would reject such abstract foundations for "liberty" as social contract theory.[22] Where social contract theorists argue from the abstraction of what reasonable *men* would do and to what conditions of civilization they would assent, feminism rejects appeals to theoretical *presumptions* about human nature. No one has ever lived in a state of nature and, therefore, despite the philosophical eloquence of Hobbes, Locke, Rousseau, or their more modern disciples, the enterprise of constructing such an abstraction may be largely irrelevant to human experience. For feminists, therefore, social contract theory, and its rejection of human interconnectedness, cannot provide useful guidance to understanding social organization and the appropriate definitions of rights therein.

To offer this observation is not to suggest that feminist jurisprudence lacks *theoretical* foundations. Arguments from empirical observation are not necessarily by their nature atheoretical. In this respect, feminist jurisprudence of the *third stage* is not unlike *legal realism* of the 1930s or *critical legal studies* of the 1970s and 1980s. In fact, it might well be argued that feminist jurisprudence melds elements of the two. Each of these approaches to understanding law asks us to look not to professed principles of society to understand its values but rather to its experience. Each offers little support for the assumptions of objectivity, neutrality, and rationality in the law. For the exponents of critical legal studies this means attention to socioeconomic power. For the legal realists it suggests only that law may be molded by events so mundane and idiosyncratic as what a judge has had for breakfast. For *third-stage* feminists, collective experience is reinforced by the personal; the values of women as a group emerge from our collective and individual experience. Seen in this light, feminist jurisprudence is certainly not alone in the twentieth century in its rejection of abstract reasoning as the foundation for a public, legal morality.[23]

Liberty as Immunity from Government

In addition to its rejection of social contract theory and other rationalist abstractions as sources of law, feminist jurisprudence also departs from traditional liberalism in rejecting the proposition that liberty is inversely related to the exercise of governmental power. Liberty is perhaps meaningfully defined as immunity from government if one is either possessed of power over others or is so self-sufficient that others cannot acquire power over her/him. Women's experience of relative powerlessness vis-à-vis the environment in which we live suggests that this popular notion of liberty is either insufficient or seriously flawed.

When government does not act in areas where other social power exists over individuals (economic, psychological, physical, medical, and so forth), the only liberty to be enhanced is the *liberty of the powerful.* The insights of feminism are not in this context unique. People of color were not served by the liberty that existed before the advent of open accommodations laws. Workers were not more "free" before we had minimum wage and occupational health and safety statutes. Similarly, women who live in abusive family relationships or who are entirely dependent financially on a father or husband do not experience *liberty* when the governmental system defines *family* as entirely private and therefore not reachable for criminal law enforcement or economic regulation.[24] In sum, while a feminist jurisprudence is capable of concluding that a meaningful concept of liberty may be furthered in some, perhaps many, contexts by an absence of public regulation, such jurisprudence would question whether the definition of liberty as immunity from government control is sufficient.

The State Action and Intent Requirements Reconsidered

Karst suggested in his application of Gilligan's findings to constitutional exegesis that a feminist approach to constitutional law would render the *intent* rule in cases on governmental discrimination irrelevant and would also significantly modify the requirement of demonstrating *state action* in cases in which equality of *citizenship* is at issue.[25] While I share Karst's view of these issues as *feminist issues,*[26] I would take his analysis further. The *web of relationships* as a community that is perceived by women, as well as the duty of care with respect to that web,[27] is only partially operationalized in Karst's analysis with respect to equality of *citizenship.* The perception of the web and of the duty of care would more generally support the principle that those who are in a position to help others have a duty to help.[28] This has serious implications for both the *intent* rule and the assumption that only *governmental* actions can be proscribed by the Constitution.

The *intent* and *state action* rules are especially important to women as a group because of the requirement that they be met in discrimination cases. *Feeney,* for example, was, in the view of a majority of the U.S. Supreme Court, fundamentally about whether the state of Massachusetts, in its adoption of its veterans' preference policy, *intended* to harm women. Feminist jurisprudence, in contrast with the orientation of a majority of the Supreme Court's justices, would ask whether the subordination of a disadvantaged group has been perpetuated by the state's policy. If a harm has been inflicted, it should be remedied by those with the power to do so, no matter the intent of the policy.[29]

The responsibility to prevent harm to others and to remedy the harm one causes, the basis on which feminist jurisprudence rejects the intent rule, would, similarly, have great consequence for affirmative action policies. In rejecting the significance of governmental *motivation,* feminist jurisprudence would judge the extent to which governments were in compliance with the equal protection clause *by the consequences of their actions.* The power of the state to adopt affirmative action programs or the power of the judiciary to order such programs in order to remedy discrimination would be based on the *outcomes* of previous selection processes employed by the state and not on the presence of nefarious motives. The duty of care, documented by Gilligan as central to women's outlook, would also support affirmative action programs themselves against the claim that they are discriminatory. All that affirmative action condones is the principle that governments (or, by extension, private employers covered by Title VII of the 1964 Civil Rights Act) have a responsibility for the *impacts* of their actions. Affirmative action programs are premised on only the principle that the states must employ criteria for selection (for employees, students, and so on) that are not unnecessarily biased in their results with respect to including women and minorities. Similarly, the argument for a constitutionally mandated adoption of "comparable worth" or "pay equity" stems from a duty of care, an obligation not to exploit, despite the states' defense that their salary practices only mimic "prevailing wage" salary practices in the private sector.

In sum, affirmative action is itself dictated by a feminist view of equal protection, a view that obligates government to take care for the needs of women as a group and not to employ selection schemes that unduly restrict the full participation of women in society. It is, thus, not only because an obstacle to lessening the subordination of women is removed by rejection of the intent rule that such a position is embraced by feminism, but as well because the intent rule, in any area of constitutional interpretation, is fundamentally about official shirking of a duty of care, a duty rudimentary to women's experience.

The *state action* requirement is, in feminist analysis, intrinsically linked to the *intent* rule, and, when appended to the liberal definition of rights as *immunities* from governmental action, these principles combine to make government seem far less significant to communal life than it is or should be deemed to be. In combination, they reinforce the proposition that government is responsible for only its *intentional* acts that contravene the Constitution (and only when it has entered an area of immunity from regulation). If, as a feminist analysis would suggest, there is a duty of care for the web of relationships that make a community, government would be accountable not only for the *consequences* of its actions but as well for the actions (or inactions) of nongovernmental actors which the government *has a responsibility to prevent (or require).*

While the state action requirement of traditional constitutional law has on occasion in the past been minimized by a finding of state responsibility for private activity,[30] it must be noted that in these cases the Court found that governmental actors were in some sense *actually* involved in the private acts in question. In a feminist analysis, the question would not be whether a governmental actor was in some manner involved in private acts depriving individuals of rights under the Constitution. The question would be *either* whether the government ought to be held *accountable* for a deprivation of rights it did not perpetrate but could have prevented through appropriate public policy, or whether we should hold powerful nongovernmental actors subject directly to the constraints of the Constitution.

I have argued previously for the principle that powerful private actors in some circumstances ought to be treated as *if they are government* with respect to safeguarding of constitutional rights.[31] While I did not at the time identify this as *feminist* jurisprudence, it is, on reflection, very much associated with such principles. It speaks to how we justify what may be intuitive notions of justice.[32] If justice must be constructed out of experience, and not from abstract principle such as contractarianism, then there must be some reason why we structured our Constitution to limit *governmental power* in particular ways. Fear of oppressive authority is the most common explanation for constitutional*ism* generically. If so, then why not extend these constitutional limitations on power to other nongovernmental actors whose potential for oppressive authority (as parents, spouses, employers, air polluters, and so forth) is as great as that usually attributed to government and as dangerous to us in their consequences? This not only speaks to why we, as a society, want to control governmental authority, but also to the principle that we value rights not just in the negative (that is, "thou shalt nots" for government) but more importantly for the positive benefits that accrue to society from their respect and exercise.

Freedom of speech provides a useful model in support of the "positive benefits" approach to rights. Freedom of communications is important not just because, in a democracy, we want to prevent government from silencing criticism and perpetuating its authority, but also because better citizens and more developed human beings result when communications are open and robust. Enhanced relationships with each other and more developed levels of scientific, social, literary, political, and artistic discourse are also important justifications for First Amendment freedoms. Under a feminist value system these would be seen as important reasons to encourage the actual exercise of the freedoms protected by the First Amendment. If this be the case, then one would not only want to hold the government accountable for *unintentional* infringements on the freedom of communication; one would also want to require that government do whatever it can to promote openness and diversity within communications, even if this means, in effect, forcing nongovernmental actors to respect constitutional rights.[33] From feminist analysis—posited on a rejection of abstractions as explanatory of constitutional rights, committed to the duty of care for the needs of others, and concerned about the web of relationships that defines human life—readily flows the principles that liberty is more than an immunity from government, that governments are responsible for the *consequences* of their actions, and that private parties may effectively undermine values embedded in our Constitution.

The Nature of Community

Gilligan's pathbreaking work demonstrated that women are acutely aware of themselves as part of a network of relationships. Where men are oriented toward the distinction between themselves and "other," seeing themselves as largely in an adversarial stance vis-à-vis others around them, women are sensitive to the web of human interactions in which the social fabric must be nurtured and reinforced. Whereas men learn to value advantage, women are taught to internalize the needs of others.[34] MacKinnon has argued that we must be especially careful not to glorify or romanticize the quality of women as *caring,* because this represents the need of the oppressed to be desirable to the oppressor.[35] In MacKinnon's view, women are caring because it is for only this quality that we are valued by men. Despite this controversial admonition, it might be suggested that, whatever *may be* the source of women's ethos and values, the fact that women appear to value the web of relationships more than men do does have implications for the ways in which we might interpret constitutional law.[36]

Having suggested that the integration of the experience and values of women into our constitutional jurisprudence would necessitate more attention to the societal web of relationships, I would, nevertheless, caution that the kind of communitarianism that emerges from Gilligan's data is not that of a community of believers nor a communitarianism of governmental repression. In Sherry's application of Gilligan's concept of the "feminine voice" to Justice O'Connor's constitutional jurisprudence, she concluded that "the community is more important than individual rights."[37] This conclusion was reached, erroneously, I would argue, in analyzing O'Connor's votes against criminal defendants in procedural due process cases. Sherry observed that "feminine jurisprudence" supports the position that a limitation on procedural rights will minimize crime in the community and is, therefore, justified in the interest of community. But the communitarian principle involved in a web of relationships is not an endorsement of hierarchical state power; its attention is rather to responsibility for the consequences of private and public actions for our personal interrelatedness. Exponents of the communitarianism that would preempt reproductive choice or reintroduce prayer in the public schools because an intense segment of the community believes that its values are being disrespected cannot claim support from feminist jurisprudence for these crusades.[38]

The jurisprudence which emerges from women's experience, an experience of relative powerlessness, is, to the contrary, uniquely sensitive to inequalities of power and to the repression, and lack of tolerance for diversity, that that has entailed. Indeed, as suggested by Zillah Eisenstein, women value social and legal respect for diversity because women are, as a group, the "other."[39] Because we have been falsely defined as homogeneous when we all share *only* our distinction from men, the heart of feminism is the freedom of women to be *different from each other*.[40] Repression of individuation, characteristic of a statist concept of community, is for feminism a distortion of community, a corruption of connectedness.

CONCLUSION

It was suggested at the outset that the foregoing analysis was designed to be "suggestive rather than exhaustive." This attempt to explore the ways in which a feminist regrounding of constitutional law would alter our understanding of the origin, nature, and purposes of constitutional rights is also *preliminary.* The insights gleaned from Gilligan's work on the voices of women with respect to *context, connectedness,* and responsibility for the *consequences* of one's behavior have been especially important in providing a framework for the intellectual enterprise in which I am engaged. These principles, when informed by the grounding of feminist thought in actual experience, rather than in abstract theory, will guide a to-date incomplete journey. The use of the word "toward" in the title was, thus, intentional.

Notes

1. Carol Gilligan, *In a Different Voice: Psychological Theory and Women's Development* (Cambridge, Mass.: Harvard University Press, 1982).

2. The discussion which follows does not assume that the characteristics of women that are addressed are common to *all* women nor associated with *only* women. What is apparent is that women, *in the main,* will express an orientation to morality and to human interrelatedness that differs from that expressed by men, *in the main.*

3. A slightly different version of this article was published in *Social Science Quarterly* 72 (June 1991): 207–20.

4. Although stage one and then stage two of feminist jurisprudence preceded the development of stage three, all three continue as coterminous "competing" philosophies.

5. *Reed v. Reed,* 404 U.S. 71; *Frontiero v. Richardson,* 411 U.S. 677; *Taylor v. Louisiana,* 419 U.S. 522; *Stanton v. Stanton,* 421 U.S. 7; *Califano v. Westcott,* 443 U.S. 76; and *Orr v. Orr,* 440 U.S. 268.

6. 388 U.S. 1.

7. In Sweden, the nation with the most advanced feminist agenda, such gender neutrality has been a prominent feature of public policy since the mid-nineteenth century. Tove Stang Dahl, *Women's Law: An Introduction to Feminist Jurisprudence,* trans. Ronald L. Craig (Oslo: Norwegian University Press, 1987), 48.

8. While the U.S. Supreme Court has, on occasion, assessed the *impact* of policies on men and women or blacks and whites when applying civil rights *statutes*—see, for example, *Griggs v. Duke Power Co.,* 401 U.S. 424 (1971), and *Dothard v. Rawlinson,* 433 U.S. 321 (1977), it has declined to find *constitutional* violations of equal protection in unequal effects of laws. *Personnel Administrator v. Feeney,* 442 U.S. 256 (1979), requiring a showing of a nefarious governmental *intent* to invalidate a *facially neutral* law, remains good constitutional law.

9. 479 U.S. 272.

10. 417 U.S. 484; 429 U.S. 125.

11. The contrast between the United States and Scandinavian countries is especially stark. In Norway, since 1966, women have been paid their full wage for eighteen weeks for childbearing (Dahl, *Women's Law,* 122), and Sweden has recently expanded such leaves for mothers and fathers to nearly full pay for up to a (combined) period of one year. In the United States not only are such paid leaves virtually unknown in most lines of employment, they are also not deemed to be the responsibility of government. The Family and Medical Leave Act, vetoed by President Bush on 29 June 1990, would have mandated only *unpaid* leaves of up to three months for, *inter alia,* the birth of a child, and would have covered only the nation's largest employers. "Bush Vetoes a Bill to Give Workers Family Leave," *New York Times,* 30 June 1990.

12. See Ann Scales, "The Emergence of Feminist Jurisprudence: An Essay," *Yale Law Journal* 95 (1986): 1381, criticizing Kenneth Karst, "Woman's Constitution," *Duke Law*

Journal (1984): 484, 494–95; and see Margaret Thornton, "Feminist Jurisprudence: Illusion or Reality?" *Australian Journal of Law and Society* 3 (1985): 16.

13. Karst, "Woman's Constitution"; Scales, "Emergence of Feminist Jurisprudence"; Elizabeth Schneider, "The Dialectic of Rights and Politics: Perspectives from the Women's Movement," *New York University Law Review* 61 (1986): 589–652; Robin West, "Jurisprudence and Gender," *University of Chicago Law Review* 55 (1988): 1–72; Suzanna Sherry, "Civil Virtue and the Feminine Voice in Constitutional Adjudication," *Virginia Law Review* 72 (1986): 543–616; Zillah R. Eisenstein, *The Female Body and the Law* (Berkeley and Los Angeles: University of California Press, 1988).

14. West, "Jurisprudence and Gender," 59–61.

15. Schneider, "Rights and Politics," 606–7.

16. 88 Wash. 2d 221 (1977), cited in Schneider, "Rights and Politics," 606.

17. Ibid.

18. Sherry, "Civil Virtue and the Feminine Voice," 582, 604; Schneider, "Rights and Politics," 593–97.

19. Schneider, "Rights and Politics," 596–97.

20. Gilligan, *In a Different Voice,* 54.

21. Ibid., 8.

22. But see Anita Allen, "Taking Liberties: Privacy, Private Choice, and Social Contract Theory," *Cincinnati Law Review* 56 (1987): 488–91.

23. Exponents of critical legal studies such as Duncan Kennedy ("Form and Substance in Private Law Adjudication," *Harvard Law Review* 89 [1976]: 1774) and West ("Jurisprudence and Gender," 12), the latter a feminist as well, stress the web of connectedness as a *human* value, ignored by liberal legalism. However, see also West's critique of the differences between critical legal studies and feminism and their "unofficial stories" in ibid., 37–41. See also David Cole, "Getting There: Reflections on Trashing from Feminist Jurisprudence and Critical Theory," *Harvard Women's Law Journal* 8 (1985): 81–91.

24. See Diane Polan, "Toward a Theory of Law and Patriarchy," in David Kairys, ed., *The Politics of Law: A Progressive Critique* (New York: Pantheon, 1982), 298.

25. Karst, "Woman's Constitution," 488, 491.

26. See my "'Intent' and Equal Protection: A Reconsideration," *Supreme Court Review* (1984): 397–457, and my "The United States Constitution: The Next 100 Years," *Beverly Hills Bar Association Journal* 21 (1987): 250–58.

27. Gilligan, *In a Different Voice,* 8.

28. Ibid., 54.

29. But see Sherry, "Civil Virtue and the Feminine Voice," 604–5.

30. See, e.g., *Shelley v. Kraemer,* 334 U.S. 1 (1948); *Burton v. Wilmington Parking Authority,* 365 U.S. 715 (1961); *Lombard v. Louisiana,* 373 U.S. 267 (1963); *Reitman v. Mulkey,* 387 U.S. 369 (1967).

31. Binion, "United States Constitution," 255–56.

32. Karst, "Woman's Constitution," 501.

33. Furthering this goal is the FCC's statutorily mandated preference for racial/gender diversity in the licensing of radio and television stations, which was upheld by the U.S. Supreme Court in *Metro Broadcasting v. F.C.C.,* 110 S.Ct. 2997 (1990). Similarly suggested here is the obligation of the same agency to require of all broadcasters that they offer broad opportunities for public access to the airwaves. While access requirements are seen by some as censorship, therefore as an unconstitutional exercise of governmental authority under the First Amendment, I believe that access, which expands our right to hear, is the antithesis of censorship.

34. Although Gilligan did not characterize the "different voice" of women as a product of differential experience and socialization, it is probably not an unreasonable conclusion,

especially given the nature of the research she cited and the explanations she provided for the findings. In no sense did she argue from biological determinism.

35. "Feminist Discourse, Moral Values, and the Law—A Conversation," *Buffalo Law Review* 34 (1985): 74.

36. Also implied by Catherine MacKinnon in *Sexual Harassment of Working Women* (New Haven, Conn.: Yale University Press, 1979), though doubtless unintended, is the assumption that the male orientation toward the world is perhaps *natural* and that women would lose the necessity to be caring and connected when male oppression is lifted. Just as useful as a hypothesis is that women would remain as we are, and male orientations, premised on the role of oppressor, would change with the end of male hegemony. See Alfie Kohn, *The Brighter Side of Human Nature: Altruism and Empathy in Everyday Life* (New York: Basic Books, 1990).

37. Sherry, "Civil Virtue and the Feminine Voice," 604.

38. A considerable weakness of communitarian thought is the easy identity it assumes between the *community* and the *state*. The former represents a sense of belonging, involving, *inter alia,* families, friends, coworkers, social organizations, and religious congregations. The juridical unit of the *state* does not necessarily correspond to these not entirely geographical concepts of community.

39. Eisenstein, *Female Body and the Law,* 8–9.

40. Ibid., 222–24.

VIII

MINORITY RIGHTS UNDER THE CONSTITUTION

★

Gary C. Bryner

Equality is a fundamental element of American political culture. It reflects one of the primary expectations of our constitutional democracy and is intricately intertwined with other values that are primary goals of democratic government. While there is a general commitment to the idea of equality, there is little consensus over exactly what that means. Some argue that equality must be given a narrow interpretation, so that efforts to pursue it do not conflict with individual freedom or rights. From one perspective, equality conflicts with efficient economic activity: the production and distribution of goods and services, to be efficient, must be free from political intervention aimed at promoting equality.[1] From another vision, the ideal of equality runs counter to the merit principle—that benefits be allocated in response to performance or expertise—or conflicts with the expectation that individuals have a right to the enjoyment of the fruits of their labor and cannot be compelled to share their property in the name of equality. Others fear that inequality threatens democracy,[2] or see it as incompatible with other important social values[3] and a violation of justice and membership in a political community.[4]

Gary C. Bryner is an associate professor of political science at Brigham Young University.

Equality is often defined as equality of opportunity, in contrast to equality of material conditions or equality of results. But the idea of equality of opportunity is ambiguous. Efforts to provide equality of opportunity can be limited to ensuring that no decisions are made on the basis of race or sex or other factors that are not relevant to the performance of the activities involved. From another perspective, however, equality of opportunity can only be achieved through positive action to expand or create educational and employment opportunities and provide the preconditions for effective choice. While some argue that equality must be individual in nature, others believe that since discrimination is group or gender based and not directed toward individual characteristics, equality must be defined in terms of a group right rather than an individual right. Still others have concluded that equality of opportunity threatens other important values such as the autonomy of families, since much of the development of individuals is a function of family life.[5]

The ideal of equality, first advanced in the Declaration of Independence, was most powerfully articulated in Lincoln's Gettysburg Address where he redefined the founding of America as a people "dedicated to the proposition that all men are created equal."[6] The Constitution's Fourteenth Amendment promise of a right of all persons to "the equal protection of the laws" has been widely accepted as part of the Bill of Rights and an essential means of ensuring that rights are secured for all persons, particularly African-Americans. America's civil rights leaders have regularly invoked the Constitution in prodding government officials and citizens alike to ensure that constitutional rights are extended to all people. Martin Luther King's speeches and writing often chided and challenged his fellow citizens to respect the constitutional rights of black Americans, to "be true to what you said on paper."[7] In his letter from the Birmingham Jail, he reminded his critics that "we have waited for more than 340 years for our constitutional and God-given rights."[8]

The current socioeconomic status of African-Americans and other ethnic minorities and women in the American economic system challenges the idea that we have been committed to equality of opportunity and fairness.[9] Poverty in America is not randomly distributed throughout the population, nor is it a natural outcome of market relationships of economically rational individuals. Blacks and other ethnic minorities and women are much more likely to be poor than are white males. The median weekly earnings of women, for example, are only a little more than two-thirds those of males, and black males earn only about three-fourths of what white males earn for the same or similar work.[10] Families headed by single women are several times more likely to be poor than those headed by single men. Women and blacks are disproportionately represented in the lowest-paying occupations and are underrepresented in most professional jobs. The unemployment rate among blacks is more than twice that of whites, and unemployment among black teenagers is usually at least three times that of their white counterparts. The labor force participation rate for black men is only about 90 percent of that for white men, reflecting the higher rate at which black males are incarcerated, are serving in the military, and have been discouraged from seeking employment.[11] By the end of the 1980s, of the six million Americans who reported they wanted work but were discouraged from seeking it, 25 percent were black.[12] Some 85 percent of black female heads of households had incomes at or below the poverty level.[13] The median family income of blacks was less than 60 percent of that for white families. Nearly one-third of blacks had incomes below the poverty line, compared with 11 percent for whites.[14] Disparities between blacks and whites in income, health care, access to bank loans, opportunities to rent or purchase housing, and many other areas continue.

The socioeconomic situation of African-American children is particularly alarming. According to the Children's Defense Fund, black children, in comparison with whites, are twice as likely to die in the first year of life, be born prematurely, live in substandard housing, and have no parent who is employed. They are three times as likely to be poor, live in a single-parent household headed by the mother, be in foster care, or die of known child abuse; four times as likely to live with neither parent and be under the direction of a welfare agency, be murdered before the age of one or as a teenager, or be incarcerated between the ages of fifteen and nineteen; and five times as likely to be on welfare.[15] The figures cited above give some indication of the yawning economic and social gap between black and white America, and, in a larger sense, between rich and poor Americans. The decay of inner cities and the emergence of an urban "underclass" that is characterized by crime, poverty, dependency, and despair is an even more sobering manifestation of the lack of opportunity. These figures are overshadowed by the growing violence and tension engulfing blacks and other minorities and whites that culminated in the riots in central Los Angeles in April 1992. Even though some progress has been made in reversing past racial discrimination, equality of opportunity continues to elude us. While these problems go beyond employment discrimination and lack of opportunity to include a maze of interrelated factors, they can be explored, in part, by examining the role of affirmative action in promoting equality of opportunity for women and minorities.

AFFIRMATIVE ACTION AND EQUALITY OF OPPORTUNITY

Is affirmative action an effective and appropriate means of securing the right of equality of opportunity for women and people of color? Does equality of opportunity require race- and gender-neutral standards, or does it demand that we go beyond that to provide some of the preconditions required for real opportunity to be guaranteed to all persons? Equal employment opportunity policy has generally been understood to include efforts to assure that decisions concerning the selection, promotion, termination, and general treatment of individuals in employment be free of considerations of race, color, national origin, religion, and sex. Specific provisions of this policy include prohibiting discriminatory employment practices, establishing mechanisms of monitoring employment decisions by federal and state and local officials, and providing for judicial enforcement for claims of discrimination. Equal employment opportunity policy rests on the idea that equality of opportunity primarily requires freedom from interference by others.

In contrast, affirmative action goes beyond a commitment to prohibit discrimination to embrace a more ambitious role for government. Terms describing hiring and promotion goals, ratios, and quotas are used interchangeably, and affirmative action has been defined in different ways. According to the U.S. Civil Rights Commission, it has three main components. First, it is remedial: affirmative action denotes efforts that take race, sex, and national origin into account for the purposes of remedying discrimination and its effects. Second, it ultimately seeks to bring about equal opportunity: it rests upon the idea that we must take into account race, sex, or national origin in order to eliminate the effects of past discrimination. And third, it specifies what racial groups are to be considered part of the "protected class" covered by affirmative action policies.[16] Affirmative action policy ranges from special outreach and training programs to hiring and promotion goals for women and minorities. Outreach and training efforts have generated little controversy since they do not visibly and directly clash with or limit the interests of nonminorities. In contrast, preferential treatment schemes that establish separate hiring, selection, and promotion channels for members of certain groups have generated considerable controversy as they raise the most difficult issues of fairness, justice, and equality.

Affirmative action has deeply split individuals and groups who were once allies in the civil rights movement of the 1950s and 1960s. Many supporters of the early movement believe that such a race-conscious policy can only reinforce prejudice. They argue that affirmative action is a corruption of the original commitment of the civil rights movement to ensuring equality of opportunity for men and women of all races. It is seen as a violation of the rights of white males and a perpetuation of racism and sexism. Critics warn that it denigrates progress made by women and ethnic minorities and causes—or at least permits—whites to dismiss that progress as the result of special help rather than merit.

Proponents of affirmative action believe that racial discrimination is so pervasive and entrenched that it can only be addressed by race-conscious remedies that directly attack discriminatory actions taken by employers. Granting preferential treatment to women and ethnic minorities in employment and educational opportunities is vigorously defended as an essential step in overcoming the present effects of past discrimination. Women and minorities will not be integrated into the work force, proponents argue, unless aggressive steps are taken to ensure opportunities for them. Executives in many corporations enthusiastically endorse affirmative action as a means of identifying talented employees that might otherwise go unnoticed.

Proponents of preferential treatment for women and minorities usually understand "goals" to require that employers need only make a good-faith effort and that compliance be conditioned by the availability of qualified applicants. Critics argue that goals quickly become hard-and-fast quotas that permit no extenuating circumstances. Conceptually, there is a clear difference between a flexible goal and a rigid quota; in practice, whether goals inevitably become or are treated as quotas has become a contentious issue. In giving preferential treatment to members of these groups, white males who appear to be otherwise more qualified are sometimes not selected in order to assure that goals for nonwhite and female employment and representation in particular job categories are met.

The debate over affirmative action and equality of opportunity has, for the most part, centered on competing views of constitutional doctrines, as discussed below. That debate will be contrasted in the last part of this chapter with a growing concern over the actual impact of affirmative action on the prospects for equality of opportunity.

THE CONSTITUTION AND EQUALITY OF OPPORTUNITY

The history and development of the idea of equality in the framing of the Constitution and, most importantly, in the post–Civil War amendments provides some perspective on the idea of equality of opportunity. Historians and others have long debated the question of whether the Constitution was a racist document, a reflection of the society in which it was framed and ratified, or whether it reflected a commitment to equality and a first step in moving the new nation away from slavery.[17] Current opponents of affirmative action argue that the Constitution is "colorblind," that race should not be a factor in government actions or, indeed, that the Constitution prohibits such considerations. They cite Jefferson's proclamation of the equality of all men and the criticisms of slavery by Madison and others as evidence of an expectation that government would treat blacks and whites the same. They read the history of the Fourteenth Amendment as an attempt to write more explicitly into the Constitution the idea of colorblindness and find in the language of the Fourteenth Amendment a simple commitment to offer to all citizens the same legal protection offered whites.[18]

While the Constitution did not use the words "slave" or "slavery" before the Thirteenth Amendment, it implicitly dealt with the status of African-Americans in several places. Most obvious is the "three-fifths" compromise (in Article I, section 2), which was an arbitrary formulation to ensure support for representation based on population. Southerners wanted slaves to be counted in determining representation, while Northerners did not want to give such a political advantage. Conversely, Southerners argued that the wealth produced by each slave was less than that produced by white men and that tax burdens should be adjusted accordingly.[19] As a result, representatives (and direct taxes) were to be apportioned "by adding to the whole Number of free Persons, including those bound to Service for a Term of Years, and excluding Indians not taxed, three fifths of all other Persons." Slaves were clearly considered as persons, but it is also clear that race was to be a factor in fashioning constitutional compromises.

The Constitution dealt with slavery in several other places. In Article I, section 9, Congress was enjoined from prohibiting, until 1808, "the Migration or Importation of such Persons as any of the states now existing shall think proper to admit," which was a roundabout way of saying, as a concession to the South, that the continued acquiring of slaves from outside the United States would be permitted for another twenty years but might be prohibited thereafter. The fugitive slave clause, set forth in Article IV, section 2, was also aimed at assuaging the fears of Southerners: "No Person held to Service or Labor in one State, under the laws thereof, escaping into another, shall, in Consequence of any Law or Regulation therein, be discharged from such Service or Labor, but shall be delivered up on Claim of the Party to whom such Service or Labor may be due." But the wording here appears to be a careful statement that slavery is essentially a state matter, regulated by state law. Indeed, the clause was inserted in Article IV, which deals with state matters, rather than in one of the earlier articles dealing with the powers of the federal government. The fugitive slave clause was a serious bone of contention between antislavery and proslavery interests throughout the pre–Civil War period and was central to the decision handed down in 1857 by the Supreme Court in *Dred Scott v. Sandford.*[20] Both those who argue that the Constitution is proslavery and those who find it antislavery would likely agree that the Framers, regardless of how ardently they supported slavery on the one hand or opposed it on the other, all recognized that race would have to be a factor in government decision making, at least for the time being.

THE FOURTEENTH AMENDMENT
AND RECONSTRUCTION

It should have been no surprise, following the carnage and upheaval of the Civil War, that any real advancement in equality did not come easily. Early postwar gestures of kindness and hope by Grant, Lee, Lincoln, and others notwithstanding, the adversaries continued to oppose each other rancorously and chaos reigned for years to come. The importance of the Reconstruction Era is so significant in the evolution of the idea of equality in the United States that it deserves a brief review.

Reconstruction actually began well before the war ended. In December 1863 President Lincoln issued his Proclamation of Amnesty and Reconstruction. Under his "10 percent plan" states were to be pardoned when at least 10 percent of state population (based on the 1860 census) took a loyalty oath and a pledge to abolish slavery was included in their new state constitutions. In 1864, for example, Maryland's reconstructed constitution won approval by referendum and emancipation took place in November. The Thirteenth Amendment, formally ending slavery, was passed by Congress by a very thin margin and sent to the states for ratification. The Emancipation Proclamation, issued on 1 January 1863, had freed the slaves, and few slaves remained by the time the Thirteenth Amendment, formally prohibiting slavery in the United States, was ratified in December 1865.

After Lincoln's assassination, Andrew Johnson recognized new governments in Virginia, Tennessee, Arkansas, and Louisiana. His proclamations provided for lenient amnesty and prewar voter qualifications, thereby failing to ensure black suffrage. One of the legacies of Johnson's Reconstruction policies was the passage of black codes that essentially restored slavery throughout the South. Southern states enacted new laws and constitutions which forbade slavery and provided some rights for blacks, such as buying and selling property, making contracts, marrying and having legally recognized children, and suing and being sued. But they went on to require labor contracts, and the contractee and his entire family were to work from sunup to sundown. They prohibited blacks from entering certain professions, breaking their contracts, owning weapons, traveling without passes, living in certain areas, congregating in groups, renting urban land, selling their crops at night, owning cattle or pigs if not a landowner, hunting or fishing on public lands, leaving the plantation, entertaining guests without permission, voting, serving on jury duty, and holding public offices. Laws prohibited interracial marriages, provided the death penalty for blacks who raped white women or stole a horse, required segregation of public transportation, allowed forced "apprenticeship" of orphans or children whose parents were deemed unable to care for them, and levied heavy poll taxes where failure to pay was deemed vagrancy punishable by whipping, pillorying, or sale of one's labor for a year or more. All blacks were required to have a current labor contract, and disputes over work or contracts were to be unilaterally decided by the contractor. Blacks were subject to arrest by any white person. Many laws aimed at freed blacks provided for vague offenses such as vagrancy, insulting speech or gestures, malicious mischief, and preaching without a license.

The legal system was entirely controlled by whites, and blacks had no right to testify in court or serve on juries. And all of these laws were put into effect while at the same time condoning wholesale extralegal acts of intimidation including beatings, torture, and murder as Southerners engaged in a ruthless campaign of terror and intimidation designed to continue to subjugate the newly freed slaves. Brutality against blacks was widespread, and in many ways conditions were worse for the freed slaves than before emancipation.

Once the Thirteenth Amendment was adopted and sent out for ratification, Republicans in Congress, angered by the violence unleashed against blacks in the South, began preparing civil rights legislation to ensure that state laws provided for fair treatment of all citizens and that laws be administered by state officials "without difference or partiality."[21] The Bureau of Refugees, Freedmen, and Abandoned Lands was created by Congress in 1865 as an agency in the War Department to help both white refugees and former slaves. Controversy enveloped its efforts as Southerners feared that the bureau stirred up black hopes of real freedom and land ownership. The bureau was originally intended to expire one year after the war ended, but eventually it became a key element in Congress's efforts to counter discriminatory black codes, unfair labor contracts forced on blacks by white landowners, extralegal terrorism and intimidation, and unfair treatment of blacks in state and local courts.[22]

In 1865, the House of Representatives also created a Joint Committee on Reconstruction that prepared civil rights legislation that would have made all persons (except Native Americans) born in the United States citizens and guaranteed to all citizens the right to make contracts, bring lawsuits, and enjoy the full and equal benefits of all laws. Congress passed that bill in 1866 and also passed a new Freedmen's Bureau Bill that authorized the bureau to provide assistance to blacks, assume jurisdiction over cases affecting them, and prosecute state officials who denied to blacks the civil rights enjoyed by whites. Johnson vetoed both bills, but his vetoes were eventually overridden. Members of Congress extended national power into state affairs to ensure that blacks were provided the same legal and governmental benefits and protections as whites. Some advocates of these laws and amendments believed in racial equality and felt that white and black Southerners had to learn to live together, while others simply held that blacks possessed basic individual rights that had to be protected by the federal government.

Johnson's veto of the Freedmen's Bureau and Civil Rights bills in 1866, the institution of black codes by the Southern states, and systematic terrorism throughout the South made further constitutional changes essential. Out of this came the Fourteenth Amendment. The reconstruction committee reported out a draft of the Fourteenth Amendment in April 1866. The House and Senate passed differing versions in May and the amendment was passed in final form in June. In July 1866 Tennessee became the first reconstructed state to ratify the amendment, but full national ratification did not occur until 1868.

Section 1 of the Fourteenth Amendment provides that "no State shall make or enforce any law which shall abridge the privileges or immunities of citizens of the United States; nor shall any State deprive any person of life, liberty, or property, without due process of law; nor to deny to any person within its jurisdiction the equal protection of the laws." (The other sections reduced congressional representation for states that denied adult males the right to vote, prohibited Southern rebels from holding federal

office and federal funds from assuming rebel debts, and authorized Congress to enact legislation to enforce the provisions of
the amendment).

Historians have vigorously disagreed over the intent of the
framers of the Fourteenth Amendment regarding section 1. The
major disagreement focuses on how broadly the amendment
should be viewed. In writing that "no State shall make or enforce
any law which shall abridge the privileges and immunities of citizens," did its sponsors intend that the Bill of Rights apply to
the states? Was the amendment designed to advance human
rights and equality, to write into the Constitution an expansive
view of natural rights, or did it have more narrow goals of preventing unequal enforcement of state laws?[23] Did the amendment reflect a fundamental shift in the nation's commitment to
fairness and justice, or was it only a modest statement that was
not expected to have any effect on northern practices of segregation and other limitations on black rights and opportunities?

William Nelson, for example, argues that there was no agreement among the framers of the Fourteenth Amendment, that
they never provided clear boundaries for what they intended the
amendment to do. They were committed to protecting basic
rights of blacks but also to maintaining the balance of power between the states and the national government, goals that were
not really compatible. What appears to contemporary observers
as an intractable conflict between individual rights and state legislative power was in the 1860s seen as much more manageable.
The framers sought to reaffirm the nation's commitment to equal
rights of citizenship while maintaining traditional deference to
state prerogatives. Proponents of the amendment "used equality
and rights principles exactly as they had used them before the
Civil War: to articulate a moral posture and, by enacting their
morality into law, to encourage others to abide by it." Amending
the Constitution "was a rhetorical venture designed to persuade
people to do good, rather than a bureaucratic venture intended to
establish precise legal rules and enforcement mechanisms."[24] The
prevailing view, according to Nelson, was that states not enact
arbitrary and unreasonable laws and that enforcement of the laws
be the same for all citizens. It was left to the federal courts to determine whether state actions were arbitrary and unreasonable.

The amendments were aimed, in the words of another scholar, at raising the newly freedmen "from the status of inferior beings . . . to that of free men and women, equal participants in the hitherto white political community."[25] The purpose was more than to provide for simple legal equality, but to permit blacks to enjoy the political, economic, and social rights available to whites. Establishing black freedom—making blacks "equal participants in the previously white-dominated American society"—was the underlying concern.[26] But the language that was used in the Fourteenth Amendment was much more expansive. This may have been due to an interest in appealing to the broad principles underlying the Declaration of Independence or a desire to be as inclusive as possible in the language used to gain the widest possible support. Appealing to the equal protection of all persons could certainly be viewed as an appropriate means of emphasizing that blacks were no longer to be treated differently. All persons were to be provided the same protections. But that does not mean that the authors of the amendment intended that race was never to be a factor in government decisions. Many proponents certainly believed that blacks and whites should be permitted at least some social separation. Few assumed a complete equality of the races to occur. They were concerned about realizing black freedom, and the experience of the Freedmen's Bureau demonstrated that they believed blacks would need some help. Some historians argue that the sponsors of the Fourteenth Amendment sought "to place the constitutionality of the Freedmen's Bureau and Civil Rights bills, particularly the latter, beyond doubt. . . . The doubt related to the capacity of the Thirteenth Amendment to sustain this far-reaching legislative program."[27]

Why were the authors of the Fourteenth Amendment not more specific in providing for the rights of blacks? That has been attributed to two factors. First, they may have been unsure exactly how to define civil rights. Southerners had been ingenious in crafting laws that limited the rights of blacks, and many Republicans believed that too narrow a drafting of language might be easily circumvented. Second, and related to the first, was their belief in natural law. Civil rights laws were only a partial listing of the broader and essentially undefinable natural rights. An approach to constitutional language that provided the kind of common-law-like flexibility and adaptability was superior to a more rigid wording. An appeal to general principles would be harder for opponents to counter than would explicit mention of race that might be used to raise fears of an integrated society. The Fourteenth Amendment was applauded as the intertwining of natural and positive law, as flexible and adaptable as the common law. It sought to incorporate freedmen "into the body politic" and to ensure the protection of their "privileges and immunities, or the life, liberty, and property of the citizen."[28] Such broad language in such a revolutionary constitutional departure, regardless of the best of intentions, has caused severe difficulty ever since.

What distinctions did the authors of the Fourteenth Amendment seek to prohibit? The context clearly indicates that they had in mind prohibiting laws that put or kept the newly freed blacks in a subservient position. They sought to end laws based on race, because those efforts prevented blacks from enjoying political, economic, and social freedom. But if abolishing discriminatory laws was not viewed as sufficient to overcome the effects of past discrimination, could blacks be given preferential treatment? Some might have argued (as contemporary observers have) that such actions would only reinforce race consciousness. But an alternative view is that the real concern is the use of race or any other characteristic to denigrate or limit individuals when those characteristics should be irrelevant. There is no need to protect individuals of the majority race in the United States, but only minorities. They are the only ones for whom race-conscious actions may be harmful. If the majority decides it wants to disadvantage its own members and advantage minorities for some legitimate purpose, is that a problem for the theory and purpose underlying the equal protection clause?

The broadest assertions of the Fourteenth Amendment's reach, vigorously denied by its sponsors, came from opponents who claimed it would establish equality "in every respect." The broad language reflected a concern that strong federal action be provided for, that the amendment serve to strengthen and unify the Republican party, and that there be some basic guarantees for blacks in the legal process. The Civil Rights Act listed the rights to be guaranteed; the Fourteenth Amendment (both the act and the amendment were being framed and debated simultaneously) was to serve as a broad statement of principle that would vindicate the legislation and insulate it from presidential veto.[29]

Democrats in Congress were concerned that blacks would be favored at the expense of whites. The Freedmen's Bureau was instructed by Congress to help both whites and blacks ("refugees and freedmen") in order to avoid Democratic criticisms of discrimination in favor of blacks. Such a fear seems hardly reasonable, given subsequent events, but it reflects the great concern of Southerners that the federal government would force the integration of Southern society. Under the first law, the Freedmen's Bureau was given virtually no funds, expected to seek donations from churches and other groups, and was to be disbanded one year after hostilities ended.[30]

Sponsors of the second Freedmen's Bureau bill sought "to protect every person in the United States in all the rights of persons and property belonging to the free citizen."[31] The law provided that whenever "any of the civil rights or immunities belonging to white persons . . . are refused or denied to negroes, on account of race, color, or any previous condition of slavery or involuntary servitude, or . . . are subjected to any other different punishment, pains, or penalties, for the commission of any act . . . than are prescribed for white persons committing like acts" the president was to extend military protection to persons so discriminated against.[32] While the Republicans were willing to write into law clear prohibitions against discrimination, commitments to laissez-faire government, state authority, and efforts to curry favor with Southern Democrats seriously degraded that effort. President Johnson's unwillingness to enforce the will of Congress in these regards led in part to Congress's effort to impeach him. Federal courts were also nonsupportive of a vigorous application of the Civil Rights and Freedmen Bureau laws.

The problem with slavery and the postemancipation legislative attempts to maintain it was not that it was a racial classification but that it deprived persons of their rights. Most whites, including the Republicans in Congress, believed that blacks were inferior to whites. They supported laws that prohibited racial intermarriage, the most sensitive of all racial issues during that period. Both races were treated alike in antimiscegenation laws; neither race was treated as inferior. Still, they sought to prohibit discrimination that treated one race or group as inferior. Blacks were equal to whites in that they all merited equal protection of their inherent rights. The Fourteenth Amendment was seen as a means of writing the Declaration of Independence's assurance of the inalienable rights into the Constitution. Distinctions were wrong not because they were based on race, but because they were a violation of basic rights.[33] The Reconstruction amendments specifically mention some rights, such as voting, while referring to other rights in the broad language of privileges and immunities. Race is not the issue; the concern is subjugating, imposing inferior status, stigmatizing, depriving persons of fundamental rights, and oppressing them.[34]

THE FAILURE OF RECONSTRUCTION

In the fall of 1868, violence against blacks began anew in the South to intimidate them from voting; hundreds were killed in Georgia and Louisiana. The Georgia legislature voted to unseat black members on the grounds that the new state constitution failed to guarantee their right to hold office. In February 1869 Congress approved the Fifteenth Amendment, which prohibited denying persons the right to vote because of their "race, color, or previous condition of servitude." A reign of terror commenced in the South in 1870 as members of the Ku Klux Klan and others used violent means to frighten blacks from voting. Hundreds more blacks were murdered throughout the South. Southern courts were utterly corrupt and provided virtually no protection to blacks.

Civil rights legislation was enacted in 1870, 1871, and 1875 by Congresses dominated by framers of the Fourteenth Amendment to protect voting rights, ensure access to public places, guarantee the right to serve on juries, and permit prosecution of violent crimes against blacks. The 1875 Civil Rights Act, guaranteeing to all persons equal access to transportation facilities, hotels and inns, and other public places, was the last Reconstruction measure enacted by Congress; no further civil rights legislation would be passed for more than eighty years. In 1876, the fate of the Reconstruction amendments and civil rights laws was sealed when Southern Democrats supported the election of Republican Rutherford B. Hayes in exchange for "home rule," a promise that the federal government would withdraw its troops from the South and no longer try to enforce the rights of freed-men and -women. Federal courts became the focus of attention, but their interpretations of federal law did little to ensure that blacks would enjoy their civil and constitutional rights.

The Supreme Court, in a series of cases heard during the last quarter of the nineteenth century, developed the view that laws could not oppress or treat unfairly and unjustly particular classes of persons. Substantive due process was the label that was even-tually attached to this judicial effort.[35] In some cases during this period, the Court sacrificed the protections promised in the Fourteenth Amendment in order to respect the power and auton-omy of the states. In a series of cases in the 1870s the Court de-veloped the doctrine that state actions were to be upheld if they were reasonable, if they could be defended as consistent with the public good, and if they were applied equally. Equal protection, at least in theory, was to be provided for basic, fundamental rights, but federal intervention into state affairs would be mini-mal, occurring only when states acted unequally in dealing with those fundamental rights.[36] Nelson concluded that the Court "did not require state legislatures to provide citizens with any rights whatever, and thus gave Congress and the federal courts no basis for declaring that any one citizen or class of citizens pos-sessed particular rights as against other citizens. All the jurispru-dence required was that, once government granted a right to some, it must not, either through affirmative action or . . . through inaction, deny the right to others." The courts were sim-ply to "determine, with due deference to other branches of gov-ernment, whether the law treated blacks, Chinese, laborers, or businessmen arbitrarily."[37] As a result, the passion for equality that infused many in the nineteenth century was tempered by a commitment to state legislative power.

In the 1873 *Slaughter-House* cases, the Supreme Court held that the amendments were primarily restrictions upon the states for the protection of blacks, rather than an extension of the power of the federal government to provide for national citizen-ship rights. Civil rights were to remain the responsibility of states. That is, the Fourteenth Amendment protected only those rights that owed their existence to the federal government specif-ically, such as access to ports and waterways, ability to run for federal office, travel to the seat of government, and protection on the high seas and abroad. All other rights remained under state control.[38]

In *United States v. Cruikshank* (1876), the Court held that the postwar amendments only empowered the federal government to prohibit violations of black rights committed by the states themselves, but not individuals, who could only be tried and punished under state laws. This made national prosecution of crimes against blacks impossible in the South and thereby gave the green light to terrorist acts where local officials either could not or would not enforce the law.[39] In *United States v. Reese* (1875), the Court declared parts of the Enforcement Acts of 1870, which provided federal forces to protect black voters, unconstitutional on the ground that the act did not specify that the denial of suffrage must be on the sole ground of race or color. A reasonable prerequisite to voting, such as a poll tax, was permissible.[40] In the 1883 Civil Rights cases, a collection of five cases challenging the enforcement of the Civil Rights Act of 1875, the Court struck down the law as an impermissible invasion of local law by the federal government. Distinctions based on race or color were, according to the Court, not violations of basic civil or political rights, and discrimination in access to public facilities was not a concern: "When a man has emerged from slavery and by the aid of beneficent legislation has shaken off the inseparable concomitants of that state, there must be some stage in the progress of his elevation when he takes the rank of a mere citizen, and ceases to be the special favorite of the laws, and when his rights as a citizen, or a man, are to be protected in the ordinary modes by which other men's rights are protected."[41] Finally, in *Plessy v. Ferguson* (1896), the Court established the separate but equal doctrine: "The object of the 14th Amendment was undoubtedly to enforce the absolute equality of the two races before the law, but in the nature of things, it could not have been intended to abolish distinctions based upon color, or to enforce social as distinguished from political equality, or commingling of the two races upon terms unsatisfactory to either."[42] The case gave constitutional protection to the rise of Jim Crow laws throughout the South that essentially reestablished black codes under the guise of the separate but equal doctrine.

THE REVIVAL OF THE FOURTEENTH AMENDMENT

Forty years later, the Supreme Court began to reverse these cases as it placed more restrictions on what states were required to do to satisfy the separate but equal standard. In 1948 the Court ruled that restrictive covenants prohibiting the sale of a house to noncaucasians could not be enforced in court.[43] In 1954 the Court, relying on sociological research on the consequences of separatism, repudiated the separate but equal doctrine in *Brown v. Board of Education.*[44] *Brown* initiated a fundamental restructuring of the Fourteenth Amendment: states could no longer use race as the basis for discriminating against individuals in state law, and the federal government could intervene in state affairs to check discrimination.

In subsequent cases, the equal protection clause has been interpreted to permit legislation and other governmental actions that make classifications and distinctions among individuals and may disadvantage certain categories of persons. Indeed, most legislation is an attempt to make such distinctions. Federal courts have generally held that classifications should be rational and serve a socially useful purpose, and they are generally willing to defer to the judgments of legislators. Some categories of distinctions, however, have triggered increased judicial scrutiny. Legislation that serves to disadvantage minorities, for example, is considered to be "suspect" and will be upheld by reviewing courts only if it is necessary to achieve a "compelling state interest."[45] It is not clear, however, if the same standard applies to efforts that benefit minorities. In *Regents of the University of California v. Bakke* (1978),[46] Justice Powell's opinion, which actually decided the case, argued that there was no distinction to be made between actions that disadvantaged minorities and majorities and that both kinds of efforts were to trigger strict scrutiny.

The *Bakke* case centered on the University of California–Davis medical school's admissions program that set aside sixteen seats in the entering class for minority students who were educationally and economically "disadvantaged" but who were also clearly qualified for medical training. The program was challenged as a violation of the rights of white males not to have decisions affecting them made on the basis of race. The Supreme Court found, according to the opinion of Justice Powell, that the strict scrutiny standard was called for here since "racial and ethnic distinctions of any sort are inherently suspect and thus call for the most exacting judicial examination." Powell argued that the purpose of the Fourteenth Amendment as understood by its framers and in recent Supreme Court cases was to repudiate "distinctions between citizens solely because of their ancestry" and was not to protect minorities against majorities. For Powell, the "concepts of 'majority' and 'minority' necessarily reflect temporary arrangements and political judgments."[47]

Powell argued that the Constitution prohibited any program that sought to assure in a student body "some specified percentage of a particular group merely because of its race or ethnic origin." There was no appropriate state interest in preferring members of racial groups "in the absence of judicial, legislative, or administrative findings. . . . Without such findings of constitutional or statutory violations, it cannot be said that the government has any greater interest in helping one individual than in refraining from harming another." "The attainment of a diverse student body," however, was, a "constitutionally permissible goal": race or ethnic background could be considered as a "plus" for particular applicants, as long as they are not insulated from "comparison with all other candidates for the available seats." The "fatal flaw" in the program, according to Powell, was its "disregard of individual rights," which were not "absolute," but could only be infringed upon when "necessary to promote a substantial state interest." The valid state interest of promoting a diverse student body could be pursued, Powell reasoned, through means other than the "assignment of a fixed number of places to a minority group."[48] Perhaps the most important implication of *Bakke* for affirmative action in employment is that, although race can be taken into account (for instance, to attain a diverse student body), it appears to prohibit the imposition of goals and timetables or quotas on hiring and promotion decisions in the "absence of judicial, legislative, or administrative findings."

In other cases, the Court has provided guidelines for what would and would not be acceptable interpretations of affirmative action under the Constitution. In *Fullilove v. Klutznick* (1980),[49] the Court upheld a 1977 federal works program enacted by Congress that set aside 10 percent of the funds provided for "minority business enterprises." The Court concluded that Congress need not act in a "wholly color-blind fashion" in remedying discrimination; "innocent parties" could be required to "shar[e] the burden" of actions to "cure the effects of prior discrimination," but that such action could only be justified under the broad remedial powers of Congress. In *United Jewish Organization v. Carey* (1977),[50] a case involving the redrawing of voting district lines, the Court ruled that the state legislature could consider the impact of redistricting on racial groups even though there had been no finding of discrimination in previous redistricting decisions.

If race is involved in state action, what kind of scrutiny should it be given? If blacks (minorities) are involved, then disadvantagement occurs and strict scrutiny is called for. But what if whites are disadvantaged? In *Bakke,* Powell argued that any time race was involved, strict scrutiny was indicated. He then, however, found that a diverse student body was a sufficiently compelling interest and that if it was narrowly tailored it was constitutional. Does the Constitution require that individuals be treated as such, with no regard to immutable characteristics, or does it require fair treatment, or something else? One commitment is to fair treatment—that individuals feel that government has dealt with them fairly. There is also a clear aversion to quotas; if they are necessary, they should be narrowly and carefully drawn, perhaps by courts, rather than by the kind of action taken by the University of California that led to *Bakke.* In *Johnson v. Transportation Agency, Santa Clara, California* (1987), the Court indicated that female employees who possess the requisite qualifications for promotion can be given preferential treatment where there is an "obvious imbalance" of men and women. Even absent legal findings of past discrimination, the Court sanctioned preferential treatment that was a "moderate flexible, case-by-case approach to effecting a gradual improvement in the representation of minorities and women in the Agency's work force."[51]

Until 1988, the Supreme Court had generally interpreted the Fourteenth Amendment in a way that upheld affirmative action programs for women and minorities as serving the compelling state interest of overcoming the effects of past discrimination. The Court required some legislative, administrative, or judicial finding of past discrimination, and the program itself was to be narrowly tailored, and it must balance the interest of the state in resolving the discrimination with and interests of the white males who would be adversely affected. But those tests were satisfied in a number of cases and affirmative action was widely endorsed by federal courts. Preferential treatment extended to the victims of past discrimination was deemed a constitutionally acceptable use of race- and sex-based distinctions. Nor was affirmative action dismissed as an effort to protect group rights in violation of the Constitution's traditional orientation toward individual rights. Women and minorities are discriminated against because of their membership in particular groups, and remedies to that discrimination must take group membership into account. But individual circumstances can and should also be considered in determining what kind of actions might be taken to increase opportunities for members of these groups. The use of preferential treatment to compensate for general, societal discrimination has been more difficult for the Court to deal with. If the discrimination is proven and if perpetrators, victims, and beneficiaries are identified, then a right to preferential treatment to compensate for this is straightforward. Whites who have been the beneficiaries of race-conscious actions in the past cannot now claim that their race is irrelevant in determining their opportunities. But what if there is no clear, specific, past discrimination, but only the effects of general discrimination in education, housing, employment, and other opportunities? Do blacks or women or other groups who have suffered discrimination in the past have a general constitutional right to preferential treatment as recompense for general, societal past discrimination that outweighs the rights of white males to be judged on race- and gender-neutral factors?

The Supreme Court's endorsement of affirmative action began to come unravelled in a series of cases in the late 1980s interpreting the Fourteenth Amendment and Title VII of the Civil Rights Act of 1964. In *City of Richmond v. Croson* (1989), for example, the Court rejected a Richmond program of reserving 30 percent of the value of city contracts for minority contractors as a violation of the equal protection clause.[52] The Court, in *Wards Cove Packing Co. v. Antonio* (1989), made it much easier for employers to protect themselves legally for using tests and requirements that adversely impacted women and minorities.[53] Other cases made it more difficult for women and minorities to challenge employment practices that adversely affected them and much easier for whites to challenge affirmative action plans, restricted legal remedies for racial and sexual harassment, and prohibited American workers abroad who were employed by United States–based firms from suing under antidiscrimination laws. Congress quickly responded in 1990 with a civil rights bill that reversed some nine different Supreme Court decisions that had weakened civil rights law and affirmative action. The bill was vetoed by President Bush. But the outcry continued and became intertwined with the candidacy of former Ku Klux Klan leader David Duke for the Republican presidential nomination and the seating of Clarence Thomas to the Supreme Court despite charges of sexual harassment. In 1991 Congress passed and the president signed a revised civil rights bill. The reversal of so many Supreme Court decisions by one law was an extraordinary political event. While the new law addressed only cases interpreting civil rights laws, as opposed to constitutional provisions, there was widespread concern in Congress that the Supreme Court had interpreted civil rights far too narrowly.[54]

The Supreme Court's rapid reversal on civil rights in the 1980s, congressional reversal of so many Court cases, and the Court's historical record of dubious interpretations of the Fourteenth Amendment have greatly weakened its ability to provide guidance concerning affirmative action. Decisions that last only a few years before they are reversed by a shift in the Court's membership do little to promote the idea that the Court is articulating fundamental constitutional principles. Rather, the justices appear as simply another group of policy makers, motivated by different ideologies and policy positions. One of the great ironies of the appointment of conservative judges is that their insistence on reversing past decisions threatens the stability and predictability of law that conservatives otherwise champion. The history of affirmative action and Fourteenth Amendment jurisprudence, along with the inherent limits of the courts in providing general guidelines for public policies from specific disputes, means that we cannot look to the Supreme Court to resolve the constitutional debate over the role affirmative action can play in promoting equality of opportunity.

The Constitution, Rights, and Public Policy

The history of the Fourteenth Amendment, Supreme Court decisions (except perhaps the most recent ones), civil rights statutes, and the whole idea of constitutional protections of minority rights all point to the conclusion that preferential treatment as a means to overcome the effects of past discrimination is constitutionally permissible. But the analysis cannot stop there. The question of whether affirmative action promotes equality of opportunity for all persons—whether affirmative action actually benefits its intended beneficiaries—remains.

There is considerable evidence that affirmative action has opened opportunities for a broad cross-section of African-Americans, including both blue-collar and executive jobs. And affirmative action has opened some of the same opportunities to women.[55] Affirmative action also promises to promote the integration of African-Americans into American society, ending "white supremacy and black inequality in all their manifestations" and ensuring "genuine equality between blacks and whites in American society." But the effects of past discrimination and racism still permeate American life, and inequalities in income and earnings, education, and political power persist. "Because the consequences of the social history of racism are so pervasive and are self-perpetuating and self-reinforcing, the system of prevention, premised as it is on adherence to racial neutrality, should not be expected to do very much to alter the condition of societal racial inequality and the disadvantaged and subordinate position of blacks."[56] We either perpetuate the effects of past discrimination or we try to overcome them. It is in society's interest to ensure that minorities and women participate equally and actively in social and economic life. While affirmative action is seen by some as unfair to white males whose opportunities are as a consequence limited, it can mean that the "burden of the consequences of the social history of racism is shared to some degree by whites, however innocent, instead of falling entirely on blacks. The real unfairness is a generational one, in that this generation is called upon to deal with the present consequences of this nation's long and tragic history of racism."[57] African-Americans and women must be assured a part in the major economic, political, social, and educational opportunities afforded other Americans.

However, some women, African-Americans, and others who have been sympathetic to affirmative action have come to conclude that it only perpetuates racism, discrimination, and notions of dependency on government and the inability to compete in labor markets. Affirmative action permits any progress made by women and minorities to be dismissed as tokenism, as benefits dispensed by the white power structure onto second-class citizens. Affirmative action causes whites to continue to harbor doubts about the ability of African-Americans to compete in and contribute to economic life. It is blamed for contributing to the increase in racial tension in the United States as the redistribution of resources and opportunities yields mistrust and hostility among whites who believe their own opportunities are sacrificed.[58] Others fear that affirmative action has captured much of the attention in addressing the employment problems of women and minorities, and, as a result, little is being done to help those who are economically isolated and trapped in pockets of poverty.[59]

Affirmative action can, by its nature, play only a limited role in addressing the problems of poverty and disadvantagement among members of minority groups in the United States. Affirmative action can help break down barriers and move women and minorities into new employment opportunities. It rests on the assumption that once those barriers are eliminated, women and minorities can compete in the labor market. Affirmative action itself, however, is not sufficient to overcome the consequences of a lack of education, preparation, and training that keep so many persons from being able to function and compete in the world of work. It is not a solution for most of the problems characteristic of an inner-city underclass, for example, and should not be dismissed because it is not a cure-all or is not able to satisfy unreasonable expectations. Affirmative action carries with it considerable risks to those whom it seeks to benefit. While it has undoubtedly helped provide opportunities for some individuals and has reinforced racism and sexism in other cases, it is exceedingly difficult to make a judgment about its overall impact.[60]

What is clear is that we need to engage in a more sophisticated debate over affirmative action and equality of opportunity. Public opinion polls regularly reflect strong opposition to favoring minorities at the expense of white males. But questions are often couched in simplistic terms such as "Which do you prefer, racial preferences or merit?" or "Should minorities be given advantages they haven't earned, or should everyone be treated fairly?" It may be too late to alter the terms of public discourse and debate over affirmative action. But for affirmative action to be successful in increasing opportunities for women and minorities, it must ultimately be viewed by most Americans as a legitimate and appropriate public policy. Affirmative action requires broad-based support in order to be successful. The vast majority of the millions of employment decisions made each day cannot be monitored by enforcement officials or challenged in court. Ensuring opportunity for all persons ultimately requires a general acceptance of that ideal. If most people believe that affirmative action is an unfair policy, an illegitimate exercise of governmental power, and a threat to their own opportunity, then affirmative action will never accomplish its purposes.

In that respect, a right to preferential treatment is not much different from other rights in that their enjoyment ultimately rests on their general acceptance in society. Courts are overcrowded, hiring a lawyer is an expense many cannot afford, and delays in seeking remedies may mean that justice is denied. Judicial enforcement of rights is important, but it cannot be substituted for general support for and commitment to the rights in society. If violations of rights are widespread, courts are overwhelmed. Development of a public culture that is committed to respecting rights is the only way rights can ultimately be made secure.[61] Similarly, a public commitment to affirmative action is necessary for it to contribute effectively to opportunity for women and people of color.

Much of the debate over affirmative action has focused on equality of opportunity versus equality of results. Opponents of affirmative action have condemned it for ignoring the goal of equal opportunity while seeking to impose equal results. It is often argued by critics of affirmative action that labor market outcomes should not be a concern of government, that equality of opportunity, and not outcomes or results, are the only appropriate policy focus. But equality of results is part of the ideal of equality of opportunity rather than its opposite. They are compatible rather than contradictory goals. People of color who have the same skill and experience as whites ought to be making the same salaries and enjoying the same promotions to senior positions. Women who perform as well as their male counterparts ought to be treated equally in the employment benefits offered them. There ought to be equal rewards for equal performance. Nor can there be true equality of opportunity to develop one's talents and abilities, to contribute to society as well as to realize one's own personal life goals, if there is not fairness in the distribution of rewards for efforts made. Nor is affirmative action sufficient to ensure meaningful equality of opportunity. It must be combined with efforts to improve education, encourage investments in economically depressed areas, and reinforce norms and values of responsibility and self-sufficiency.

Public policy has evolved from an emphasis on nondiscrimination to an emphasis on preferential treatment, largely as a result of experience demonstrating that a reliance on sex- and race-neutral efforts has been insufficient to break down existing barriers and increase opportunities for women and minorities. The goal of nondiscrimination seems, for now, to be a premature one. It may simply not be possible to escape race- and sex-conscious remedies in countering the effects of past racial and sexual discrimination.

Notes

1. Peter L. Berger, *The Capitalist Revolution: Fifty Propositions about Prosperity, Equality, and Liberty* (New York: Basic Books, 1986).

2. See, for example, Arthur M. Okun, *Equality and Efficiency: The Big Tradeoff* (Washington, D.C.: Brookings Institution, 1975).

3. Samuel Bowles and Herbert Gintis, *Democracy and Capitalism: Property, Community, and the Contradictions of Modern Social Thought* (New York: Basic Books, 1986).

4. Michael Walzer, *Spheres of Justice: A Defense of Pluralism and Equality* (New York: Basic Books, 1983).

5. For an excellent summary of this debate, see James Fishkin, *Justice, Equal Opportunity, and the Family* (New Haven, Conn.: Yale University Press, 1983).

6. See Garry Wills, "The Words That Remade America," *The Atlantic,* June 1992, 57–79.

7. Quoted in Clayborne Carson et al., eds., *Eyes on the Prize: A Civil Rights Reader* (New York: Penguin, 1991), 413.

8. Quoted in Juan Williams, *Eyes on the Prize: America's Civil Rights Years, 1954–1965* (New York: Viking Penguin, 1987), 188.

9. For a thoughtful review of the state of race relations in contemporary America, see Thomas Byrne Edsall with Mary D. Edsall, *Chain Reaction: The Impact of Race, Rights, and Taxes on American Politics* (New York: W. W. Norton, 1991).

10. U.S. Department of Commerce, Bureau of the Census, *Statistical Abstract of the United States, 1987* (Washington, D.C.: Government Printing Office, 1987), 402.

11. Ibid., 376.

12. Louis Uchitelle, "America's Army of Nonworkers," *New York Times,* 27 September 1987.

13. Marian Wright Edelman, *Families in Peril: An Agenda for Social Change* (Cambridge, Mass.: Harvard University Press, 1987), 2.

14. Richard Bernstein, "King's Dream: America Still Haunted by Problems of Black Poor," *New York Times,* 17 January 1988.

15. Edelman, *Families in Peril,* 2–3.

16. There is some disagreement over what groups are the target of affirmative action, although blacks and women are of central concern. Under Title VII, for example, the primary equal employment opportunity statute, minority groups include blacks, Hispanics, Asians or Pacific islanders, and American Indians or Alaskan natives. Under public works legislation that sets aside 10 percent of funds for minority-run enterprises, groups included are blacks, Spanish-speaking persons, Orientals, Indians, Eskimos, and Aleuts. Federal agencies that have primary responsibility for policy in this area define protected groups as blacks (all racial groups of Africa except North Africa), Hispanics (Mexicans, Puerto Ricans, Cubans, Central or South Americans, and those from other Spanish cultures), Asians/Pacific Islanders (from the Far East, southeast Asia, Indian subcontinent, and

Pacific islands), and Native Americans (original people of North America who maintain their tribal identity). But none of these definitions indicates what percentage of an individual's ancestors must fall within one of these groups in order to trigger the requirements of the law or how far ancestry can or should be traced back.

17. For an introduction to the topic and a set of essays that pursue competing views of this question, see Robert A. Goldwin and Art Kaufman, eds., *Slavery and Its Consequences: The Constitution, Equality, and Race* (Washington, D.C.: American Enterprise Institute for Public Policy Research, 1990).

18. Such arguments are important, since an appeal to the intent of the Framers and ratifiers of the Constitution and constitutional amendments can be a powerful claim of legitimacy. The process of ratification is important in a constitutional democracy since it is the accepted means of making basic policy decisions. Not only does an explicit constitutional provision provide a basis for imposing legally binding responsibilities on government, but it is evidence of a general acceptance of the position in question. While there may be other constitutional rights such as privacy, a formal, explicit action to recognize a right or principle gives it a higher place in the constitutional system. This is not to ignore the great difficulties involved in ascertaining the intent behind a constitutional amendment or provision. There are many framers and ratifiers, representing a variety of concerns, values, and priorities. But there may also be sufficient consensus over the basic purposes of a constitutional provision—general agreement over the problem to be solved—that a constitutional intent is evident. An inquiry into the intent of the authors of legislation is the beginning point for virtually all judicial interpretations of law. While many questions cannot be answered through an examination of intent, some can. Did the authors of the Thirteenth Amendment really mean to abolish slavery? Few would argue no. Did they intend to integrate newly freed slaves into society as equal members? The historical record is less clear here, but many did not.

19. Don E. Fehrenbacher, "Slavery, the Framers, and the Constitution," in Goldwin and Kaufman, *Slavery and Its Consequences,* 6–8.

20. 60 U.S. (19 How.) 393.

21. Harold M. Hyman and William M. Wiecek, *Equal Justice under Law: Constitutional Development, 1835–1875,* New American Nation Series (New York: Harper Collins, 1986), 396.

22. Kenneth M. Stampp, *The Era of Reconstruction 1865–1877* (New York: Vintage Books, 1965), 131–32.

23. Much of the historical debate is summarized in William E. Nelson, *The Fourteenth Amendment: From Political Principle to Judicial Doctrine* (Cambridge, Mass.: Harvard University Press, 1988).

24. Ibid., 9.

25. Arthur Kinoy, "The Constitutional Right of Negro Freedom," *Rutgers Law Review* 21 (1967): 387–88.

26. Robert A. Sedler, "The Constitution, Racial Preference, and the Equal Participation Objective," in Goldwin and Kaufman, *Slavery and Its Consequences,* 137.

27. Judith Baer, *Equality under the Constitution: Reclaiming the Fourteenth Amendment* (Ithaca, N.Y.: Cornell University Press, 1983), 75.

28. Hyman and Wiecek, *Equal Justice,* 410.

29. Eric Foner, *Reconstruction: America's Unfinished Revolution, 1863–1877,* New American Nations Series (New York: Harper Collins, 1989), 257.

30. Hyman and Wiecek, *Equal Justice,* 315.

31. Ibid., 413.

32. 14 Statutes at Large 173 (1866).

33. Baer, *Equality under the Constitution,* 95, 102.

34. Ibid., 256–58.

35. Nelson, *Fourteenth Amendment*, 9–10.

36. Ibid., 155–81.

37. Ibid., 196.

38. 83 U.S. 36, 71–72.

39. 92 U.S. 542.

40. 92 U.S. 214.

41. 109 U.S. 3.

42. 163 U.S. 537.

43. *Shelley v. Kraemer*, 334 U.S. 1.

44. 347 U.S. 483.

45. For a review of this judicial doctrine, see Michel Rosenfeld, *Affirmative Action and Justice: A Philosophical and Constitutional Inquiry* (New Haven, Conn.: Yale University Press, 1991), 135–62.

46. 438 U.S. 265.

47. Ibid.

48. Ibid.

49. 448 U.S. 448.

50. 430 U.S. 144.

51. 480 U.S. 616.

52. 109 S.Ct. 706.

53. 490 U.S. 642.

54. The Civil Rights Act of 1991, S 1745, PL 102–166, 105 Stat. 1071. The 1991 law addressed the following major cases: *Patterson v. McLean Credit Union,* 491 U.S. 164 (1989); *Wards Cove Packing Co. v. Antonio,* 490 U.S. 642 (1989); *Price Waterhouse v. Hopkins,* 490 U.S. 228 (1989); *Lorance v. AT&T Technologies, Inc.,* 490 U.S. 900 (1989); *Martin v. Wilks,* 490 U.S. 755 (1989); *Jett v. Dallas Independent School District,* 491 U.S. 701 (1989); and *Independent Federation of Flight Attendants v. Zipes,* 491 U.S. 754 (1989). This is not the first time Congress has reversed civil rights decisions. Other civil rights cases effectively overturned by Congress include *General Electric Co. v. Gilbert,* 429 U.S. 125 (1976), overturned by the Pregnancy Discrimination Act of 1978, 92 Stat. 2076; *United Air Lines, Inc. v. McMann,* 434 U.S. 192 (1977), overturned by the Age Discrimination in Employment Act Amendments of 1978, 92 Stat. 189; *Grove City College v. Bell,* 465 U.S. 555 (1984), overturned by the Civil Rights Restoration Act of 1987, 102 Stat. 28; and *Smith v. Robinson,* 468 U.S. 992 (1984), overturned by the Handicapped Children's Protection Act of 1986.

55. See the essays by Randall Kennedy, Cornel West, Ronald Brownstein, Kenneth S. Tollett, and Paul Starr in "Race, Liberalism, and Affirmative Action (I)," *The American Prospect* (Spring 1992): 13, 116–28.

56. Sedler, "Racial Preference," 126.

57. Ibid., 127.

58. For a review of this debate, see Paul Starr, "Civil Reconstruction: What to Do without Affirmative Action," *The American Prospect* (Winter 1992): 7–14.

59. See, for example, William Julius Wilson, *The Truly Disadvantaged: The Inner City, the Underclass, and Public Policy* (Chicago: University of Chicago Press, 1987).

60. Stephen L. Carter, *Reflections of an Affirmative Action Baby* (New York: Basic Books, 1991); and Shelby Steele, *The Content of Our Character: A New Vision of Race in America* (New York: St. Martin's Press, 1990).

61. For more on the importance of public culture, see Richard Vetterli and Gary Bryner, *In Search of the Republic: Public Virtue and the Roots of American Government* (Totowa, N.J.: Rowman and Littlefield, 1987).

(

IX

RIGHTS AND HUMAN FLOURISHING

★

A. D. Sorensen

Human existence everywhere is typically conceived as primarily a mode of collective and individual self-direction aimed at a favorable life outcome. Everywhere people normally believe that living is better than not living; that, within certain horizons, life has various possible outcomes, some of which are preferable to others; and that human beings together and individually have some ability, in relation to other determining factors, to control life's outcome so that on balance it can turn out at least tolerably well or worthwhile. So in the main, people everywhere pursue some view of human good in a self-directed way.

How persons conceive themselves as self-directed beings in pursuit of some view of a good life constitutes the basic conception in the organization of any political society. Every political society sets out to define, develop, and organize the abilities of its members so that they can, primarily in a self-directed way, favorably affect how their lives turn out in a larger cause-effect world. The general hope of members of a political society is that life may turn out well, and its central claim is that it helps make some such outcome possible. Indeed, the self-direction of its members along the paths it prescribes and permits constitutes the very soul of any political society. In the long run its viability

A. D. Sorensen is a professor of political science at Brigham Young University.

depends on the merits of its promise of a worthwhile life as an object of self-direction, and on its capacity to make good on it.

So, as we would expect, the legal role of government in an established political society involves primarily helping to protect and promote that society's vision of a life worth living as a mode of self-direction. That is finally what makes a government relevant and effective in the society of which it is an indigenous part. Of course, a political society typically favors some parts of its membership over others in its promise and promotion of a worthwhile life; and whatever its primary design as an order of self-direction, overt and covert mechanisms of social and political control work powerfully to uphold that favoritism. Indeed, a view of self-direction or a conception of human good itself can define and organize how persons live so that relations of domination of one part of society by another become second nature to all involved. Still, the basic conception that forms any political society concerns a mode of self-direction and a view of human good.

The soul of the United States as a political society is its particular mode of self-direction and the promise of a life worth living which it holds out. That mode of self-direction has become embodied in our system of federal and state constitutions and its ongoing authoritative interpretations expressed in law and public policy. The basic concepts that compose the main body of our constitutional system, and our political society's mode of self-direction, are powers and rights. In our federal Constitution, certain powers are delegated to the federal government and certain rights are enumerated which limit the power of the federal and state governments. These powers and rights help compose a larger set of powers and rights which are, in the Ninth and Tenth Amendments, exhaustively classified as "delegated" and "reserved" powers and as "enumerated" and "retained" rights. Together, rights (both enumerated and retained) and powers (both delegated and reserved) compose our own political society's main moral-legal formula of self-direction—one in which the people collectively and individually determine the outcome of their lives in self-directed ways. Because we conceive powers and rights as possessions of the people, we think of ourselves as a free people and our way of life as the free life. The free life is the primary moral-legal value in our constitutional system.

In our constitutional tradition, a basic notion of what being a free people means is that the people as individuals have the right to choose and carry out their own plans of life without interference from government. That helps explain why our constitutional system is organized the way it is, why rights appear in it as they do, and why it does not in the main include any particular vision of the good life which everyone must pursue. The law does not so much answer the question of how people should live as it does put them in a position to answer it for themselves. This is not to say that we as a people do not have a view of what the human good might be. From before the Founders' time until now, the leading conception of human good in our political society has been human happiness. But again, the purpose of government and law has not so much been ·to make people happy as it has been to secure a framework of freedom within which they can pursue happiness for themselves. One way to express this point is to say that in our political society human freedom, as our mode of self-direction, takes priority over human good.

In this essay I offer an interpretation of our political society's formula of human self-direction with its promise of a worthwhile life. My main concern is with the role of rights—particularly those mentioned in the Bill of Rights—in that formula. I claim that to understand the proper role of rights in our political society, we must first understand the sense in which human self-direction takes priority over human good and how this priority makes possible human flourishing, as well as making human flourishing the end of human living. Indeed, in my view, the genius of our political society lies in its promised mode of self-direction (which, I would add, has not yet been fairly or fully actuated) and the unique opportunity for human flourishing it holds out. But as is fitting to say at bicentennial time, there is a real possibility that we will lose our vision of human self-direction with its promise of human well-being. Much depends on how we understand and implement rights in defining and organizing our common lives. We particularly need to be aware of tendencies, inherent in the free life itself, for people to pursue their interests under the protection of rights in ways that weaken the genius underlying our political system.

In what follows, I first consider, as an ideal, the fundamental relations between human self-direction and human good in our political society. As I mentioned, these relations both make possible human flourishing (human happiness) and make human flourishing the point of human existence. Then I examine the proper role of rights, as basic concepts in our Constitution and public morality, in defining and organizing how people live so that they might pursue human good in a self-directed way and flourish. Finally, I review some ways in which the free life with its opportunity to flourish might decline in the name of rights.

THE FREE LIFE AND HUMAN FLOURISHING

Everywhere (as already noted) human life is conceived primarily as a mode of self-direction in pursuit of human good. Human self-direction and human good are inseparable. There could be no self-direction without human good, but there could also be no human good without self-direction. This is true of our political society. In our society, within the interdependency of self-direction and human good the basic value is the intrinsic worth of persons as free beings. As the basic value in this relationship, the worth of persons takes priority over human good.

This means, first of all, that each person is to be the primary agent in his own life with respect to any view of human good as a way of living that life. Being a primary agent involves the person's ability to distinguish, as a being aware of himself, between the unique opportunity to be as a person (his own life) and alternative ways of realizing that opportunity (one or more views of human good). Because of this ability, a person can consider what his life is like, assess how well that life is turning out, and perhaps critically evaluate the way of life itself with an eye to living somewhat differently. What being a primary agent in relation to human good means is that the person may rightfully decide whether to abide by some view of human good as a way of realizing one's life. It means that it is the person himself who rightfully must be persuaded without coercion to adopt or continue to embrace a view of how he might best live. He is rightfully the final receiver of reasons for accepting or rejecting a version of human good.

The priority of the worth of persons as free beings over human good involves a second concept. It is that the person's life has high, intrinsic value, as his unique opportunity to live, prior to human good as a view of how to live that life. This suggests two additional points. First, it indicates that a way to live should be worthy of a person's life if that way is to be acceptable. Not just any way of living—any view of human good—will do. It must be deserving of the person's existence. Second, the idea that the person's opportunity to live has intrinsic value prior to a view of a good life implies that the person exists to live as a person and that a view of human good serves to make that possible. In other words, the worth of persons provides the reason for participation in good: the point of pursuing and realizing human good is so that persons can live for the sake of living as persons. We might say that human good exists for the sake of the person rather than that the person exists only for the sake of the good.

The intrinsic worth of persons as free beings and some view of human good represent the basic values in the morality of freedom and the morality of some version of the good life, respectively. Again, though interdependent, the former morality takes precedence over and provides the context for the latter. Let me briefly explain. When the morality of the free life, with its focus on the intrinsic worth of persons, defines and orders the lives of people, it generates deep appreciation for free human existence, including mutual respect and concern among persons as primary agents with unique lives to live. This organization and esteem for the life of freedom form a community of free persons which in turn helps make possible an enhanced human community that is envisioned by a view of human good and its morality. As reflection seems to reveal, only when people recognize and appreciate each other first as free beings (as the morality of freedom requires) can they enjoy the larger sense of community promised by versions of the good life and its morality. It seems that full human community can exist only when all receiving and giving originate in respect for persons as primary agents in their own lives and concern that they realize their unique opportunities to live in a worthwhile way accepted by them. This basic respect and concern are the roots from which enhanced forms of human care grow and derive their strength. Typically we cannot truly care for another as a whole person unless we have respect and concern for the person as a free being. In other words, a community of free persons provides the context within which enlarged communities of care can occur and constitutes the center part of those communities—which is to say that the morality of freedom forms the core of a good life and its morality.

How the free life conceives the relation between the intrinsic worth of persons as free beings and human good, in conjunction with certain supportive conditions (which I will not consider here), makes human flourishing possible. In the first place, human flourishing involves being alive to good and successfully pursuing it. It entails doing and undergoing things as a person which are intrinsically good. But human flourishing can occur only if the person participates in good as a free being having intrinsic worth.

To begin with, the person cannot flourish through the pursuit of good unless that person freely chooses to pursue it. It is simply self-contradictory to say that what the person does and undergoes as a result of compulsion constitutes flourishing. To flourish one must realize things intrinsically good because one finds them to be good.

However, to realize good in this way, it is not enough that the person willingly participate in good. To flourish, willing participation must originate in the self and not another. One cannot flourish if one lives primarily under the direction of another, however willing one is. Being such a person—really a servile person—places beyond one's experience so much that is good in human life and necessary to flourishing. For one thing, being a servile person cuts one off from relations of love and friendship among equals. It also precludes so many small as well as large acts of creation that spring from one's own thought or imagination. To be more general, if a person does not seek good because it is intrinsically good, but for reasons supplied by another, then she is not alive to it in a way that helps constitute the opportunity to flourish. She cannot pursue or realize good for itself, which is necessary for flourishing, unless she herself wills the good rather than because someone else wills her to will it. To flourish, the person must be the primary initiator of involvement in a life that is good.

In order to be the primary agent in one's own life, one must incorporate certain ethical qualities that are part of having intrinsic worth as a free person. First, one cannot be the primary agent in one's life unless being such is conceived by self and others as right. The ethical property of rightness helps form the very capability of being the primary agent in one's life. Shift the operation of that ethical quality to someone else, and that other person becomes the chooser and initiator in how one lives; the result is some sort of servility.

Further, if the person is to flourish, the exercise of ability as primary agent must itself be intrinsically good. The person's *own* participation in bringing about good—that it is the *person herself* so engaged in contrast to not being involved—must be desirable in itself to that person in order for the person to flourish. The very goodness of being alive and a primary agent serves to unlock the flourishing that is potential in the pursuit of good. In other words, unless participation in good is itself right and good— right and good for the person as first agent in that person's own life—the person cannot flourish. A link between human good and human self-direction necessary for human flourishing remains unformed.

Furthermore, the idea that the person is the primary agent in how he lives involves a distinction noted earlier, between the unique opportunity to live and ways one may choose to realize that opportunity in pursuit of human good. When the person lives as one having intrinsic worth, the unique opportunity to live has intrinsic value for that person. The primal concern as primary agent is to live life well or in a worthwhile way. The implicit worry is that one might waste one's life—an unpleasant possibility underlined by mortality. So not just any way of living will do. It should be one which can satisfy one's primal concern as chooser of how to live.

Unless the person's opportunity to be has high intrinsic value to her, and, given that, unless the way she decides to live fulfills her primal concern as agent to live well, she cannot flourish. Either an impoverished sense of her own existence or a way to live with little worth would preclude her flourishing. But even if she becomes involved in a life truly worth living, she will not flourish by accomplishing the good within it if her own opportunity to be has little value to her, or if to her how she lives seems unworthy of that opportunity.

It is also necessary, if the person is to flourish, that she realize human good as her own agent by being a producer or creator of value. To flourish she must be creative or productive as a self-directed being. Indeed, it seems that being a creative or productive person is part of the idea of being a free person—one who can determine the outcome of her own life in a self-directed way. Further, the person must find being a productive being intrinsically good in order to flourish. For example, a person cannot flourish by being productive if her end in life is consumption. But it is also not enough that she bring about something of value in a self-directed manner; she must find doing so of intrinsic value to her. Moreover, if she is to flourish, the creative or productive work the person does must help fulfil her desire as primary agent to realize her valued life in a way that counts to her.

It is only as participants in human community that people can flourish. For one thing, to firmly experience the worth of one's own life, the value of one's role as agent, and the good one engages in, one must live in a world in which that worth, value, and goodness receive common recognition. Moreover, in order for persons to flourish, that recognition must be nonegoistic. In other words, there must be mutual recognition of the intrinsic worth of the person as a free being and the goodness of how he lives as a person in order for that worth and goodness to become full realities—in order for him to enjoy that full ethical aliveness that makes possible human flourishing.

The respect and concern that persons have for one another as free beings constitute an aliveness to good without which individuals cannot flourish. Of course, if people are to flourish, the respect and concern for persons as free beings must be enlarged and deepened to become care for them as whole persons. A life without human community in this enhanced sense, made possible by each caring for the other in her wholeness, is an impoverished life indeed. But as observed earlier, only when people recognize and appreciate one another first as free beings can they enjoy the larger sense of human community. Only when giving and receiving originate in respect for persons as primary agents having lives of intrinsic worth can giving and receiving occur with full care for persons in their wholeness. And without having such care for others, the person cannot flourish.

Much of what has been brought out so far about human freedom and human flourishing may be summarized by saying that, in order to flourish, persons must be alive to good as free beings who cherish free human existence. Their being alive to or caring for things that are good has as its core their being alive to or cherishing human life and its freedom. Now the intrinsic value of human life has a twofold structure which is essential to the viability of the free life and the chance to flourish it offers. It is something of great value that must be perpetuated to posterity by the living as well as being enjoyed by them. So when the intrinsic value of human life operates in defining and ordering how people live, they naturally conceive themselves as beings who perpetuate their own kind by caringly creating new life, nurturing it to full and hence free personhood, and otherwise providing for it. Of all the good works of a community of free people, creating and providing for their own kind is typically the most significant. If persons did not deeply care about the continuation of human life and its freedom in light of human mortality, they would not be sufficiently alive to the goodness of human existence to flourish. To flourish, a people must esteem human life itself and its chance to be free as a profound good to be perpetuated.

Now that I have somewhat explained how the free life makes possible human flourishing, we can say why the aim of the life of freedom is human flourishing. The reason has to do with the fact that the intrinsic worth of persons as free beings takes priority over human good. As noted earlier, that priority implies that the point of free human existence is to be much alive to good and to pursue it for the sake of living as persons. When persons realize this aim and escape major suffering, they flourish. Indeed, to flourish and to be much alive to and realize good without considerable suffering are the same thing. So we may say that the point of the free life is to flourish. It is natural for people for whom the worth of free persons is prior to human good to desire flourishing as their reason for being.

One might conclude that to live flourishingly for its own sake makes the person an egoist—one whose final aim in life is to realize his own self-interest (e.g., his own happiness) exclusively. But that is not necessarily so. A person can be a nonegoist for its own sake, and, as well, desire to *flourish,* by virtue of being a nonegoist, for *its* own sake. To be a nonegoist, the person need not be indifferent as to whether *he* is a nonegoist as against being something else or not existing at all. He (the nonegoist) can want to be the primary agent in his own life and find that intrinsically good. He can consider his unique opportunity to live as something intrinsically valuable and desire to realize it in a way that counts. He can embrace being a nonegoist as the best way to live in order to live his life in the most worthwhile way. And he can, on reflection, accept being a nonegoist as the right way for him and others to live for reasons that transcend his own self-interest. There is no inconsistency here; apparently no facts make it impossible.

Furthermore, the fact that the person flourishes by reason of being a nonegoist and finds his flourishing good in itself does not change matters. Indeed, he can consider flourishing to be the point of human existence and acknowledge appreciatively that he (as a nonegoist) is realizing that end. For, as a nonegoist, he does not serve others so that they might flourish (as one thing) in order to flourish himself (as another thing). He does not separate his own flourishing from the well-being of others. He wants others to be nonegoists and to flourish for their sakes. Again, all this seems factually and logically possible. He perceives his flourishing and their flourishing as one.

RIGHTS AND THE MORALITY OF THE FREE LIFE

The role of the free life's morality—our common morality—is to help define and organize our political society's mode of self-direction in relation to a view of human good. This means, in view of my remarks so far, that its function is to help make possible the life of freedom with its opportunity for human flourishing. Rights are basic concepts in the morality of the free life. To understand their proper role in our political society, we must see the place they have in that morality. First, I will describe generally the morality of freedom. Since such a description can become rather extensive and detailed, I will present only a brief and general description here, only barely sufficient to indicate the place rights have in the free life's morality. Then I will indicate how I think rights figure into that morality, and finally I will consider relations between rights and human flourishing.

The morality of the free life helps make possible human flourishing for the sake of persons primarily by promoting the growth and securing the operations of its general value—the intrinsic value of human life and its freedom—in the lives of people. For when that value defines and organizes how people live, they cherish free human life as something to be realized by the living and perpetuated to future people. As explained earlier, the deep esteem for human life that is free—for both its enjoyment and perpetuation by the living—forms the core ingredient in being alive to human good and realizing it. And being alive to good and successfully pursuing it, along with supportive conditions such as certain material things and good health, constitutes the possibility of human flourishing.

The morality of freedom engenders and preserves high esteem for free human life chiefly by means of its rules and precepts that determine, mainly implicitly, how people understand social life and conduct themselves within it. Its most general imperative tells a people that they ought, as soon as it is practicable, to establish the free life among themselves and perpetuate it without decline out of profound esteem for free human life. This general norm with its twofold requirement contains more particular ones that I will bring out so we can see the role rights play as part of our common morality.

Consider first the requirement that a people highly esteem the life of freedom and organize themselves so they can enjoy it. To live the free life in a way that affords the opportunity to flourish, the following things are necessary. First, concern for persons as free beings must order the lives of people so that each can *develop* the capabilities of freedom—notably the capacities to choose and act as the primary agent in one's own life. A person must possess these capabilities if she is to form and carry out a plan of life and to participate in the political process as ways of being alive to human good and pursuing it. For the most part, these capabilities will be developed as persons grow up in a free society. (There will be more to say on this later). Second, for people to enjoy the free life, their concern for persons as free beings should motivate them to organize things so that each has the environmental opportunity to live as the primary agent in her own life—most notably the opportunity to participate in the political process and join in free economic intercourse with others in order to produce goods and services or procure the income to achieve life projects. Finally, people can enjoy a life of freedom and a chance to flourish only when their respect for each other as free beings secures an area of negative freedom—an area free from unjust coercive interference from others—within which they may conduct their personal and political lives.

To summarize, a life of freedom becomes possible only when people organize their lives so that each adult has the capabilities, opportunities, and autonomy to take part in politics and pursue her own course in life. These ingredients of freedom supply the primary content of the norms and precepts that make up the morality of freedom's general requirement that the free life be enjoyed by all adult persons. So that the role of rights can later be described, I will now outline these rules or precepts, beginning with the general requirement that the free life be enjoyed and then proceeding to more particular precepts, stopping at that point where fundamental rights enumerated in the Bill of Rights appear. Each norm mentions the respect and concern for persons as free beings which help form the opportunity to flourish.

A. General norm addressed to persons capable of the free life: People ought to organize themselves out of deep respect and concern for individual persons as free beings, so they can enjoy fully the life of freedom.

  1. Second-level norms
     a. People ought to order their lives, out of a deep respect and concern for one another as free beings, so that each person enjoys fully and equally personal freedom—the freedom to choose and carry out a plan of life.
     b. People ought to organize how they live, out of a deep respect and concern for one another as free beings, so that each person enjoys fully and equally political freedom—the freedom to participate in the political process.

  2. Third-level norms
     a. People ought to deeply respect each person's negative freedom—an area within which the individual can conduct her personal and political life without unjust coercive intervention from others.
     b. People ought to organize themselves, out of deep concern for persons as free beings, so that adult persons possess the capabilities necessary to take part in politics and to pursue individual plans of life.
     c. People ought to organize themselves, out of a deep concern for persons as free beings, so that they have the environmental opportunity to be self-

determining—most notably so that they can enter into free economic intercourse with others to be productive for its own sake, and to create the goods and services or procure the income which enables them to be self-determining.

d. People ought to organize themselves, out of deep concern for persons as free beings, so that persons have the environmental conditions necessary to participate in the political process.

3. Fourth-level norms (some major examples)

a. People should deeply respect each person's negative freedom—freedom from unjust coercive interference by others—to think, speak, and publish concerning political and other matters.

b. People should deeply respect each person's negative freedom to associate with others for political and personal reasons.

c. People should deeply respect each person's negative freedom in the choice and practice of religion.

d. People should organize themselves, out of deep concern for each other as free persons, so that each has an opportunity as a voter to participate in the political process without unfair discrimination.

e. People ought to organize themselves, out of deep concern for persons as free beings, so that each has an opportunity to enter free competition with others for jobs in the economy without unfair discrimination.

f. People should deeply respect each person's negative freedom to form a family, procreate, and raise children within the limits set down by the morality of the free life.

Consider now the requirement that the free life, with its opportunity to flourish, be ongoingly passed on to near future people without decline out of profound esteem for human life and its freedom. Of course, to perpetuate the free life, new human life itself must be created and nurtured so that it develops the desires and capabilities of free persons. Also, succeeding generations of new life must be provided with the political and economic infrastructure and natural environment so that a life of freedom can be carried on without decline—again, out of a profound care for new human life itself. Let me once more outline the norms and precepts related to the general imperative that the free life be perpetuated, beginning as before with the most general norm. As I mentioned, my purpose is to provide a framework within which to indicate the role rights play in our public morality.

B. General norm addressed to a people who now can or do enjoy partly or fully the free life: The people ought to pass on the free life to posterity out of profound esteem for human life and its freedom.

1. Second-level norms
   a. People ought to ongoingly promote and protect the life of freedom for near future people out of deep concern for human life and its freedom.
   b. Persons ought to create new life out of profound care for human life itself.
   c. Persons who create new life ought to caringly nurture it to free personhood.
   d. People ought to protect new life against arbitrary killing out of deep respect for human life.
   e. People ought to organize themselves, out of deep concern for new life, so that the cultural and material framework exists within which it will be able to carry on the free life.

2. Third-level norms (major examples)
   a. The people ought to organize themselves, out of profound care for new generations of free life, so that individuals within each generation have equal educational opportunities to develop the capabilities of free beings.
   b. The people ought, out of profound care for new human life, to establish or preserve the institutional framework within which that life can enjoy political freedom.
   c. The people ought, out of profound care for new human life, to establish and preserve a system of

free economic intercourse so that new life can become productive and self-determining.

d. The people ought, out of profound care for new
human life, to establish and preserve the material
infrastructure and physical environment that will
help enable new life to carry on the free life without decline.

e. The people ought, out of deep care for new human
life, to establish and preserve the esteem for
human life and freedom, passing that esteem on to
succeeding generations.

Let us consider now the role of rights in our political society.
Their general function should be to help accomplish the aim of
the morality of the free life—which is to define and organize the
lives of people so that they, out of profound esteem for free
human life, both enjoy and perpetuate it and have an opportunity to flourish. The scope of that function depends on what concept of rights we consider. My main concern here is with those
rights mentioned in the Bill of Rights, both those "enumerated"
and those "retained." I shall consider first how those rights
might figure into the morality of the life of freedom and then
how they help make possible human flourishing by generating
respect and concern for free human life itself. I maintain that
rights should always be construed so that they facilitate and do
not impede accomplishing the aim of the morality of freedom.

Traditionally, the rights enumerated in the Bill of Rights have
been interpreted as negative rights that limit only governmental
power. At first those rights limited only federal power, but later
certain provisions of the Bill of Rights came to be applied to the
states through the Fourteenth Amendment. The First Amendment
forbids Congress to pass laws abridging the freedom of speech,
the press, assembly, and religion, as well as laws regarding an establishment of religion. The Second Amendment guarantees people's right to keep and bear arms; the Third protects them
against the housing of troops in private homes; the Fourth forbids unreasonable searches and seizures and requires that war-
rants to search or arrest be issued only upon probable cause. The
Fifth, Sixth, and Seventh Amendments mainly pertain to rights
of persons accused of federal crimes. The Fifth Amendment also

prohibits the taking of private property for public use without just compensation. Finally, the Seventh Amendment requires a jury trial in certain civil cases.

How the fundamental rights of the Bill of Rights figure into the morality of the free life can be generally indicated by reference to the outline of that morality provided earlier (that outline is not worked out in enough detail to where the right to bear arms, the right to trial by jury, the right not to have soldiers quartered in one's home, and the right not to be subject to unreasonable searches and seizures might emerge). Generally speaking, basic rights secure an area of freedom from the coercive influence of government in which persons may participate in the political process and carry out their own plans of life (see norms A2a; A3a, b, c, & f). These rights are correlatives of the "oughts" that appear in these norms, but only insofar as government is concerned. Accordingly, norm A2a (for example) could be restated to read: Individual persons have a right to negative freedom from government so they can conduct their personal and political lives, implying that government ought not to interfere coercively with such conduct. Similarly, norm A3c could be construed as saying that persons have a right to pursue the religion of their choice without intervention from government, implying that government ought to respect freedom of religion.

Enumerated rights do not cover fully the area of freedom from governmental intervention that should be secured if persons are to enjoy and perpetuate the life of freedom. For example, the Bill of Rights does not explicitly forbid laws that establish a particular secular view of the good life; nor is the autonomy of the family protected; nor is the right to live of new human life secured (see norms A1a; A2f; B1c). Furthermore, the Bill of Rights does not directly protect persons from forceful interference in their lives by private groups and persons. Finally, there are major parts of the morality of the free life which negative rights, whatever their scope, do not touch (see, for example, norms A2b; B1c & e; B2a & d).

So, though being free from intervention in our lives by the federal government is an important part of the free life, other major dimensions must be protected and promoted as well if the life of freedom is to be enjoyed by all persons and passed on to posterity. This fact should influence legal interpretations of the

Bill of Rights so that it helps secure the life of freedom rather than hinder it. Indeed, from the viewpoint of the morality of the free life, it would be an abuse of power if enumerated rights were interpreted and implemented by government in ways that seriously impeded the free life's enjoyment and perpetuation.

The Ninth Amendment indicates that the people have other rights besides those specifically mentioned in the Bill of Rights. What those rights are depends, in my view, on how the morality of the life of freedom is to be understood. Certainly, there is room in that morality for positive rights as well as further negative rights. As for other negative rights, it would be natural to construe the general requirements in the morality of the free life which secure negative freedoms to be the correlatives of negative rights (see norms A2a; A3a–d & f; B1c). For example, the norm A2a, which says that all people (not only government) ought to respect each person's negative freedom, would read: Every person has a right to be free from unjust coercive interference by all other people in the conduct of his personal and political life, implying that all people (not just government alone) ought to respect negative freedom. Other norms that protect negative freedom may be similarly interpreted.

Positive rights may well be given a large role to play, as part of the morality of freedom, in defining and organizing people's lives so that they may realize and perpetuate the free life. Think of those norms that require that new life have a chance to develop the capabilities of free persons and prescribe that the political and economic systems be maintained which make carrying on the free life possible (see norms B1c–e; B2a–d). Think also of those norms that indicate that persons have an equal opportunity to vote and compete for jobs and that those without means who must acquire new capabilities in order to become self-determining again be provided with a chance to do so (see norms A2b–c; A3e). Such requirements might be understood as the correlatives of positive rights. (Space does not permit a discussion of that possibility here).

But even if positive rights and an expanded set of negative rights are included in the morality of the free life, there still remain important norms outside the purview of rights. Among these norms are those that require that a people protect the free life for future people and that persons create human life itself (see norms B1a–b). It seems that persons who do not yet exist do not have rights. But even though that may be the case, the requirement to perpetuate free human life has very high priority in the morality of freedom and places stringent limits on what may be done by reason of rights. In other words, from the viewpoint of the free life's morality, persons are not free to weaken or undermine the perpetuation of the free life.

Having located the place rights might have in the morality of freedom, let me now consider the part rights might perform in making possible human flourishing. Earlier I observed that human flourishing is made possible by being alive to good and successfully pursuing it, and that being alive to the high intrinsic value of free human life forms the core part of being alive to good. To flourish the person must be, and find it intrinsically good to be, a primary agent in the world; she must experience her own unique opportunity to live as something of intrinsic value; she must pursue a way to live (a view of human good) worthy of her existence and accept it as such; she and others must have deep respect and concern for one another as free beings; and she must cherish human life and its freedom as something to be passed on to future peoples. The aim of the morality of the free life involves fostering this esteem in which free human life is held and enabling persons to live freely so that they for their own sakes might flourish.

As my review of the place rights may have in the morality of freedom reveals, rights play an important role as part of that morality in forming the opportunity for human flourishing. They help generate esteem for free human life so that persons can be alive to good and organize things so they can freely realize it. Both positive and negative rights, as forms of respect and concern, help establish the rightness and goodness of being a primary agent with a unique opportunity to live. Negative rights safeguard an area of freedom from the coercive intervention of others within which human good may be successfully pursued. Positive rights organize people so that persons can develop the capabilities and have the opportunities to realize human good. Both kinds of rights, when operating as they should, help create the human community without which flourishing cannot occur. As noted earlier, human community is formed by the care each has for the other in his wholeness. But human community exists only when all givings and receivings stem ultimately from the respect and concern for each person as a free being with his own life to live.

To conclude, the main canon for interpreting the proper role of rights in our political society is that rights should operate so that persons can enjoy equally and fully the life of freedom and perpetuate it without decline. According to this canon, it would be wrong to construe rights in a way that (for example) establishes or preserves unequal opportunities to develop and exercise the capabilities of personal and political freedom; or that sustains overt or covert domination of one class, race, or sex by another; or that justifies bartering the future of the free life in order to better indulge ourselves now. That rights have been and continue to be so misconstrued cannot be denied.

RIGHTS AND THE DECLINE OF THE FREE LIFE

Every political society has implicit within itself possibilities of its own decline. In order to define and organize the lives of persons, morality and law must set limits and boundaries beyond which persons can but ought not to go. They close off certain human possibilities so that others might be open. For example, in order for persons to pursue a favorable life outcome in a self-directed way, others must be prohibited from interfering coercively and arbitrarily in that pursuit. The upshot is that, built into every political society by way of its ethical-legal limits and boundaries, are possibilities of its own demise.

This is true of our political society. In defining and ordering persons' lives, the morality of freedom sets bounds and thereby creates possibilities for the free life's degeneration. Since rights are basic moral ideas in our political society, and given that certain tendencies exist for persons to live beyond the limits set by the free life and to justify doing so, people are prone to move beyond those bounds in the name of rights. When this occurs, rights foster the decline rather than the actuation of the free life.

There is not space enough here to work out thoroughly ways in which the free life may degenerate from within. So I will focus on certain aspects of what seems to be the central possibility of decline in the free life as we understand it. That possibility involves the individualism which characterizes our political society's view of self-direction and of human good. In the free life, each person is proprietor—the primary agent—over his own life as something of great value. The person's primal concern as proprietor is to live life well, or in a worthwhile way, and to flourish. Inherent in the nature of the person thus conceived is the tendency to be egoistic. By egoist, I mean one whose dominant or final aim in life is to realize his own self-interest exclusively—which in our political culture usually means his own happiness. This natural egoism may work itself out in certain ways in the name of freedom rights and thus weaken or even undermine the free life. I wish to examine somewhat how that might occur.

Recall that the viewpoint of the morality of the free life is nonegoistic. From its perspective, all persons have equal intrinsic worth as free beings (its aim is that everyone enjoy the life of freedom) and emerging future generations have worth equal to present generations (its aim is that the free life is perpetuated without decline out of profound concern for free human life). Furthermore, only when persons assume this nonegoistic point of view can they flourish. As observed earlier, to flourish persons must be very much alive to good, but to do so they must be alive to the intrinsic value of human life and its freedom, as something precious to be enjoyed by all and passed on to posterity. The growth of egoism among a people undermines the nonegoistic view of the free life and hence the opportunity to flourish. Let me indicate some ways it does so. As I do, let us bear in mind that human self-direction (e.g., the free life) and human good (e.g., human flourishing) are inseparable. What wears away the one weakens the other.

Imagine what impact the development of egoism would have on human community. As observed earlier, when the morality of freedom defines and organizes how people live, it creates mutual respect and concern for persons as free beings of intrinsic worth. This mutual respect and concern forms a community of free beings which provides the framework within which persons can choose the course their lives will take and out of which richer communities of care can emerge. Unless persons form a community of free beings thus understood, they cannot flourish.

The "egoization" of people's lives undermines human community. In the first place, it destroys the care, respect, and concern that makes possible human community and that forms the context within which the worth of persons as free beings and the goodness of their lives become actual to the degree necessary for human flourishing. The egoist has intrinsic worth in his own eyes and his living has intrinsic value for him, while others have instrumental worth for him or no value at all, depending on how they figure into the pursuit of his self-interests. One consequence is that the egoist cannot enjoy human community with others as free beings having intrinsic worth for him. If a person does not enjoy human community in this sense, then his opportunity to participate in human good and to flourish is very greatly reduced.

But also the egoist's own worth and value in her own eyes is greatly diminished. For one thing, even when others regard her as a being of intrinsic worth, it seems doubtful that she can receive that regard in a way that substantiates her intrinsic worth as a person. She cannot receive the messages of others that she has intrinsic worth because they do not have intrinsic worth to her. And when others around her are themselves egoists, then because they regard her as having only extrinsic value for them, her own worth is not grounded and made real in the recognition of others. In either case—whether others regard her nonegoistically or egoistically—the result is that the egoist's worth in her own eyes diminishes and hence her possibility to flourish through participation in human good is greatly impoverished.

Given the place of rights in our public law and morality, we should expect the egoization of political society to be reflected and fostered by such rights. That is, we should expect that among egoists the primary role of rights will be to order their lives so they might peacefully pursue each his own self-interests. We should expect egoists to understand rights as a way to demand what is due one without ultimate regard for others. In this situation politics will likely involve conflict between groups of interests over interpreting and implementing rights, each trying to gain an advantage for itself. Consequently, freedom rights tend to be unstable in their operation, their relations become notably incoherent, and their numbers tend to proliferate.

As lives become egoistic, productivity and creativity are likely to decline as ways of participating in human good. The central aim of life becomes more the consuming of value than the producing or creating of value. The latter becomes merely a means to the former—something of instrumental value only—and thereby loses much of its power to help make possible human flourishing. When this occurs, persons understand rights as a means to secure and enhance their opportunity as consumers. In these circumstances, we have reason to expect government will more and more be counted on to make available means of consumption that the person previously provided for himself through free intercourse with others. So in general, individual self-determination, along with the significance of being productive and creative, will decline as critical parts of being a self-directed person with an opportunity to flourish.

When consumerism becomes a foremost part of the free society's mode of self-direction and view of human good, then typically so does carnal-mindedness, meaning that persons tend to conceive human good to be the maximum satisfaction of material and physical desires. The result is still further impoverishment of the possibility of human flourishing. Here again we should expect rights to be interpreted so they can play a fostering role in securing the person's position in political society as a consumer of material goods and services, including opportunities to be gainfully (not always productively) employed as a means to that end.

If our political society becomes egoized, particularly if consumerism and carnal-mindedness characterize its mode of self-direction and idea of human good, then it seems likely that persons will carry on their lives in ways that neglect the perpetuation of the free life itself. This tendency strikes at the very heart of the free society—or any political society, for that matter. For the continuation of a political society depends on succeeding generations working to perpetuate their way of living as an integral part of enjoying it. But from the egoistic point of view, and especially from the perspective of the carnal-minded, perpetuating the free life constitutes for many a sacrifice of their lives and their means, both of which are "scarce resources." So in the natural pursuit of their egoistic ends, they tend to care insufficiently for the continuation of the free life. They are more willing to waste and pollute, neglect the young, pass on to future people great debt, and in general impoverish the free life with its promise of flourishing—all in the pursuit of their self-centered ends.

Both human flourishing and, of course, the viability of our political society depend on the people finding the free life to be something of profound value to be perpetuated as well as enjoyed

by them. In fact, perpetuating human life and its freedom constitute a most significant way in which persons in a political society
like ours—or in any other political society, for that matter—can
be alive to and realize human good. Indeed, people cannot flourish when they no longer deeply appreciate human life as something to be caringly created and provided for. When this occurs,
human living in general is impoverished.

If our political society were to neglect the perpetuation of
human life and its freedom, we should expect rights to play a
role in it. We should expect rights to be interpreted in ways that
allow the living to pollute and waste, lessen their regard for new
life, fail in nurturing the young, burden future generations with
the debts from prodigal living, and in general impoverish the
culture that makes possible the free life.

A Concluding Remark

How well the free life fares over the next two hundred years in
our political society depends on how its mode of self-direction
and opportunity for human flourishing fare. If we expand and
further actuate the ideal of the free life with its promise of
human well-being, then the next two hundred years may well
surpass the previous two hundred in human freedom and human
flourishing. But if the people fail in this regard—particularly, if
instead they protect and promote the tendencies toward decline
inherent in the free life itself—then we should not expect our
progeny to be very free or happy. Much depends on the future of
rights—on whether they are properly understood and implemented so that persons can freely pursue good and flourish.

X

THE FUTURE
OF RIGHTS

★

Gary C. Bryner
A. D. Sorensen

More than any other part of our federal Constitution, the Bill of Rights symbolizes our identity as a people. We think of ourselves, above all else, as a free people, and we are free primarily because we possess rights. So it is appropriate as we commemorate the ratification of the Bill of Rights to reflect on the meaning and significance of rights in making possible our freedom. In doing so, our main concern will be the future of rights. Like the Founders, we as a people want to be free; we want our posterity to be free; and most of us, at least, believe that rights are essential to freedom in the future.

This discussion of rights and the future of freedom involves three things. First, we need a means of evaluation, a general overview of the role that rights should play in making possible the free life—for considering the past and future of rights. We next review critically portions of the history of rights in our country. How successful has our political society been in realizing the life of freedom for all persons? What part have rights assumed in making possible the free life? To what degree have they fostered a life of freedom and to what extent have they hindered it? Finally, we preview the future of rights. What remains to be accomplished in actuating the free life? Do rights have a large role to play? If so, should we hold to the prevailing view of rights or must we revise it in major ways in order to further establish and preserve individual freedom? Answers to these questions require that we consider, in a rather fundamental way, the nature of the free life and the role of rights in making it possible.

SECURING THE FREE LIFE

The original Bill of Rights includes the first ten amendments of the federal Constitution. The First through Eighth Amendments enumerate rights that limit the powers of the federal government and thereby help establish an area of freedom for persons subject to that power. The Ninth and Tenth Amendments concern all powers and all rights ultimately possessed by the people, which those amendments classify as "delegated" and "reserved" powers and "enumerated" and "retained" rights. That these rights and powers are possessed by the people is implied by the language of the Ninth and Tenth Amendments and the Constitution as a whole. As that language indicates, it is "we the people" who should in the end delegate and reserve, enumerate and retain power and rights.

In our political tradition, all governmental powers, whether delegated or reserved, ultimately belong to the people in the form of rights. Let us refer to these rights as "power rights" in distinction to the "enumerated" and "retained" rights mentioned in the Ninth Amendment, which we will call "freedom rights." When we think of the Bill of Rights we always think of freedom rights and usually only of the enumerated ones. For some purposes this makes good sense. But to understand the full significance of the Bill of Rights as was envisioned by the Founders and most people since, we must consider all rights held by the people— both power rights (delegated and reserved) and freedom rights (enumerated and retained)—because it is only by virtue of the total set of rights that we can be a free people and our way of life can be a free life. In particular, the rights enumerated and the powers delegated in the federal Constitution should be examined in conjunction with the powers of state government and the rights enumerated in state constitutions. We will consider, in the most general way, what part this overall system of rights and powers should play in actuating the free life.

The free life, or being a free people, is the basic value underlying our Constitution. While the Declaration of Independence articulated the purpose of government—the securing of rights—the Constitution's task was to provide a means of accomplishing that purpose. Freedom rights and power rights work together; their job is to help define and order how people should live so that they can collectively and individually determine the outcome of their lives in a self-directed way. That is what being a free people and enjoying the free life means. Because it is the basic value on which our Constitution rests, the free life constitutes the fundamental imperative of our public morality. That imperative indicates that all things considered the free life—a life in which the people are individually and collectively self-directed primarily by virtue of power rights and freedom rights—ought to be actuated.

The Constitution itself embodies this norm—as do all current state constitutions—and provides a legal mechanism for its implementation. It is this value that we will later use in evaluating disputes concerning rights in our political society and in prescribing what their future should be. But first we must indicate what we think actuating the free life means and what role rights (both freedom and power rights) play in it.

What constitutes the free life? A life of freedom is a mode of self-direction. It is a way of defining and organizing how people live so that they can collectively and individually determine the outcome of their lives in self-directed and favorable ways. The free life is composed of two basic components: the relative ability of persons to determine life's outcome in self-directed ways, and the aim of these choices—a vision of the good life. These two components are inseparable. Without some view of human good, there could be no self-direction; but without human self-direction there could be no human good. In our political society, human self direction takes priority over human good. People should be free, within certain general limits required by the maintenance of the free life itself, to carry out their own view of the good life. This priority of human self-direction over human good helps explain why our fundamental law does not so much answer the question of how people should live as it puts them in a position to answer it for themselves.

Because of this feature of our law (and because of limited space), we shall not be concerned here with the nature of the good life in discussing the future of rights. We shall focus on the concept of self-direction in a free society, what it means to actuate it, and what roles rights play in that actuation. As we do, we shall examine only the core ingredients of self-direction and, at first, only in a very general way. Our concern is to provide a fuller picture of the free life, but many of its temporal and community aspects will be left in the background.

What does the actuation of the free life as a mode of self-direction mean? Human existence is typically conceived of as a mode of collective and individual self-direction situated in a larger cause-effect world. In order for any mode of self-direction to become well established, certain general requirements must be satisfied. In the first place, a political society must be organized so that persons develop the capabilities to choose and act. Second, it must generate and procure enabling conditions necessary for exercising their capabilities. Third, an area of autonomy within which persons can choose and act without compulsion must be secured. Finally, persons must be situated in the larger cause-effect world so that they affect the outcome of their lives in an overall meaningful way. If a political society fails to realize any one of these requirements, then its mode of self-direction would fail. Or, if a political society's organization was seriously inadequate in providing for any one of those requirements, its overall mode of self-direction would be significantly weakened. All of this is true of our political society. In order for the free life's mode of self-direction to become well established, people must be organized so that the above requirements are satisfied. If any requirement just discussed is inadequately provided—for example, if a significant number of people cannot develop the required capabilities, or procure the needed enabling conditions, or enjoy the prescribed area of autonomy, then the free life as a mode of self-direction remains to that degree unrealized and our political society fails to satisfy the basic moral-legal imperative that justifies its existence.

If we assume that every person in a free society has equal as well as high intrinsic worth, then the free life requires that every adult person should enjoy full and equal status as a free being. What do full and equal status as a free person mean? We can in large measure answer this question by considering the two basic

freedoms in our political society. They are the freedom to participate in the political process (political freedom) and the freedom
to choose and carry out a plan of life (personal freedom).

To participate freely in the political process, a person must
possess the capabilities, have access to certain enabling conditions, and be free from coercive interference by others. In discussing what free and equal political freedom means in view of
these components of it, space permits us to examine only two aspects—the freedom to take part in the election process and the
freedom to enter the race for elected public office.

In the first place, to establish political freedom, persons must
have the opportunity to develop the capabilities of political freedom. Since each person has equal intrinsic worth as a free being,
each should have an equal chance to develop those capabilities. In
our society, having an equal chance to develop the capabilities of
political freedom would involve mainly making available an
equal and quality education for all persons throughout the nation. In particular, it implies that education opportunities should
not vary significantly according to arbitrary characteristics, such
as race and sex, or according to differences of wealth between
areas of the country.

Furthermore, for political freedom to be fully actuated, persons should have equal opportunity to exercise their capabilities
as voters as well as seekers of elected office. What equal opportunity involves here has to do with the very purpose of the electoral
process itself. That purpose is both to enable persons to participate in the politics of self-government for its own sake and, in
doing so, to enable them to choose those most qualified to represent them in establishing and preserving a free society. The
means for doing this, as they have emerged in our political society, include everything from voting in party primaries to voting
in national elections. The organization and facilities for conduct-
ing these kinds and levels of elections constitute vital enabling
conditions for the enjoyment of political freedom, for exercising
the political capabilities persons should have an equal chance to
develop.

As for equal opportunity in voting, the imperative to actuate
political freedoms requires that adequate means to vote exist and
that all adult citizens have roughly equal and reasonably easy access

to them. This requirement of equal opportunity appears to us to be clearly rooted in the idea of the equal worth of free persons.

Equal opportunity to compete for elected office is related to a basic purpose of the election process mentioned earlier, which is to select the most qualified representative to protect and promote a society of free people. Accordingly, persons have equal opportunity to run for elected office when (and only when) qualifications for office serve as the main criteria that govern the process and outcomes of competition for office. More particularly, this means that qualifications for office guide who should enter the race for elected office; that the subsequent process of competition works to disclose the qualifications of candidates; that in the end voters select persons for office according to who is best qualified; and that extraneous considerations, such as race, sex, or wealth, do not figure significantly into the competitive process and its outcomes.

To conclude, when viable opportunities exist to vote and compete for public office according to qualifications—opportunities comprised of human capabilities, enabling conditions, and area of autonomy—and when persons have equal access to these opportunities, then they set the course for political freedom, fully and equally actuated. We turn now to the other basic freedom, the personal freedom to choose and carry out a plan of life. Like political freedom, personal freedom helps form the free life's mode of self-direction. As such it involves human capabilities, enabling conditions, and individual autonomy which together constitute the opportunity of personal freedom. Here, too, the fundamental imperative to actuate the free life, which underlies and is incorporated in our constitutional system, requires that persons come to enjoy, fully and equally, personal freedom.

As with political freedom, personal freedom can only be actuated if all persons have adequate means to develop the capabilities of personal freedom, which, in our current political society, primarily means an equal chance for a good education. Furthermore, to exercise the capabilities of personal freedom, persons must possess enabling conditions of various kinds. The near-universal means of procuring enabling conditions is money income. In a free society, the primary way persons generate enabling conditions and procure the money income that controls them is by engaging in free economic intercourse with others for that very purpose. This process of free intercourse is an integral part of how persons live as self-determining and self-directed beings in a free society.

In order for all persons to enjoy personal freedom, they must have an equal opportunity to participate in economic intercourse with others. Only then can persons in a free society live their lives in a self-directed way. Here, as in other areas of freedom, opportunity involves the coming together of personal capability, relevant enabling conditions, and individual autonomy. Equal opportunity involves, as we have already observed, having an equal chance to develop the capabilities of personal freedom. Equal autonomy means that all persons enjoy the same high degree of absence of restraint by government and others in how they choose to live. That leaves the question of how the enabling conditions necessary for exercising the developed capabilities of personal freedom figure into equal opportunity.

We have already noted that, in a free society, persons generate enabling conditions and acquire the money to control them through free economic intercourse with others. But enabling conditions serve as a means of participating in that economic process itself. There are three ways in which control over enabling conditions helps make participation possible in free exchange with others. One is when persons first seek to enter into the economy as a producer or creator of values. What equal opportunity means precisely here could involve us in a rather long discussion. But the general idea goes something like this: We shall assume that in a free society the positions available in the economy for a person to be productive call for different capabilities and vary in the rewards they offer, including income. If personal freedom is to be fully and equally actuated, each person should have the enabling conditions that make it possible to compete, in a fair process of selection, for positions in the economy for which he or she has the capability. How society might be organized to ensure this outcome cannot be examined here, but it very likely would require that society, through government, provide enabling conditions for some of its less fortunate members so that they can enter the economy as creators of value and can become self-determining. Once persons are successfully engaged in creating or producing value in free exchange with others, then they may be able to change or better their position in the economy. This is the second way in which enabling conditions make it possible for persons to be self-determining by participating in free exchange with others. But because such exchange results inevitably in unequal income, the ability to change or better one's economic conditions will be unequal.

Finally, because of circumstances beyond their control, some persons may lose their positions in the economy and therefore may lose their opportunity to be self-determining. When this happens, these persons need certain enabling conditions such as food, shelter, and some income to sustain themselves until they can become self-determining once more. Here again we should expect the free society, most likely through its government, to support people in these situations so that personal freedom might be more fully realized.

However, some persons, even when they do secure the means to sustain themselves through work, have insufficient means to enjoy a life of freedom of even minimum quality. This appears to be an unavoidable outcome of free economic intercourse. The standard of living of those caught temporarily or permanently in this situation should be elevated by social assistance to the point where they can live a minimally decent life as a free being.

So, as far as enabling conditions of personal freedom are concerned, persons have equal opportunity to be self-determining when they control enabling conditions sufficient for them to enter into free intercourse with others and there obtain at least a minimally decent level of living. When they also have an equal and good chance to develop the capabilities of personal freedom and enjoy an equal and broad area of autonomy in deciding how to live, they realize fully and equally personal freedom.

So far we have focused on what it means to actuate the life of freedom by making it possible for persons to enjoy opportunities for self-direction fully and equally. But there is another basic part to actuation rooted in the intrinsic value of human life and its freedom. It is that the free life is something of profound value that must be perpetuated by the living beyond their own existence as well as being enjoyed by them. Some such precept helps form the common identity of human beings everywhere. People everywhere see themselves as mortal beings of a kind that perpetuate themselves.

Our political society should not only define and organize people so that they might enjoy the free life but, at least equally importantly, it should define and order their lives so that they perpetuate it. The central concern in perpetuating the free life involves creating new life itself, nurturing it to full personhood, and otherwise providing it with the particular means and general cultural and physical environments necessary to realize a quality free life. Since creating new life and caring for it should be—and normally will be—an integral part of enjoying a life of freedom, what was said earlier about people realizing personal freedom fully and equally also applies to creating new life and its development. The process of developing the capabilities of personal freedom, protecting a broad range of autonomy in which to express them, and acquiring the necessary enabling conditions for doing so should be conceived and arranged so that persons have, as a significant part of their opportunity to be free, the desire and ability to help perpetuate the free life, particularly by creating and caring for new life itself. The most important institution involved in this process is the family. It is primarily by means of the family that people create new life and nurture it to full free personhood, but all major institutions share in the responsibility of protecting and providing for succeeding generations of persons so that they might have the opportunity to live freely.

THE ROLE OF RIGHTS IN A FREE SOCIETY

Now that we have considered the free life as a basic value of our political society and what it means to actuate it, we can examine the meaning and significance of the rights referred to in the Bill of Rights. To do this, we must consider the people's power rights (delegated and reserved), their freedom rights (enumerated and retained), and the general relations between them. In particular, the rights enumerated and the powers delegated in the federal Constitution should be examined in conjunction with the powers of state governments and the rights enumerated in state constitutions. We will consider, first, in the most general way, what part this overall system of rights and powers should play in actuating the free life.

Consider first the part power rights (both state and federal) should play when we assume that their primary purpose is to protect and promote the free life. Given this purpose, it would seem that the power rights the people themselves possess prior to government are limited only by the value of the free life itself. That value limits the power rights of the people in two ways. The most obvious way is that power must be used to promote and protect the life of freedom and not to weaken or undermine it. But the free life also limits power even when its employment would actually increase the extent to which people can realize a life of freedom. The use of power ordinarily should not violate the freedoms of individual persons in order to enlarge the overall freedom of the people. The second kind of limits stem from the intrinsic worth of people as free beings, which requires that the individual as a free person enjoy a certain inviolability that must not ordinarily be overridden in the name of human good, even when that good is the life of freedom itself. There will be more to say about how the free life limits the usage of power to realize the free life as we consider freedom rights. We shall consider, first in the most general way, what part this overall system of rights and powers should play in actuating the free life.

The rights of power are limited further by the nature and organization of the constitutional system itself. In the first place, the powers of the national government are limited to those delegated and implied powers conferred upon it by the constitution. Additionally, the constitutional system circumscribes power by how it organizes it, dividing it as it does between levels of government and between branches of government at each level. All such limits should be understood as facilitating the overall purpose of power by restricting powers so that they will more likely be used to foster the free life rather than to undermine it or prevent it from being actuated. These limits, like all constitutional restrictions, should not be construed in ways that keep government from using whatever power it has to secure the free life as an end in ways consistent with freedom as a limit on power.

The main way government uses power rights to foster the free life is by determining and upholding primary moral-legal norms which themselves define and order a life of freedom. Think of political freedom, for example. In order for persons to have the opportunity to vote and to compete for elected office, their lives must be defined and ordered so that they can develop their political capabilities, possess the enabling conditions to exercise them, and be free from coercive interference by government and other people. All this comes about only through the operation of certain primary norms that help constitute the opportunity to vote and to compete for elected offices. Various legal norms require certain persons to set up voting booths in accessible locations and honestly tabulate the votes, limit financial contributions to candidates for office, protect voters from harassment, and so on. Much the same is true of personal freedom: a system of moral-legal norms must operate in defining and organizing how people live so that they may enjoy full and equal opportunity to choose and carry out their life projects, including doing their part to perpetuate human life and its freedom. To repeat, the principal role of power rights is to further personal and political freedom by interpreting and upholding the primary norms which order things so that those freedoms become possible.

The fundamental moral-legal imperative of the free life serves as a standard that a system of primary norms must satisfy to be acceptable. Such a system must not only secure an area of individual autonomy but must also help organize things so that individuals in succeeding generations can live freely. It is as part of such a system of primary norms that freedom rights play their role. In conjunction with other moral-legal concepts, they should help fully actuate the free life. Doing that depends on the kinds of freedom rights included in the system of primary norms and the range of operation those rights have. According to one view, freedom rights are negative rights that limit governmental power so that persons enjoy an area of autonomy within which to enjoy political and personal freedom. Another view recognizes both negative and positive rights and can see them as the basic moral-legal concepts in the primary system of norms which orders the free life. But whatever view of freedom rights we accept, the fundamental imperative underlying our constitutional system is that rights should function so that individuals in succeeding generations of persons enjoy fully and equally the life of freedom.

We can see the place freedom rights should hold in a larger system of moral-legal norms required to organize persons so that the free life can be fully and equally enjoyed by succeeding generations. The larger normative system should order things so that persons have an equal chance to develop the capabilities of freedom, have equal access to enabling conditions necessary for exercising those capabilities, and are unhindered by coercive interfer-

ence from government and other persons. The part played by
negative freedom rights consists of securing an area of autonomy
free from governmental dictations. Freedom rights thus understood do not protect persons from purely private power and of
course do not require that persons have the positive means to develop and use the capabilities of freedom. So in order for the free
life to be well established, other moral-legal norms in conjunction with negative rights must function to organize things to
that end.

To better grasp the roles negative freedom rights should play
in our free society, let us recall the conclusion reached earlier
about the proper role of governmental power (power rights). We
concluded that the primary purpose of our federal system of
power (delegated and reserved powers together) is to protect and
promote the free life in ways consistent with the value of the free
life itself. As we just noted, negative freedom rights are to function as an integral part of a larger system of moral-legal norms
whose purpose is to organize things so that the free life is fully
established and preserved. Given the purpose of governmental
powers in this function of negative rights, it follows that negative rights should limit governmental power so it will most likely be used within its range of effectiveness and consistency with
freedom to foster the realization and perpetuation of the life of
freedom.

Consider what that implies about how negative freedom rights
should *not* be interpreted and implemented. Generally speaking,
negative rights should not be construed in a manner that pre-
vents promoting the free life in ways consistent with the free life.
For example, those rights should not be interpreted so that they
stop government from using powers to regulate primary and secondary education in order that persons in different school dis-
tricts have good, equal chances to become capable as free persons.
Nor should such rights be construed to keep government from
regulating the economy to ensure that minorities have equal opportunity to participate in free intercourse with others in productive activity and are considered for jobs and promotion without
discrimination, so that they can be self-determining. Nor should
negative rights permit living generations to sacrifice the future
quality of the free life in order to better satisfy their own self-
interests, so that, for instance, existing economic interests can

seriously pollute the environment or waste nonrenewable resources. When negative rights are interpreted in any of these ways the result is that some persons or groups receive preferential treatment under law in their enjoyment of life in our free society, meaning that they have privileged opportunities to develop their abilities of personal and political self-direction and to exercise them in ways that hinder or undermine the continued realization of the free life for others. This is contrary to the fundamental imperative of a free society.

The other view of freedom rights we want to notice conceives rights as a basic norm in organizing how people live so that the free life may be actuated, so that succeeding generations of individuals fully and equally realize the free life. For freedom rights to play the major role in achieving this end, both positive and negative rights must operate in ordering people's lives. Negative freedom rights protect people from coercive interference by private persons and groups as well as by government. Positive rights require that people be given an equal chance to develop into free persons and an equal opportunity to enjoy personal and political freedom fully. Both positive and negative rights must work together to integrate the perpetuation of the free life with the enjoyment of it by the living. The textual basis of this larger view of rights is the Ninth Amendment. People have both enumerated as well as retained rights (some of the latter being enumerated in state constitutions), which together are sufficient to order their lives so that a life of freedom can be realized by the living and their posterity.

The view of freedom rights as negative limits on government power has been the prevailing view since before the Founding. But the other view has frequently been debated in the past and in recent years has received considerable attention in legal circles and has gained ground in constitutional interpretation. The contemporary situation is one in which negative rights come under strong attack for not adequately serving the purposes of our political society. Some critics even think that theories of rights in general should be replaced by theories of human good and human community. What the future of rights will be in our country may depend very much on how this debate turns out. Should negative rights continue to play their dominant role in securing the life of freedom? Or should a larger view—one which includes positive as well as negative rights—operate to that end? Or should rights cease to play a major part in defining and ordering our political society? Before offering our own view of future rights, we turn to a critical review of portions of the history of rights to gain perspective.

THE EVOLUTION OF RIGHTS IN THE UNITED STATES

Negative and positive rights have played an important role in promoting the preconditions of the free life in America, although not always expressed in those terms. Personal capabilities, the first element of the free life, are usually defined as attributes largely determined by innate characteristics and personal environment rather than government action. There are limits to what society can do to promote equality of opportunity, since individual ability is so greatly affected by inherited ability, family upbringing, and other values. We cannot, as James Fishkin has argued, have both family autonomy and real equality of opportunity.[1] Enabling conditions may be made available, but personal capabilities are required for the free life to flourish. However, one cannot draw lines too precisely; personal capabilities, for example, are also affected, indirectly, by the existence of the enabling conditions necessary for the free life.

The second element of the free life, ensuring individual autonomy, has been widely viewed as a primary purpose of government, and negative rights have widely been seen as the vehicle for achieving it. The limitations on governmental power provided for in the Bill of Rights were aimed at the national government and, with a few exceptions—such as the 1798 Alien and Sedition Acts, which prohibited criticism of the government, and the Civil War, when civil liberties were curtailed—the federal government was not a major threat to individual freedom and autonomy during its first century. While the second hundred years has seen many more threats to individual rights from the exercise of governmental power, there has nevertheless been a fairly high level of confidence in the ability of the Bill of Rights, interpreted and applied by a strong, independent judiciary, to check the power of the federal government and preserve individual autonomy.

Much more controversial and problematic has been the role of the Bill of Rights in protecting individual autonomy in the face of actions against state governments. In 1833 the Supreme Court ruled, in effect, that the Bill of Rights did not apply to state governments.[2] Despite the passage of the Fourteenth Amendment and its promise of national citizenship, the Supreme Court was slow to use the Bill of Rights to protect individual autonomy against actions taken by the states. The First Amendment was incorporated into the Fourteenth Amendment in a series of cases in the 1920s and 1930s; the rights of the accused were incorporated in the 1960s, and a right to privacy that was rooted in the Bill of Rights was articulated in the 1970s. This incorporation of the Bill of Rights required that the federal government, particularly federal courts and marshals, take action to restrain state governments. Similarly, the federal government began intervening in state affairs to protect the individual rights guaranteed ethnic minorities under the Fourteenth Amendment. By the end of America's second reconstruction, it was clear that the federal government was required to take affirmative steps to ensure individual autonomy.[3]

Despite the progress made in recent years, individual autonomy has never been adequately secured for all persons. There is inevitable tension between individual autonomy and majority rule. The power of the majority to work its will is usually overwhelming, and challenges to that power are infrequent. The modest progress in protecting individuals against arbitrary or unfair government power under the Bill of Rights has largely left untouched the problem of private actions that impinge on individual autonomy and the promise of the free life. Civil rights legislation permits individuals victimized by racism to sue individuals who have violated their rights, and the courts have provided other opportunities for suits against private parties, but new threats to individual autonomy regularly arise. Individual autonomy remains an unrealized ideal of American society and an unfulfilled condition for the free life for many ethnic minorities, people with nontraditional lifestyles, and people who find themselves outside of majoritarian society and culture.[4]

The third element of the free life, the enabling conditions required for individuals to exercise choice and develop their personal capabilities, has been at least as problematic. The creation of national regulatory agencies in the 1880s and again during the early 1900s signaled the beginning of a constitutional revolution that recognized the role of positive rights in ensuring individual freedom that culminated in the New Deal. Congress's constitutional authority to regulate interstate commerce was expanded when it created the Interstate Commerce Commission in 1887. The Progressive Era triggered the first round of federal social regulatory legislation. Widely published exposés of practices in the food and drug industries led to the Food and Drug Act of 1906 that prohibited shipping across state lines food and drugs that were misbranded or adulterated. A number of regulatory agencies were created between 1915 and 1927 to regulate commercial and financial activities.

The most significant results of this burst of regulatory activity were to challenge the primacy of the common law in regulating economic affairs and to expand the role of the federal government in the economy. The weakening of the hold the common law had on regulating markets was a critical step in legitimizing government intervention in economic and social activity; market exchanges were no longer seen as natural, neutral ways to facilitate private choices but part of a social structure that distributed benefits and burdens in certain ways. The rise of federal regulatory agencies recognized that the coercive power of the national government could reach private decisions. These changes, however, were quite modest. Their major impact was to lay the framework for the real constitutional revolution of the New Deal.

The Great Depression and the New Deal engendered a whole generation of regulatory agencies and social welfare programs. This dramatic expansion in the role of the federal government in creating a national welfare, regulatory state constituted a constitutional revolution of profound importance. In 1941 Franklin Delano Roosevelt issued a call for the worldwide recognition of the "Four Freedoms"—freedom of speech and expression, freedom to worship God, freedom from want, and freedom from fear.[5] While the speech was primarily aimed at world affairs and the growing threat of the Fascist powers, it also signaled an expansion of the role of government at home. Three years later, as victory in the war appeared inevitable, Roosevelt returned to this theme:

This Republic had its beginning, and grew to its present strength, under the protection of certain inalienable political rights—among them the right of free speech, free press, free worship, trial by jury, freedom from unreasonable searches and seizures. They were our rights to life and liberty.

As our Nation has grown in size and stature, however—as our industrial economy expanded—these political rights proved inadequate to assure us equality in the pursuit of happiness.

We have come to a clear realization of the fact that true individual freedom can't exist without economic security and independence. . . . In our day these economic truths have become accepted as self-evident. We have accepted, so to speak, a second Bill of Rights under which a new basis of security and prosperity can be established for all—regardless of station, race, or creed.

New, positive rights were needed:

The right to a useful and remunerative job in the industries or shops or farms or mines of the Nation;

The right to earn enough to provide adequate food and clothing and recreation;

The right of every farmer to raise and sell his products at a return which will give him and his family a decent living;

The right of every businessman, large and small, to trade in an atmosphere of freedom from unfair competition and domination by monopolies at home or abroad;

The right of every family to a decent home;

The right to adequate medical care and the opportunity to achieve and enjoy good health;

The right to adequate protection from the economic fears of old age, sickness, accident, and unemployment;

The right to a good education . . . .[6]

While the New Deal fell far short of establishing programs that assured the enjoyment of these rights, it created a new realm of expectations for government intervention in social and political affairs. Intervention was defended as being consistent with individual freedom as a way to ensure that individuals enjoyed real equality of opportunity. That goal of equality of opportunity was not new; Roosevelt's contribution was in arguing that government had a much expanded role to play in ensuring that all citizens enjoyed the preconditions for that opportunity.[7]

Legislation establishing social security, unemployment compensation, the Federal Housing Administration, the Civilian Conservation Corps, and a host of regulatory agencies all reflected the idea that new rights had been recognized and government had a duty to ensure that those rights were realized. While this constitutional revolution engendered vociferous criticism as a violation of the old order, which it surely was, it was just as aggressively defended as an essential response to the failure of a free-market economy, regulated by the common law system of liability, contracts, and torts, to ensure that all Americans enjoyed an equal opportunity to make meaningful life choices.

Roosevelt's revolution was resumed twenty years later when Lyndon Johnson launched the Great Society, another effort to realize economic and social rights for all Americans. Welfare and health care programs were created and expanded. Public housing, urban renewal, funding public education, ensuring adequate food, and protection of civil rights became central responsibilities of the national government. The revolution was secured when Richard Nixon embraced these programs and supported Congress in recognizing even more rights—the rights of workers to a healthy and safe workplace, the rights of consumers to safe products, the rights of all Americans to clean air and water, the reproductive and workplace rights of women, and the rights of those accused of crimes.

This extraordinary revolution in the role of government was widely viewed as consistent with individual rights and often defended as promoting equality of opportunity. While a narrow view of equality of opportunity might minimize governmental intervention in society, a richer notion of equality of opportunity, like the ideal of the free life, requires governmental intervention. Individuals need to have some minimum level of resources before they can effectively make choices and pursue opportunities. A commitment to equal rights of all Americans required that government intervene aggressively to limit the exercise of private power that interfered with individual rights and to provide the material preconditions for the exercise of individual choice.

Government was to ensure that individuals were given the resources necessary for individuals to live meaningful, self-determined, self-directed lives.[8]

While poverty was the target of much of the Great Society, the lack of opportunity that women and ethnic minorities suffered from was an even more pressing problem. Affirmative action programs required active government intervention in private organizations to ensure that the effects of past discrimination were overcome, that victims of past discrimination were put in the place they would have been had discrimination not occurred, and that traditional barriers limiting the life choices of women and ethnic minorities be eliminated. Affirmative action and nondiscrimination regulations, as much as any other government policy, recognized the need for government to take positive steps to ensure the rights of all persons and reinforced the idea that aggressive government programs are consistent with individual rights.[9]

Individual freedom is threatened by unsafe workplaces, inadequate health care, substandard housing, dangerous chemicals in the environment, poor air quality, polluted water, dangerous consumer products, and racial and sexual discrimination. Government intervention to ensure rights can empower people to live free lives. It can expand personal autonomy by increasing the choices available to individuals. The creation of new rights in the 1930s and the 1960s was a powerful means of securing the preconditions for a life of freedom for all persons.

Political rights, like individual rights, were also expanded during the past fifty years. The minimum voting age was lowered to eighteen years of age by the Twenty-Sixth Amendment, ratified in 1971. Barriers aimed at limiting voting by ethnic minorities were dismantled through ratification in 1964 of the Twenty-Fourth Amendment, which prohibited a poll tax, and the 1964 and 1965 Civil Rights acts reduced the use of literacy tests and other efforts to reinforce discrimination in voting practices. Implementation of these provisions required that the federal government take aggressive action to challenge the practices of state governments.

However, in 1981 the Reagan administration challenged this expansive commitment to rights. It institutionalized some of these challenges through spending cuts in social programs, making it more difficult to become eligible for federal programs, and reduced regulation. Congress began reversing some of the Reagan inroads throughout the mid-1980s. Presidential candidate George Bush promised a kinder, gentler America, including more support for regulation and welfare, as a way to insulate him from some of the critics of the Reagan era, and the Bush administration expanded some regulatory and welfare programs. This temporary respite came to a halt as the 1992 presidential campaign began and concerns of economic growth and international competitiveness overwhelmed other policy issues. However, the most significant consequence of the Reagan and Bush attack on the regulatory-welfare state will likely be the appointment of hundreds of conservative federal judges and several Supreme Court justices who have begun to restrict the reach of the new rights. Courts played a fundamental role in the expansion of rights through activist judges, who embraced new rights with enthusiasm, and as an inevitable result of a host of new laws that effectively created new rights. Some retrenchment has occurred, but the statutory basis of many rights places significant restraints on a conservative judiciary. This tension between an interventionist Congress and conservative courts is at the heart of the debate over the future of rights in America.

A market economy with minimal government intervention allocates individual opportunities and life choices in particular ways. These allocations are not natural or objective but are a consequence of certain preferences and beliefs. Some of these allocations are unfair to others and can be altered through public policies. Individual preferences also change as new information is provided and new opportunities are opened to individuals. Government intervention to help provide the enabling conditions for a life of freedom have helped to enlarge the scope of participation in the free life, particularly for women and ethnic minorities and for people who temporarily find themselves out of work or unable to compete in the labor market. These efforts have usually been defended as essential in ensuring the right of Americans to enjoy real equality of opportunity. While the right to equal opportunity can be viewed as a minimal commitment on the part of government not to interfere with market exchanges, the prevailing notion has been a much richer one—one that requires active government involvement to ensure that the preconditions of effective choice and opportunity are available to all persons.

There is great enthusiasm throughout the world for rights. The United Nations Declaration of Human Rights and the U.S. Bill of Rights have been widely invoked as the rallying cry for revolutions in eastern Europe and throughout the world. There has been a tremendous outpouring of enthusiasm for rights and a great yearning for freedom secured by rights. Rights appear to be at the heart of transforming political societies throughout the world. Much of the power of rights has been visible in challenging autocratic governments, in loosening the power of totalitarian regimes, and in freeing individuals from the oppressive reach of corrupt governments. It is less clear if rights will serve as the basis for transforming conditions in the less developed world, where forty thousand children die each day from disease and malnutrition. Can claims for government action that rest on positive rights of ensuring the preconditions for a free, self-directed life be the basis for addressing global poverty, hunger, and disease? Can positive rights be the basis for expanding opportunity for those who lack it?

While rights may possess the evocative power to transform societies, their impact in the United States has been modest at best. Widely reported evidence in the United States of disparities in income, the extent of poverty, chronic disadvantagement, continuing racism and sexism, and a whole host of other social problems are clear evidence that not everyone enjoys the preconditions of the free life as defined here. Discrimination continues to be pervasive, and women and ethnic minorities continue to lack the same kinds of opportunities afforded others.[10] Children continue to be ravaged by poverty and social problems that prevent them from developing the skills and other preconditions for the free life and real equality of opportunity.[11] The United States falls far behind the rest of the wealthy world in recognizing the right to some minimum level of food, shelter, education, and health care.[12] Even a minimal quality education, long recognized as a right enjoyed by all Americans, is not available to millions among the poor.[13] Despite the progress made, the preconditions for the free life are not available to many people.

THE FUTURE OF RIGHTS

An expansive view of the free life that includes the right to at least some level of enabling conditions is an attractive one for several reasons. Once these conditions are understood as rights, they must be provided even if resources are limited or there are other demands that must be met. Rights, and their corresponding duties, cannot easily be withheld or withdrawn. Invoking rights is politically powerful, given the central role rights play in helping to define the nature of our political society.

However, the case for this expansive view of the compatibility of positive rights and the free life has been challenged. The expansion of the welfare state and new rights in the 1960s and early 1970s, for example, has been attacked from several directions. Conservatives have argued that the creation of new rights endangers traditional ones. There are limits to what rights can be effectively protected. The expansion of rights results in an inflation of rights that ultimately devalues all of them. The shift to positive rights also increases the likelihood of competing rights; the rights of individuals to freely contract with each other collides with the right to be free from discrimination on the basis of race or sex, for example. In a broader sense, rights conflict with the power of the majority to shape societal values. The expansion of the rights of women to control their pregnancies, the rights of sexual preference, the rights of criminals, and the rights of publishers to produce pornography, for example, threaten traditional values championed by conservatives.[14]

From a perspective of economic efficiency, public choice theorists argue that most government intervention is ultimately intended to insulate some interests from the competition of markets. Regulation that is justified in the name of protecting individual rights only protects inefficient producers and rewards seekers of special benefits. Government itself is the greatest threat to individual choice and the efficient allocation of scarce resources that flow from those choices.[15] Other critics of existing public policies argue that the clear majority of government programs benefit the well-off rather than the poor.[16]

Liberals have also joined in the criticisms of the expansion of rights. Liberal theory is naturally uneasy with strong government. Governments that are powerful enough to ensure a wide

range of rights are also powerful enough to restrict individual behavior or to impose a vision of the common good inimicable to
individual freedom. The welfare state, in relying on broad grants
of discretionary power to administrative agencies, can become a
system of privilege and access for special interests rather than a
way to promote individual liberty.[17] The regulatory welfare state,
some critics argue, contains the seeds of its own destruction: government is expected to control the harmful consequences of conduct. But under some conditions, any conduct can be harmful;
and government is then expected to regulate all behavior that
might have any negative impacts. Great expectations are engendered that are impossible to fulfill, and the legitimacy essential
to effective government suffers.[18]

Communitarians argue that rights exaggerate individualism,
undermine community, and make more difficult collective efforts.
For them, rights are divisive, individualistic, and competitive and
fail to provide an appropriate, effective basis for society. Liberals
and conservatives have criticized social programs for perpetuating dependency. One of the most influential critiques of welfare
concluded that programs developed in the 1960s and 1970s
served to "make it profitable for the poor to behave in the short
term in ways that were destructive in the long term. . . . We
tried to provide more for the poor and produced more poor instead."[19] Welfare policy has not been able to liberate the poor,
but, instead, has perpetuated their dependency. For many, affirmative action has come to symbolize the way in which the new
rights have outstripped their support in society. White workers,
caught in an economy that is undergoing tremendous changes,
see preferential treatment as harmful to their own interests. Race
has "provided a mechanism to simultaneously divide voters over
values, and to isolate one disproportionately poor segment of the
population from the rest of the electorate."[20]

Despite these problems, we are convinced that rights can play
an essential role in identifying the positive actions government
can take to provide the enabling conditions for the life of freedom. The challenge is to do so in a way that does not itself
threaten the free life, that is consistent with the idea of equality
of opportunity and empowers people so that they can eventually
provide those enabling conditions for themselves. Rights need
not be divisive, but can be a means of identifying and reinforcing

shared values and commitments. Rights need not insulate individuals from each other, but can be part of defining membership in a political society and reinforcing shared commitments.

We argue that since the purpose of government is to ensure that individuals realize the free life, government should be involved in ensuring that the preconditions of the free life are made available to all. A society that offers real equality of opportunity to only *some* of its citizens falls short of satisfying this basic criterion by which governments can be assessed. Since rights play a central role in defining the powers of government, are central to our political traditions, and are a powerful expression of our fundamental political commitments and values, they will inevitably occupy a central place in our political discourse about how we can realize this goal.

If rights are to play a transforming role in ensuring real equality of opportunity, they will have to be thought of in different ways—not just as restraints on government but as ways of promoting the preconditions for a life of freedom for all people. Rights can be viewed as a means of empowering individuals to live self-directed lives. They can serve to increase our interrelationships with each other, reinforce our responsibility for each other and for the kind of society that we are part of, and assert the moral and social responsibilities we have in common. Rights can help foster common concerns and values and commit ourselves to ensure that each person enjoys the preconditions for realizing a meaningful life, for enjoying real equality of opportunity.

One way to foster this richer notion of rights might be to couple it with increased participation in the political system. Political participation itself is an empowering exercise and can contribute to a sense of community and shared values. Participation in public debate over the nature and scope of rights and the policies needed to ensure them can foster support for the decisions ultimately made. Active involvement in the political system can engage individuals in thinking about common concerns and public interests.

It may be, however, that such an expansive view of rights is not possible, given divisions in our society, alienation from politics as usual, and the current distribution of social, economic, and political power. But the appeal of the idea of the free life, of real equality of opportunity, is also significant. It might serve as a force for awakening an interest in democratic politics, in the possibility of citizens coming together to make decisions about the kind of society in which they wish to live.

A commitment to the rights required to secure the free life for all persons can provide guidance in determining what policies government should undertake. Indeed, we argue that the primary criterion by which public policies can be judged is their compatibility with the realization and perpetuation of the free life. However, there has been little explicit discussion of the ideal of the free, self-directed life and the role of rights in realizing it. We continue to invoke the rhetoric of rights. We rely on a discourse of rights to discuss the values and concerns that are of most importance to our political, collective lives. But the controversies surrounding rights place into question the future of rights and their contribution to the flourishing of the free life for present and future generations.

Government provides the infrastructure for the development of opportunities: public education, mass media and communications, and so on. Government provides for economic and commercial infrastructure: currency, credit, contract enforcement, protective regulation, transportation, communication, foreign trade. Government intervention can provide for public health, environmental quality, and preservation of natural resources that are essential for human survival as well as for personal enjoyment and recreation. Government provides a social safety net, a minimum level of income, services, and support for individuals and families: welfare, health care, food stamps, and so on.

Government has, throughout history, socialized the risk of engaging in modern industrial and commercial society. The primary focus of traditional tort law, for example, has been to protect industrial owners against liability for work conditions or product safety. Victims were required to demonstrate negligence on the part of these defendants. But tort has made a dramatic shift toward socializing risk through no-fault and enterprise liability doctrines that give to consumers the kind of protection long afforded owners of corporations. Similarly, changes in divorce law have expanded the options for women. Rehabilitative alimony, for example, has been ordered by some courts in divorces where women have supported their husbands during professional training programs; these women have been awarded alimony sufficient to give them the opportunity to pursue their own professional training. It is clear that we have a long tradition of and commitment to public policies that benefit certain groups and interests; the challenge is to expand those policies to respond to the rights of all members of the polity and not just some of them.

Some policies may go beyond providing infrastructure to provide special privileges for certain recipients. The line between providing benefits that are in the public interest (or a public good) and granting narrow privileges is hard to draw, since private interests that receive the subsidies to provide the services or goods are benefitted in both cases. But there is a general check against egregious violations of these norms and they are usually challenged over time. If the goal of government is the fostering of the free life, and the free life is dependent on the securing of positive and negative rights, then government must provide for positive and negative rights. Policies that contribute to the right of individuals to live freely and realize their life chances are to be encouraged; policies that do not foster independence and the freedom to make and realize life choices are to be discouraged. The key tasks are to identify what government actions are required to secure these rights, ensure that the rights are extended to all persons (particularly those who have not been included in earlier efforts), and ensure that the preconditions for the perpetuation of the free life are secured for future generations. This is no easy task. It is difficult to assess public policies in terms of how well they contribute to the rights that are part of the free human life, or to identify policies that threaten these values.

Public policies can be assessed by examining the extent to which they contribute to this vision of the free life. Rather than debating whether individuals have a right to welfare payments, adequate housing, affordable health care, a job, and clean air, we can begin with the question of how government can foster the self-directed life. Below are some illustrations of how the general principle might be applied to specific policy issues. The application of this principle, we believe, deserves careful debate and discussion. We provide some illustrations below as an invitation to that debate.

In the area of welfare, for example, there seems to be a consensus that the welfare system needs to promote independence on the part of program participants and help integrate them into the work force. Welfare needs to be oriented toward helping recipients develop the characteristics that will enable them to become productive, self-sufficient members of society. This basic commitment has been at the heart of the experiments of states with welfare reform and was embraced by the authors of the 1988 Family Support Act. But there is still little agreement over how to accomplish that. Some argue that all AFDC recipients should be required to work, while others believe that work should be encouraged and facilitated but that women should remain free to decide to stay home with their children if they wish. Some argue that recipients should be encouraged or forced to take work as soon as it is available, with a minimum of training and counseling, while others believe recipients should be able to enroll in long-term educational programs if they so choose. Should welfare be primarily oriented toward moving women as quickly as possible into the work force, or should it be a means of providing educational opportunities that have not been available in the past?

Programs aimed at helping AFDC recipients can merge with those aimed at women who are working full- or part-time and still remain poor. Part of the debate over welfare focuses on whether state agencies should include a wide range of services such as prenatal health care, child care, and parental leave or should limit themselves to providing assistance until work is found. It makes little sense to orient welfare toward work and then ignore the problems that women face when they try to support their families. The key component of welfare policy should be efforts to help provide the skills and qualities that will lead to independence and self-sufficiency.

In the area of environmental quality, there is increasing awareness of the interaction of ecological and environmental considerations. Without a commitment to protecting natural resources, long-run economic activity is simply not possible. With a commitment to preserving environmental quality, the viability of future generations is threatened. More immediately, since pollution is waste, if it can be reduced then so can costs. Traditional regulatory programs usually trap pollutants at the end of the pipe and simply transfer them into another medium: air pollutants are transferred into solid waste or leached into the water supply rather than eliminated. If pollution is reduced or eliminated through changes in production or materials used, then economic and environmental goals can be achieved in tandem. Individuals are protected from the adverse effects of pollution, and scarce economic resources are efficiently used. Effective environmental regulation in the face of health-threatening pollution is essential in procuring part of the precondition of a free, self-directed life for current and future generations.

Affirmative action can play an important role in helping women and ethnic minorities realize a self-directed life by ensuring that opportunities are open to them. Affirmative action has been most effective in opening up opportunities for those who have the background and preparation to compete in the labor market but will only benefit those who can meet job qualifications. Other limitations on employment opportunities for ethnic minorities that are rooted in poor educational opportunities, crime- and drug-infested neighborhoods, isolation from economic opportunities, and other problems must be addressed directly and cannot be expected to be remedied through affirmative action. Affirmative action efforts that require that candidates meet minimum qualifications and are combined with programs to provide for remedial training when necessary are less likely to clash with those who fear that the rights of white males are being trammeled in order to promote minorities and women.

Health-care options are complicated, given the tremendous costs of health care in the United States. But the role of access to adequate health care to the self-directed life is an essential one. While many of the issues of how to control costs, ensure quality, and fund expanded coverage are most difficult, some policy direction can be given from a commitment to protecting rights. Access to at least some minimum level of health care needs to be provided to all persons, regardless of their ability to pay. The real test of policy is how well it meets the needs of all individuals, rather than how well it satisfies the demands of the insurance and health-care industries. Individuals should be given some opportunity to choose from whom they will obtain health care. Canadian health-care providers are private, for instance, and Canadians are free to choose among them. That choice could be provided to Americans. Health-care insurance needs to be transferable so that employees can be free to leave one place of employment for other opportunities without losing protection.

Financing positive rights is a challenge. Reliance on an ever-increasing federal budget deficit for funding these and other programs may be attractive in the short run but are inconsistent with a sense of responsibility to future generations. Future generations that are burdened with heavy debts that resulted from consumption (rather than investments that can produce benefits to subsequent generations) reduce their opportunities and choices. Tax policies that raise funds to finance these public policies may reduce the freedom individuals have as they are compelled to pay taxes. But these contributions can be justified on at least two grounds. First, they are in the self-interest of all, since public policies are designed to promote the life chances and opportunities of all; and public investments in these preconditions for opportunity are part of the commitment we have to each other as part of living in a complex, interdependent society. Second, government taxing and spending policies inevitably support some interests and preclude others. The key is to promote policies that contribute to the preconditions for the free life, either by temporarily providing them directly or by acting as a catalyst to encourage their development by others. Everyone can contribute to the resources needed for those policies; but in a progressive income tax scheme, some contribute more than others, and those at higher income levels could simply keep their money and buy the resources they need to exercise the choices they want. But real equality of opportunity requires that everyone have at least a minimum level of infrastructure so that they can enjoy at least some measure of freedom to make life choices. Those with more resources would enjoy more freedom; the social commitment is to ensure some level of freedom for all persons. Personal ability will still largely determine outcomes, but everyone will have at least some minimum opportunity to develop those abilities. In this respect, freedom and equality are not opposites but essential elements of the fostering of free human existence.

CONCLUSION

Should rights be at the center of the debate over what government should be about? The commemoration of the Bill of Rights provides an occasion to reconsider how government can protect and preserve rights. But simply invoking rights does not resolve the debate. The future of rights depends on the extent to which they can play an active, vibrant role in public discourse, in helping to provide guidance as we debate basic questions of what governments should and should not do. One way to return rights to a central place in the debate over what government should and should not do is to refocus on the idea that the primary purpose of government is to ensure that individuals can live free, self-directed lives.

A simple invocation of traditional rights, or arguments that rights and responsibilities must be discussed in tandem, may not do that and may even deflect us from asking the more fundamental questions of whether public policies promote the free, self-directed life or run counter to it. If we return to the argument made at the beginning of this essay—that the purpose of government is to secure human freedom, to make free human existence possible—then the primary task of the public policies pursued by government is to secure freedom for the current generation and ensure that conditions will be conducive for the freedom of future generations. This criterion should guide policy makers in determining what public policies are to be pursued by governments. The rights to be secured by government are those that are central to ensuring free human existence, the freedom of individuals to live self-directed lives. Securing these rights requires that governments take affirmative steps. The free human life requires some preconditions. Government cannot provide all of these preconditions but can and must provide many of them in order for individuals to be able to realize the free life. This vision of government is not new but has not always been defended in terms of the perpetuation of the free life.

For rights to continue to play a central role in our political life, they must help determine what restraints are to be placed on governmental power as well as to what ends that power is to be used. A theory of rights that focuses on their contribution to the realization of the free life provides some guidance for dealing with the policy debate, a way to sort out issues and develop an analytic framework for making choices. It provides for criteria that can be used in assessing policy proposals and evaluating existing efforts. It enriches the idea of freedom to incorporate the concerns of how to provide for the good life and how to address criticisms of the libertarian commitment to freedom that does not incorporate broader social concerns, without requiring that government define the ends of social and individual life. It is future-oriented and looks to the challenges ahead of us and how a commitment to rights and, in particular, the right of human freedom, might be pursued. Rights are the vehicle for making public policy because such a focus can ensure that policies are consistent with the goal of promoting human freedom that is the ultimate purpose of government.

Notes

1. James S. Fishkin, *Justice, Equal Opportunity, and the Family* (New Haven, Conn.: Yale University Press, 1983).

2. *Barron v. Baltimore*, 7 Peters 243 (1833).

3. See, generally, Charles W. Eagles, *The Civil Rights Movement in America* (Jackson: University of Mississippi Press, 1986); Juan Williams, *Eyes on the Prize: America's Civil Rights Years* (New York: Viking, Penguin, 1987).

4. For a less optimistic view, see Norman Dorsen, ed., *Our Endangered Rights: The ACLU Report on Civil Liberties Today* (New York: Pantheon, 1984).

5. Samuel I. Rosenman, comp., *The Public Papers and Addresses of Franklin Delano Roosevelt* (New York: Random House, 1938–50), 9: 663–72.

6. "Message to the Congress on the State of the Union," 11 January 1944, ibid., 13: 41.

7. See, generally, James MacGregor Burns and Stewart Burns, *A People's Charter: The Pursuit of Rights in America* (New York: Knopf, 1991), 237–67.

8. For an elaboration of these arguments, see Cass R. Sunstein, *After the Rights Revolution: Reconceiving the Regulatory State* (Cambridge, Mass.: Harvard University Press, 1990), esp. chap. 1.

9. For useful debates over affirmative action and equal opportunity, see Norman E. Bowie, ed., *Equal Opportunity* (Boulder, Colo.: Westview Press, 1988); Ellen Frankel Paul, Fred D. Miller, Jr., and Jeffrey Paul, *Reassessing Civil Rights* (Cambridge, Mass.: Blackwell, 1991); and Russell Nieli, *Racial Preference and Racial Justice* (Washington, D.C.: Ethics and Public Policy Center, 1991).

10. Douglas G. Glasgow, *The Black Underclass* (New York: Vintage, 1980).

11. Marian Wright Edelman, *Families in Peril: An Agenda for Social Change* (Cambridge, Mass.: Harvard University Press, 1987).

12. Lisbeth R. Schorr, *Within Our Reach* (New York: Anchor Press, 1988).

13. Jonathan Kozol, *Savage Inequalities: Children in America's Schools* (New York: Crown, 1991).

14. These ideas are developed more fully in Gary Bryner, "Constitutionalism and the Politics of Rights," in *Constitutionalism and Rights,* ed. Gary C. Bryner and Noel B. Reynolds (Provo, Ut.: Brigham Young University, 1987), 7–32.

15. See, generally, James M. Buchanan, *Freedom in Constitutional Contract* (College Station: Texas A&M University Press, 1977).

16. Neil Howe and Philip Longman, "The Next New Deal," *The Atlantic Monthly,* April 1992, 88–99.

17. See Theodore J. Lowi, *The End of Liberalism* (New York: W. W. Norton, 1979).

18. Theodore J. Lowi, "Liberal and Conservative Theories of Regulation," in *The Constitution and the Regulation of Society,* ed. Gary C. Bryner and Dennis L Thompson (Provo, Ut.: Brigham Young University, 1988).

19. Charles Murray, *Losing Ground: American Social Policy 1950–1980* (New York: Basic Books, 1984), 9.

20. Thomas Byrne Edsall and Mary D. Edsall, *Chain Reaction: The Impact of Race, Rights, and Taxes on American Politics* (New York: W. W. Norton, 1991), 5.

Index